Wellspring

Wellspring

365
Meditations
to Refresh
Your Soul

KAREN MOORE

Abingdon Press
Nashville

WELLSPRING:
365 MEDITATIONS TO REFRESH YOUR SOUL

Copyright © 2011 by Abingdon Press

This book is printed on acid-free paper.

ISBN-13: 978-1-4267-4232-3

Library of Congress Cataloging-in-Publication Data has been applied for.

Scripture quotations unless otherwise indicated are from the Common English Bible. Copyright © 2011 by the Common English Bible. All rights reserved. Used by permission. (www.CommonEnglishBible.com)

11 12 13 14 15 16 17 18 19 20 — 10 9 8 7 6 5 4 3 2 1

MANUFACTURED IN THE UNITED STATES OF AMERICA

One writer said,
"The real voyage of discovery consists
not in seeking new landscapes,
but in having new eyes."
This book is dedicated to each one
who seeks the Living Waters of Grace with
new eyes and with the heart of an adventurer.
May you be continually refreshed, and may
God's blessings overflow just for you!

—Karen Moore

January

I was hungry and you gave me food to

eat. I was thirsty and you gave me a drink.

I was a stranger and you welcomed me.

Matthew 25:35

COME TO THE WATER

All of you who are thirsty, come to the water!
—Isaiah 55:1

As you celebrate the beginning of a brand new year, it feels like time is back on your side. With a new burst of energy, you're able to reassess your priorities, look at where you've been and where you want to go, and you're invited once again to drink from the well of living water. Slip away then from the muddy shores of the past and step into today where you can make a clean start. You may still be parched from yesterday, or a bit thirsty from all that you have left undone, but you're not going on alone from here.

Thomas Fuller once said, "We never know the worth of water till the well is dry."

Let us seek to understand the "worth" of living water this year for we have a fountain of joy to drink from, a well that is everlasting. We only need to come and take a daily dip into this pool to be refreshed and renewed continually.

As you change the date on your calendar to reflect a new year, clear the dryness in your throat by refreshing yourself with God's living Word and his everlasting waters. Allow him to wash over you with the goodness and love he has already prepared. It's a New Year and a new chance for you to quench your thirst. Come to the water!

IN THE FLOW

Dear Lord, as I start another year, remind me that you are with me every step of the way. Wash away the things in my past that I no longer need and renew my life and my Spirit in your precious Name. Amen.

How to Be Happy

Even if the forest falls and the humbled city is laid low, those who sow beside any stream will be happy, sending out ox and donkey to graze.
—Isaiah 32:19-20

What does it take for you to feel happy? Isaiah offers a little insight into raising your happiness quotient when he says, "sow beside any stream and you will be happy." Sowing beside a stream puts you in the flow and connects you to the Source of all that brings life and sustains you. It means you have chosen to plant your values and your dreams, your hopes and aspirations in a place where they can be nurtured and grown. It is a place that fills your spirit with expectant joy.

St. Augustine reflected on happiness in this way. He said, "Where your pleasure is, there is your treasure; where your treasure is, there is your heart; where your heart is, there is your happiness." When your heart is connected to the One who can wash you anew, cause you to come clean and to start again with honest effort and joy, you have every ingredient for happiness.

The New Year has just begun. Happiness is ready to embrace you, ready to reveal its secrets as you walk into the waters of the Living Savior. He will guard your heart and mind and keep you steadily on the path of true joy. Be happy today.

In the Flow

Father in Heaven, help me plant my hopes and dreams firmly in your care this year. As I seek to find greater happiness through you and the treasures you place in my heart, hold me close. Amen.

GO AHEAD, TAKE A CHANCE!

*Send your bread out on the water because, in the
course of time, you may find it again.*
—Ecclesiastes 11:1

It's not easy to figure out when to take a risk or when to start
something new. Even making an effort can seem overwhelming,
and yet, something nags at you, insisting that it's time, that today is
a new day and even if you didn't make it work before, you can now.
Think of the Nike slogan that implores you to "just do it!"

Procrastination may make sense in terms of giving your
new ideas thoughtful consideration. Weighing the odds is a
worthwhile use of your time. Getting uncomfortable, though, is
a challenge, but the writer of Ecclesiastes doesn't really care. He
says get it done. With a little due diligence, in the course of time,
you may reap a reward, and you may win the day.

If you don't cast your bread on the waters, you know that
nothing can return to you. If you simply cast the bread and
walk away, you won't be expectant. You won't recognize the
opportunity or be ready for the win. So go ahead. Take a chance
on becoming all that God meant you to become and show him
and the rest of the world what you've got. It will renew your spirit
and you'll be in a refreshing stream of opportunity.

IN THE FLOW

*Lord, I let things pass me by over and over again. This year, help me
take a chance and step up to the plate to get things done. Amen.*

THE DRINK THAT REFRESHES

*Both fresh water and salt water don't come
from the same spring, do they?*
—James 3:11

About this time of year, we love the idea of sandy beaches and
warm salty water. We imagine the sounds of seagulls and ocean
waves and shells along the shore. We love it until we need a
nice cool drink. Hmmm . . . imagine being surrounded by
blissful breezes and burning sands, but no cold refreshing drink.
Everything is saltwater. It looks like water, sounds like water, but
it can't refresh you from the inside. It only leaves you feeling
drier and thirstier.

Life can be like that. We don't notice whether we're being
nourished because for the moment we're being satisfied. Once
the illusion fades, we catch the reality like we just walked on
a jellyfish. We are almost startled to realize we need a taste of
something that will truly sustain us, something more.

Your current faith may sustain you very well, or it may just
keep you afloat on an endless sea of uncertainty. It may be time
to drink more deeply and receive greater refreshment.

There is a beautiful beach, a place where you can play and
hang out in the sun. All you have to do is ask and you'll be there,
filled forever after with the cool, refreshing Spirit that will never
leave you thirsty again.

IN THE FLOW

*Lord, thank you for being the only living water that quenches the
thirst of your children. Thank you for giving us all we need. Amen.*

GOD GAVE YOU TODAY

This is the day the LORD acted; we will rejoice and celebrate in it!
—Psalm 118:24

Do you ever get so caught up in your routine that you forget what day it is? You have to remind yourself whether you're going to work, or maybe sleeping in because it's Saturday? Some of us may even forget that we didn't "invent" today. In fact, we wouldn't be here at all if God had not acted on our behalf a very long time ago. The psalmist is right to point this out to us. God made this day. Now what will we do to show him how glad we are that he did?

Since it's the beginning of the year, let's be more mindful of what God has done each morning when we rise. We can begin the day, even before we put a foot on the floor, saying "Thank you, Lord." We can put a smile on our faces and celebrate the fact that we are surrounded by the abundance he provided.

Every action causes some kind of reaction. God acted. Now it's your turn. This is the day the Lord made so that you could . . . what? What can you do to cause God to celebrate a little? What can you give back today that will connect your heart more closely to his?

Take a moment and give God a very intentional response. Don't hesitate to show him what you can do. It will be good for both of you. Praise him, praise him for today!

IN THE FLOW

Lord, I get caught up in the to-do list of my daily life and I forget to be grateful. I thank you for all you do to make it possible for me to live more fully and richly. Bless this day and walk with me. Amen.

Hitting the Jackpot

Generous persons will prosper; those who refresh
others will themselves be refreshed.
—Proverbs 11:25

Have you ever considered what you'd do if you won the lottery or somehow managed to win or receive an unexpected, but fabulous fortune? After you got over the excitement of the event and paid off your house and all your loans, you might start thinking about giving to others. You might start to imagine how good it would feel to share your good fortune.

The good news is this. You've already won the lottery. You already have a vast fortune to share with others. It may not be showing up in your bank account, but it's there. It's the spirit of generosity that came into your life the day you started following Jesus. It's the day you said, whatever I have, I'm willing to share.

You have been blessed with an abundance of treasure, and the more you give that treasure away, the more blessed you are. C. S. Lewis reminded us that "nothing is really ours until we share it."

It's a new day and the perfect moment to look at what you have to give away. It may just be a moment of your time, a smile, a kind word to the taxi driver, but whatever it is, share it. Love is never witnessed by a clenched fist, but only through an open and generous hand.

In the Flow

Father, you have blessed me beyond measure. You have filled my home and heart with joy. Cause me to never forget what you've done for me and to always remember to give in any way I can to others. Amen.

Setting Priorities . . . Again!

Instead, desire first and foremost God's kingdom and God's righteousness, and all these things will be given to you as well.
—Matthew 6:33

The start of a new year is a good time to take a look at your priorities, to examine more closely where you are willing to put your effort and energy. What's at the top of your to-do list?

Most likely, you'll find a lot of things there like working hard for that next promotion, studying to get through a course at school, or exercising to get your weight under control. At the beginning of a year, we're usually pretty focused on improving ourselves and our lot in life.

Matthew recommends that we go back to our to-do list to see if we've remembered to put God at the top of it. He says that when we start there, we're getting it right. In fact, we're getting the message that there's really nothing worth doing if God is not a part of the equation.

Today, put your grocery list aside for a bit and scratch out the stuff that keeps you busy and look for the stuff that keeps you in the business of life, the life God called you to. He can only help you, guide you, and bless you if you invite him into your story. Call him, he's always available to you.

In the Flow

Lord, I know that I get so busy with life I forget to even mention your name in passing. I forget that you are the reason I get to do anything at all. Be with me today and lead the way to all that you would have me do. Amen.

IT ALL BEGINS WITH YOU

*I was hungry and you gave me food to eat. I was thirsty and
you gave me a drink. I was a stranger and you welcomed me.*
—Matthew 25:35

It's easy in our culture to gloss over the needs of our neighbors
and those who are still strangers to us in the world. We can pass
by the homeless and imagine that they just weren't very good
at managing their money or they really should join AA or some
other "will somebody else please fix them" program. We may
even give to United Way or some other such agency through the
place we work. That makes giving so easy we don't even have to
think about it. To us, it's just a loss of income anyway.

So how can we recognize the opportunity we have to act like
Jesus? How will we differentiate the mindless-though-helpful
giving from the kind that causes us to stop and notice what we're
actually doing? When you give with a full intention, from the
heart, is that more of the idea that Jesus had in mind?

Giving is always a choice. Whether you put your heart and
mind into it is also a choice. Feeding others is not simply a
matter of buying a meal. It's a function of inviting them to the
feast of a gracious God who gave everything for our good.

Giving begins with you. It keeps you in the flow of blessing
in ways that nothing can measure. Is anyone thirsty in your midst
today? Be their blessing.

IN THE FLOW

*Lord, show me how I can open up my heart and be more generous to
others. I know that you have been more than generous to me. Amen.*

WOW! THAT WAS STUPID!

Patience leads to abundant understanding, but impatience leads to stupid mistakes.
—Proverbs 14:29

It's a New Year, and you have set new goals for yourself. So, what happens if things take a little longer than you expected? What happens to your faith when you have to wait things out?

We live in a world of instant gratification. When the Internet goes down for five minutes, we're irritated. We're used to getting information now and we don't like it very much when we have to wait . . . for anything!

Look at what happens if you get caught in a traffic jam for fifteen minutes, or you're in line at the grocery store with the sweet little lady who has twenty-seven coupons. At first, you're a little annoyed, maybe a little antsy, and then just out and out angry because someone else is taking up your precious time. After all, you're pretty important and you have things to do.

Impatience leads to all kinds of problems. You try to go around the traffic jam, only to get caught in even greater congestion elsewhere. Today, watch the flow and energy around you. Observe your willingness to slow down enough to recognize that prayerful patience will reap greater rewards. The reward will surely help limit those stupid mistakes.

IN THE FLOW

Lord, I know that I am not always patient. Help me realize that you can use me a lot more when I slow down and think of you. Amen.

FOR GOD SO LOVED YOU

God so loved the world that he gave his only Son, so that everyone
who believes in him won't perish but will have eternal life.
—John 3:16

Can you really take that in? Are you able to comprehend
what it actually means that the God of the universe, the One
who created everything and who has the only real power and
authority over heaven and earth, actually loves you? Wow! Who
are you?

Who you are may not be nearly as important as what you are.
You are his child, his object of affection. You are the one he sent
his only Son to redeem because he couldn't stand the thought
that anything would ever happen to you. You mean the world to
God and he is doing everything he can to prove himself to you.

Today, take a moment and imagine what it really means to be
loved by God. Embrace the idea. Pray and ask God to help you
understand it more fully. Then, remind yourself that such love
deserves to be shared. You're in a relationship and it's the biggest
one that you'll ever be part of. It's bigger than your spouse, it's
bigger than your partnership at the firm or your membership in
the church. It's you and God, one to one.

God so loved you that he acted on your behalf a long time
ago. You have every opportunity to act on God's behalf today.

IN THE FLOW

Dear Lord, I can hardly take in the idea of your great love. I know
that it is a gift of your spirit and I treasure it. Help me to be worthy
of your love in all that I do. Amen.

What's Your Reality?

Faith is the reality of what we hope for,
the proof of what we don't see.
—Hebrews 11:1

Reality TV is a funny concept. It invites us into a personal encounter with someone we've never met and before long, we're in a virtual relationship. We think we're part of their lives and they are part of ours. The problem is that neither of you knows the other, and chances are good you never will. It's simply not reality.

Sometimes we want faith to be a bit like a reality TV spot. We want to plug in and connect with it, and ultimately make the right choice and come out with the happy ending. We want it to be easy.

The writer of Hebrews reminds us that faith is about a reality we hope for, an outcome we believe in and move on even when we don't have proof. It's a lot like love or appreciation of the arts. No one else can really understand your choices or how you feel, but it's your reality.

Look at the things you have faith in. Furthermore, look at the things you don't have faith in and check in with your Creator. He is the only reality. He is the proof of what you don't see. Have faith in him and faith in yourself and the things you hope for will begin to come to you according to his will and purpose. Open your heart so that greater faith can flow through you to others.

In the Flow

Lord, I thank you for the gift of faith. Sometimes I have a lot and I feel on fire for you. Other times, I have a little and I look to things in this world to give me answers and direction. Help me see all that you want for me with eyes of faith. Amen.

WHEN YOU'RE SMILING

A joyful heart brightens one's face, but a
troubled heart breaks the spirit.
—Proverbs 15:13

Remember the old song that suggested "when you're smiling, the whole world smiles at you"? Proverbs 15 agrees.

Today, notice the difference in your attitude when you encounter someone with a smile. A smile invites you in and suggests that friendship is possible. A smile says all is well and the world is a beautiful place today. A smile puts you on holy ground.

A frown, on the other hand, breaks you down and leaves you feeling uncertain, unavailable, unloved even. Your troubles weigh in and prevent you from seeing all that is good. Of course, you'll have days when a smile is simply not going to carry you along, but do what you can to make those days as few as possible. Imagine the smile God has on his face when he thinks of you. It just may help you to have a lighter and brighter countenance. After all, your smile is what others embrace.

A smile is like a welcome glass of cool water on a warm day. It refreshes you and strengthens you. It warms you as you follow in the footsteps of the One who loves you more than anything. Yes, you really can smile because God loves you.

IN THE FLOW

Lord, I may not always feel like smiling, but I realize that with you
in my heart, I always have a reason to smile. No matter what I'm
going through, help me to hold on to the hope and joy I have in you.
Amen.

WHAT ARE YOU THINKING?

*From now on, brothers and sisters, if anything is excellent
and if anything is admirable, focus your thoughts on
these things: all that is true, all that is holy,
all that is just, all that is pure, all that is
lovely, and all that is worthy of praise.*
—Philippians 4:8

Have you ever gotten caught in a gripe session? You know, the kind where everyone is grumbling and complaining about life and it appears that there is absolutely nothing to be glad about? How do you feel after that session is over? Do you feel energized and ready to get back in the game of life or do you feel like just letting everything go because there's really no point anyway?

What you think about and what you take into your consciousness from others is vital to your well-being. When you're around toxic conversations and toxic people, you suffer the consequences. You feel depleted of hope and energy.

Snap out of it! The writer of Philippians has some good advice. Don't think about every bad possible outcome you can imagine and try to cope with living. Be intentional about what you allow into your heart and mind. After all, you own that space and you need to protect it. Think about good, true, and beautiful things. It will make a big difference in your day.

IN THE FLOW

Lord, help me steer clear of the people who see only the dark side of life. I have you, the Light of the World, in my heart. Amen.

PASS ON THE BLESSINGS

*Finally, all of you be of one mind, sympathetic, lovers of
your fellow believers, compassionate. . . . You were called
to do this so that you might inherit a blessing.*
—1 Peter 3:8-9

Someone needs what you have to give today. It may be a small
gift of encouragement through your words or your greetings. It
may be a gentle heart that listens with compassion. It may be
your clever sense of humor and your ability to chase away the
clouds of gloom that threaten their day. You are God's hands
and feet, his eyes and ears.

Emily Dickinson reflected on this need in her own way when
she wrote . . .

They might not need me; but they might.
I'll let my head be just in sight;
A smile as small as mine might be
Precisely their necessity.

Your smile, your thoughts, your helping hands are just
what somebody else needs today. Bless others and God will
immediately bless you. Show his face and shine his light
everywhere you go today. You are blessed to be a blessing.

IN THE FLOW

*Lord, you know the needs of each person I will encounter today.
Help me see them as you see them. Help me offer them the gift of
your blessing. Amen.*

STAND FIRM . . . TAKE A BOW!

You must stand firm, unshakable, excelling in the
work of the Lord as always, because you know that your
labor isn't going to be for nothing in the Lord.
—1 Corinthians 15:58

You've probably done a few thankless jobs in your life. You know, those are the jobs where you trudge in to work every day, do what you must with as much energy as you can manage, and trudge home again wondering why you keep doing it.

Paul, in his letter to the Corinthians, tells us that when you see what you do as doing work for the Lord, you have every reason to celebrate. His Spirit will supply all the energy you need and your heart will be light because of the joy you experience.

God has every desire and intention for you to be happy in your work. If you find yourself in the slow lane, trudging your way, begrudging your day, then it might be time for a change. Ask God to help you know whether he wants you in the job you're in. If you're working for him, there will always be a reward. In fact, your future is guaranteed and the benefits are awesome.

IN THE FLOW

Lord, I know that I don't always feel sure I'm doing the right work.
I know I don't give all that I can when my heart isn't in the flow of
things. Help me see your hand in the work I do and shine your light
so others can see your good works and rejoice. Amen.

What's in Your Wallet?

*No one can serve two masters. Either you will hate the one
and love the other, or you will be loyal to the one and have
contempt for the other. You cannot serve God and wealth.*
—Matthew 6:24

Credit card companies would have you believe that the kind
of credit card you carry makes a difference. Perhaps! It's not
always easy to recognize the seductive power of being able to
spend money that isn't really yours. If your circumstances ever
make it necessary for you to live on those credit cards, you start
to discover what kind of hold they actually have over you.

Perhaps you don't think you have money issues because
you don't even use credit cards, but look again. It doesn't take
much to become slaves to our money. We build a lot of our lives
around it . . . saving, spending, planning, and dreaming. It sounds
harsh, but the truth is in your wallet. What keeps you moving
forward? Is it your prayer life, your commitment to the things
God designed for you to accomplish, or is it something else?
What seduces you into believing you can do it all on your own?

There's nothing wrong with your credit card as long as you
give credit where it's due. As long as you are diligent enough to
recognize whether you own it or it owns you.

You're the child of a King and everything in this world is
open to you from your Father's hand. Go to him for anything
you need. Serve him with your whole heart.

In the Flow

*Lord, it's so easy to be seduced by the things of this world. Please help
me see the truth in all I do. Amen.*

WHERE ARE THE WISE?

Where are the wise? Where are the legal experts? Where are today's debaters? Hasn't God made the wisdom of the world foolish? In God's wisdom, he determined that the world wouldn't come to know him through its wisdom. Instead, God was pleased to save those who believe through the foolishness of preaching.
—1 Corinthians 1:20-21

What suggests that a high IQ directly leads to wisdom? Where do we find those who are the real sages, the ones worthy of our listening ears? According to Paul, we are wise when we come to know God, and in that wisdom, we understand more of what makes us worthy in his sight. The things that stand out in this world, the beautiful people, the brilliant ones, the wealthy ones, may or may not have wisdom. Those who are not as inclined toward a kind of brilliance that sets them apart in worldly ways, may yet be the wiser.

God sets his people apart and he has placed them in every arena of life. He has equipped his own with a kind of wisdom that will brilliantly lead others to his door. That's wisdom. That's what sets the wise at heart truly apart.

Be wise and seek him in every way you can today.

IN THE FLOW

Lord, I have glimpses of wisdom, moments of brilliance, but I know that I don't stay in those spaces unless you lead me there. Grant me greater wisdom in the things I do that please you. Amen.

WATERS OF JOY

You will draw water with joy from the springs of
salvation. And you will say on that day: "Thank the
LORD; *call on God's name; proclaim God's deeds among*
the peoples; declare that God's name is exalted.
—Isaiah 12:3-4

What makes you happy? Sometimes it's the special things, the holidays, the moments that are rare and treasured. Other times, it's simply being able to do the everyday, mundane things with ease. Drawing a glass of water from the well, more than likely your kitchen sink, may not seem like a reason to be happy, unless you have been without water for a few days.

Sometimes we forget how happy we are about the little things that life brings. When we do remember, though, Isaiah offers us a way to let God know how pleased we really are. First of all, he tells us to thank God. Thank God for each and every moment that stirs our hearts with joy. Call him.

God's phone is never unplugged or too busy. You can call him any time even when you're not in need. You can call him just to share your love. Now that's a good reason to be happy.

IN THE FLOW

Lord, thank you for the things that make my life happy and secure.
Thank you for loving me just as I am. Help me give all the credit to
you for the things that are so good in my life. Amen.

Clinging to the Vine

Now choose life—so that you and your descendants will live—by loving the LORD your God, by obeying his voice, and by clinging to him.
—Deuteronomy 30:19-20

Life is full of amusement to those who observe it philosophically. It is a reason to laugh out loud. For those who filter everything through the lens of the heart, through the things that touch every nerve in their being, it can be overwhelming, even tragic. Life is not easy for the sensitive of heart. Yet, for those who seek God first, who cling to the Vinedresser and press forward, it is indeed a victory.

The Vinedresser presents you with daily choices, designed to help you experience more of what he has for you. He offers you an abundant journey as you listen to him and to voices that resonate with you and stay steadily on the path. Every day, perhaps even every hour, you are asked to choose. What will you cling to?

Believers in Christ may differ in the degree, the practice, or the intensity of their system of belief, but they all have one thing in common. As believers, they all have the victory through Jesus. This is your day to proclaim the victory and to let others know your choice.

Live today in the joy of the Lord.

In the Flow

Lord, you have opened your arms to me, ready to guide me on to the victory that comes from knowing you. Help me keep making the choices that will bring me safely home. Amen.

YOUR INNER BEAUTY

You are the one who created my innermost parts;
you knit me together while I was still in my mother's womb.
I give thanks to you that I was marvelously set apart.
Your works are wonderful—I know that very well.
—Psalm 139:13-14

You are wonderful! You are the divine craftsmanship of an expert. You are the best version of you that there could be. How is that possible? Because you were divinely inspired and God knew you before you were ever born.

You're God's masterpiece and nothing can change that. You were and are marvelously set apart.

What does that mean to you? It means turn up your light and let your inner self, your beautiful self, lead the way and live for him as though living is the only mission you have on earth. Live as though what you do is important to God because it is. What you do matters. What you think and believe and dream matters. God sees you and he loves you from the inside out.

IN THE FLOW

Dear Father, I know you formed me and loved me before I was even a light in my mother's eyes. Help me take that in and realize how important I am to you. Help me shine from the place of my innermost being and bring your light to those around me. Amen.

WE ARE FAMILY

Keep loving each other like family. Don't neglect to open up your homes to guests, because by doing this some have been hosts to angels without knowing it.
—Hebrews 13:1-2

You may not have the same last name or the same address, but the writer of Hebrews encourages you to treat everyone who comes to visit or stay the night as family. Opening your heart and home to honored guests changes the dynamic of your relationship instantly. You create an atmosphere where everyone under your roof is your family.

What's so good about that? For one thing, you get to have authentic experience. You get to be yourself and your guest does too. You get to share your personal stories, your faith stories, and other matters in ways that resonate with truth and create opportunities for further discussion. You talk about things in a family that you can't begin to discuss with strangers.

You may not find yourself in the presence of angels, or then again, you may, but the point is to treat everyone like family. In fact, if you treat people with love, you'll be serving them as an angel of friendship, fellowship, and joy. Nothing could make your Father happier than to see you treat his other children so well.

IN THE FLOW

Lord, help me always be a warm and generous host to anyone who finds their way to my door. As you have so lovingly welcomed me into your family, let me return the favor by the way I embrace those who spend time in my home. Amen.

STILL CALLING HIS FOLLOWERS

As Jesus walked alongside the Galilee Sea, he saw two brothers
. . . throwing fishing nets into the sea. . . . "Come, follow
me," he said, "and I'll show you how to fish for people."
—Matthew 4:18-19

If Jesus stopped by any of our towns today to call his followers,
would he venture into the heart of commerce? Would he go to
Wall Street and look for the biggest investment gurus or set his
sights on a physician from the local hospital? It's interesting to
try to imagine who he might deem to be worthy disciples, and
yet one thing is clear: You would be on his list. He would call
you to follow him. Today, more than anything else he wants
to help you cast a bigger vision for your life, fill your nets to
overflowing with the good things of God, and help to heal your
wounds in any possible way. Jesus is still calling.

If you're already following him, think for a moment how
that affects your daily decisions, your daily purpose. How do you
align yourself with his will for your life? How often do you truly
allow him to lead?

The trouble with followers sometimes is that they try to
scoot ahead of their leaders, sometimes taking a wrong trail.
Wherever you are today, pause a moment and reflect on who is
leading your life. Are you following Jesus even now?

IN THE FLOW

Lord, as I go about my business today, help me seek your guidance
and direction. Help me be a wise and loving follower. Amen.

Waiting for Forever!

With the Lord a single day is like a thousand years and a thousand years are like a single day. The Lord isn't slow to keep his promise, as some think of slowness, but he is patient toward you.
—2 Peter 3:8-9

When you were a kid, it seemed time went so slowly. You waited for Christmas and your birthday and the big vacation with the family. Now that you're a little older, days and nights may seem to melt into each other and make you wonder how anything can get done when there is so little time.

Peter reminds us essentially that with God, time is not really an issue. In fact, he invented the whole concept of time and it appears that he had no limitations for himself. But for us, time is a mystery.

The thing we have to notice is what happens to our patience or our ability to wait when time drags on. When everything about life is suddenly grounded and nothing moves, when everything stops, then you might feel somewhat dismayed.

Today, pay closer attention to your time and how you spend it. How much of it did you dedicate to God?

In the Flow

Lord, I admit that I get frustrated by time. I either don't have enough of it, or I have a little too much on my hands and then I get impatient. Remind me that you are the arbiter of my time, the one who knows how I best need to live my life. Amen.

FAITH—WHAT'S ENOUGH?

*Jesus said to him, " 'If you can do anything'? All things
are possible for the one who has faith." At that the boy's
father cried out, "I have faith; help my lack of faith!"*
—Mark 9:23-24

Most of us can empathize with the poor father who struggled
with his faith in the story Mark has noted here. We want to
believe. In our best moments, we do believe. In our worst
moments, we question what we believe. We're not always certain
we have enough of this thing called faith.

Alas, we can't buy more faith on the open market, but we
may be able to buy into the concept, the idea, the fact of faith
in such a way that we do indeed receive more of it. Perhaps faith
is something like love. The more of it you give away, the more
of it you use, the more you have. If so, why don't we look for
every opportunity to share our faith, to ground our faith, to
substantiate our faith in such a way that lack is never a problem?
When someone we love is ill, we call on our faith knowing that
with God all things are possible.

Take a moment and measure your faith quotient today. Is
it enough to get you through every twist and turn the day may
take? If not, start the day with one request. "Lord, help my lack
of faith."

IN THE FLOW

*Lord, help me depend on faith and on you in such a way that
nothing can really shake it, nothing can take it away from me. Help
me know that with faith in you all things are possible. Amen.*

YOU LOOK LIKE YOUR FATHER

*Instead renew the thinking in your mind by the Spirit
and clothe yourself with the new person created according
to God's image in justice and true holiness.*
—Ephesians 4:23-24

Most of us take it as a compliment when someone tells us we look like a parent or a favorite relative. We want to reflect the people we love in a positive way. How wonderful when we reflect the likeness of our Father, the God who made us in his own image.

How do we do that? What can we do so that others will see his mannerisms in our walk and talk, see his glow in our faces? One of the keys to changing our image is right here in this verse. It says that we must renew our thinking; we must renew our minds by God's Spirit.

When you're excited about life and the way you look, you also have a tendency to dress differently. In fact, you may be motivated to buy a new outfit to reflect the new you. You're more apt to want to look appealing to people in every way because you're happy about the way you look.

It's a great day to clothe yourself in God's image, to wear his smile for all those who see you, and share his heart with each one you meet. Change your thoughts, change your clothes, and create a style all your own . . . one that reflects your love for your Father.

IN THE FLOW

Lord, I do want to look and act and be more like you. Help me think about you in such a way that I naturally reflect you in the things I do. Help others see your face any time they look at me. Amen.

LET YOUR CONSCIENCE BE YOUR GUIDE

*Some people have ruined their faith because they
refused to listen to their conscience.*
—1 Timothy 1:19

We live in an era where people often act without any trace of conscience. Moral guidelines are given only a perfunctory look, and virtue is no longer espoused as a thing worthy of our attention.

Whatever happened to having a conscience? Jiminy Cricket taught some of us that it was good to let your conscience be your guide. Add to that the idea that the Holy Spirit taps into our conscious selves and tries to offer clear and clean direction. We're not alone here but we act as though we are. We act as though the things we do have no consequence and whether we please God or not is simply not on the radar.

First Timothy warns us that we can actually ruin our faith, perhaps even lose our faith, when we aren't willing to listen to God. The still small voice speaks to us, and it serves us well to listen. Today is a new day and no matter how closely you were listening yesterday, make it your intention to do so now. See what the spirit of God wants you to know and feel the direction being offered for your soul. Listen carefully because it will do your heart a lot of good.

IN THE FLOW

*Lord, help me tune into my conscience, trusting and believing that
you are working to help me live according to your will and purpose.
Amen.*

THE RACE OF GOD'S GRACE

I also observed under the sun that the race
doesn't always go to the swift,
nor the battle to the mighty, nor food to the wise,
nor wealth to the intelligent, nor favor to the knowledgeable.
—Ecclesiastes 9:11

The writer of Ecclesiastes reminds us that the sun shines on everybody and it doesn't necessarily just shine on the people who deserve it. When we prepare for a race, a new job, or an opportunity that puts us out in front of others, we may forget one thing. We may forget how much our ego is also invested in the outcome. We may even start to become people who believe life owes us and that we're entitled to the good stuff.

What we're entitled to is God's grace, given freely, no matter who we are. Others may get ahead of us, but it could be by accident as the passage suggests, or it could be by design. After all, the Creator of the universe has every tool at his disposal for good or ill. He can bring out the rain and the sun whenever he chooses.

Today, as you examine your effort at the things you do, don't worry about who else might win at the game you are playing. Just trust and believe that it's important for you to be the best you can possibly be. Your Heavenly Father knows why.

IN THE FLOW

Lord, help me stop comparing myself to others, and be willing to
bring only my best to you no matter what. Amen.

YOU LOOK MARVELOUS!

*Don't try to make yourselves beautiful on the outside, with
stylish hair or by wearing gold jewelry or fine clothes. Instead,
make yourselves beautiful on the inside, in your hearts,
with the enduring quality of a gentle, peaceful spirit.
This type of beauty is very precious in God's eyes.*

—1 Peter 3:3-4

If God were to create a magazine with all the beautiful people
in it, who would we see there? More than likely we'd see the
images of people like Mother Teresa and Martin Luther King,
Jr. We'd see the caretakers, the peacemakers, the givers and the
generous. We'd see the ones who knew what beauty really was as
it emanated from within. We'd see those who have gone before
us with peaceful hearts and kind souls.

You're precious to God. You're beautiful too. As you
walk through today, imagine yourself on the front cover of his
magazine. You're already in his book. May your heart leap with
joy at the very thought.

IN THE FLOW

*Lord, sometimes I forget what beauty really is. I'm grateful that you
see me and love me just as I am. Amen.*

WATCHING OUT FOR THE OTHER GUY

Everything is permitted, but everything isn't
beneficial. Everything is permitted,
but everything doesn't build others up. No
one should look out for their own
advantage, but they should look out for each other.
—1 Corinthians 10:23-24

We're inclined to think that we can do whatever we want as long as it doesn't hurt someone else. That may not be a bad rule of thumb, but it doesn't help us become more caring for others. Paul's comments to the Corinthians were aimed at getting them to be more mindful of one another, to make it a practice to watch out for the other guy.

We all appreciate it when someone takes us under her or his wing and takes care of something we need, offering us a helping hand, a gift of food or a place to stay. The outcome is that both people benefit, the giver and the receiver.

As you go about your life today, pay attention to those in your care, who need what you do for them, who benefit from your attention. The more you offer them a hand, the more God will bless your efforts. He sees your heart and applauds the good things that you do.

IN THE FLOW

Lord, help me be more aware of the needs of those around me. Help
me open my heart and my hands and let me genuinely minister to
the needs of others. Amen.

FINDING THE SUPERHERO IN YOU

Therefore, imitate God like dearly loved children.
Live your life with love, following the example of
Christ, who loved us and gave himself for us.
—Ephesians 5:1-2

Don't you love watching children at play when they are pretending to be superheroes? The superheroes don their capes and vow to protect the innocent, always ready to defend and fight for the right. They definitely make the world a safer place.

We can't really pretend to be God, but we can imitate those traits that we recognize as being a part of his holiness. We can follow the examples that we have recorded in Scripture of what it means to love others as we love ourselves. We have biblical heroes who serve the people of God and who serve as examples for us to follow.

Today, "pretend" to be a little kinder, a little more generous, and a little more conscious of God's great love than you were the day before. Chances are, it won't be long before it's not a pretense at all, but the truth of who you are.

IN THE FLOW

Lord, help me today to try to walk further in your shoes. Help me lean into you so much that I can show your love and your light to everyone I meet. Amen.

A Matter of Contentment

*I know the experience of being in need and
of having more than enough;
I have learned the secret to being content
in any and every circumstance,
whether full or hungry or whether having plenty or being poor.
I can endure all these things through the power of the one
who gives me strength.*
—Philippians 4:12-13

How often do you find yourself feeling fully content? You send your children off with love, do your work in peace, and take what comes with calmness and ease. It's a wonderful place to be in.

Sadly, it's a difficult place for most of us to achieve. We stay out on the skinny branches all alone wondering if we can survive or if wolves will come and tear us apart. We're always slightly on edge.

Paul reminds us that we don't have to be. He says that he doesn't let what is going on outside affect what is happening to him on the inside. He's free to find the good in every opportunity. He's able to see that he is not alone. He sets his focus on Jesus and accepts the strength that he then receives.

As you look out at the world today, remember, you have the option of giving your day over to the One who can provide the strength to sustain you and bring you contentment.

In the Flow

Lord, strengthen my steps today as I look to you. Help me trust and to lean on you for all that I am. Help me breathe in the peace that only you can give. Amen.

February

*A*bove all, show sincere love to each other,

because love brings about the forgiveness of

many sins.

1 Peter 4:8

THIS THING CALLED LOVE

*May the Lord cause you to increase and
enrich your love for each other
and for everyone in the same way as we also love you.*
—1 Thessalonians 3:12

Love is such an awesome concept, it's often hard to define. Sure, we think we have a grasp of what it means to love. After all, we love our spouse and our children and others in our family. We have a reasonable sense of love.

But it may be time to turn up the heat. What would it take to increase your real understanding of love?

Like most things, love thrives on attention. In fact, it often demands attention. It grows with genuine interest and effort. It takes shape through good times and bad times. James Bryden said, "Love does not die easily. It is a living thing. It thrives in the face of all life's hazards, save one—neglect."

God is interested in how we experience love, and he does not want us to neglect it. His love for us is steady and strong and he wants ours to be like that with others and with him.

Love is a living thing, and you and God share a love that is a match made in Heaven. Today, pour on the love everywhere you go.

IN THE FLOW

Lord, your love for me and others is beyond me, beyond my understanding. I know it's real, though, and I know that more than anything I want our love for each other to grow. Please help me embrace all you want me to know about love. Amen.

KEEP YOUR HEART PUMPING!

*May the love cause your hearts to be strengthened, to be
blameless in holiness before our God and Father when
our Lord Jesus comes with all his people. Amen.*
—1 Thessalonians 3:13

We talk about how to keep our hearts healthy, at least in the
physical sense. We recognize the sadness of heart disease as it
destroys people's lives. As true as it is in our physical nature,
it's also true in the spiritual sense. What are we doing to avoid
spiritual heart disease? What are we doing to strengthen our
hearts on a daily basis?

The heart muscle pumps as long as it can no matter how
we take care of it. The problem comes in when we neglect it for
too long, when we eat all the wrong things and never exercise,
or when we act as though what we do has no consequence. The
truth is what we do matters, especially in matters of the heart.

That heart-thumping evangelist Jonathan Edwards said this:
"See that your chief study be about your heart: that there God's
image may be planted; that there His interests be advanced . . .
that there the love of holiness grows."

The heart has a big job to do. Today and every day, check in
with your spirit and make sure your heart is being nourished. Ask
God to keep your heart and your mind in Christ Jesus. That way,
you'll always have a healthy heart.

IN THE FLOW

*Whatever else I do today, Lord, help me be aware of my heart.
Protect it, shape it, and strengthen it according to your will and
purpose. I thank you for loving me so much. Amen.*

LOVE SAYS, "I'M SORRY!"

Above all, show sincere love to each other, because love
brings about the forgiveness of many sins.
—1 Peter 4:8

Love is a multifaceted thing and one of its best attributes is that
it allows us to forgive each other when we mess up. Imagine if
you got a scratch on your hand, then you got a bruise on your
ankle, and then a scrape on your knee. Now imagine what you'd
look like in a pretty short order if those scrapes and scratches
didn't heal. What if you had to walk around wearing every one of
those bruises for the rest of your life?

Fortunately, God designed us so that we can fall down, get
a few scrapes, dust ourselves off, and walk on again. In a pretty
short time we'll be healed and good as new.

The same opportunity is yours when it comes to healing
the bumps and bruises in your relationship life. The people you
love sometimes cause you to feel a bit bruised. Sometimes they
cut you to the quick, and you feel like even a bandage won't fix
it. The truth is, love can fix it. Love is the one thing that can
make everything that goes haywire, okay again. Love means you
know just when to say, "I'm sorry," and just when to receive an
apology from someone else.

It's a new day and a new opportunity to heal a bruise and
make things whole again with someone you love.

IN THE FLOW

Lord, I thank you that you love me so much you forgive me over
and over again. Remind me often to do the same for others and to
remember that it's good to say, "I'm sorry." Amen.

LOVE . . . THERE'S NO FAKING IT!

Love should be shown without pretending.
—Romans 12:9

No matter how we address the idea of love, one thing remains true, you simply can't pretend to love something you don't. Sure, you can try it on, test it out, and see if it happens, but eventually you'll set it aside because it simply wasn't genuine. It simply wasn't the real thing.

Of course, great imitations are out there, those experiences that seem real or pass as love for a time, but then can't sustain, and so fade away. As a way to gauge this for yourself, put God into the equation. What if his love wasn't genuine? What if he was only pretending to love you? Where would you be?

God can never be anything but genuine and real. He is love. He can only be love. We fall far short of that mark, but he loves us anyway. He says to keep trying. Keep following my example and I'll help you get a sense, a better idea of what real love is all about. He has provided us with amazing examples.

Mother Teresa said this about love: "Spread love everywhere you go: First of all in your own house . . . let no one ever come to you without leaving better and happier." You can't fake that kind of love. Share the authentic, genuine, unmistakable love in your heart and make it real in all your relationships.

IN THE FLOW

Lord, you are such a great teacher. Teach me to love fully and completely, genuinely and joyfully for your sake and the sake of others. Let me spread love every place I go today. Amen.

February 5

The Problem . . . With Love

*We even take pride in our problems, because we know
that trouble produces endurance, endurance produces
character, and character produces hope.*
—Romans 5:3-4

The truth is this. Love is not the problem, it's the solution.
Certainly soap operas and Harlequin romances carry on about
the problem of love, but maybe love isn't the problem at all.
Maybe if we handle any problem with love, the right kind and
degree of love, we have reason to hope.

Hope keeps us going and growing. When we show our
willingness to endure the hard things, to grow past fears and
obstacles, and to keep our eyes on the One who can change
things, it makes a difference. Handling a problem with love
instead of fear brings us into the place where change is possible.
It brings us face to face with the Holy Spirit, who can then
intercede for us and bring us back to safety and peace.

It's been said that "the will of God will never take you
where the grace of God cannot keep you." You can handle your
problems with despair, or you can handle your problems with
God's love. May your heart be filled with hope as you seek every
solution through love!

In the Flow

*Lord, I don't always know how to tap into your love. I try hard to do
anything I can to fix a problem and then I come to you exhausted
and weary. Help me come to you first and fill me with hope. Amen.*

OH, FOR GOODNESS' SAKE!

*Let's not get tired of doing good, because in time
we'll have a harvest if we don't give up.*
—Galatians 6:9

If you're the kind of person whose heart goes out to nearly everyone you meet, who tries to do a kind deed, or several, every day, and who pays attention to the things members of your family all want, you may get a little weary. After all, you're taking on a big job and you do that job without hesitation. You're gifted at goodness! So, what happens when you just can't do one more good deed even if it rings your doorbell and demands attention?

Chances are, you don't really think of all those benevolent things you do in this way, but it's also a good chance that you do grow tired of being the one who reaches out first. You may simply begin to wonder if what you do makes any difference at all.

God sees you, and he sees what you do. Those are good reasons to keep going all by themselves. Another reason is that he has given you a spirit of giving. Yes, there's a lot of work to do. But, one day, there will be a harvest and you will have the joy and pleasure of seeing some of your work as it plays out on the heavenly broadcast coming sometime soon.

Don't give up! Your good deeds make a difference to every person's life you touch. So, for goodness' sake, take a bow! You deserve a little standing ovation today.

IN THE FLOW

Lord, you know it does my heart good to do the things I can for others. Thank you for giving me a spirit of compassion and giving. Guide me to give in ways that please you. Amen.

LOVE IS THE BEST INGREDIENT

Better a meal of greens with love than a plump calf with hate.
—Proverbs 15:17

Most of us like to entertain, or at least we like to eat. Good food is conducive to good conversation. Friendships blossom, love grows, people are happy. So why do we need a proverb to remind us about this fact?

If you've ever taken part in a meal where everyone sat stone cold and was silent, where no amount of tasty gourmet delights could change the atmosphere in the room, then you understand the point here. You can eat grilled cheese with someone you love and feel like it was a gourmet treat or you can eat roast duck with someone you don't care for and hardly be able to swallow the mint sauce.

The lesson here is also a good reminder about the attitude we may have toward life. We might think we'd be happier if we had more money or a bigger house or prettier clothes. We might think love comes with more status in a job or in the community. The truth is that love doesn't care about how much money you make or how often you eat at a fancy restaurant.

Love cares about just one thing . . . your heart. If your heart is right, right with God and full of love, salad greens will be morsels from heaven because all will be right with the world.

IN THE FLOW

Lord, I know that I aspire to having more material things and a better job, but help me be grateful for what I have and for the people who love me. Amen.

COMPLETE IN LOVE

If you love only those who love you, what reward do you have?
Don't even the tax collectors do the same? And if you greet only
your brothers and sisters, what more are you doing? Don't even the
Gentiles do the same? Therefore, just as your heavenly Father is
complete in showing love to everyone, so also you must be complete.
—Matthew 5:46-48

Matthew reminds us that love isn't just about the people we're comfortable with, or the people who make us happy, or the people we relate to in some special way. Love is about our neighbors. It's about people we haven't met and never will. It's about doing what we can in the name of love for humankind. That's complete love, not excluding anyone simply because we don't have a personal kinship with them.

The ancient philosopher Tertullian said, "It is our care for the helpless, our practice of loving kindness, that brands us in the eyes of many of our opponents. 'Look! . . . How they love one another! Look how they are prepared to die for one another."

Love is an action word and it is our mission to become better lovers, better givers, and better caretakers of others. That is what completes us. Reach out in love today.

IN THE FLOW

Father, I am a neophyte in the arena of love. I love those who are near me, but I often neglect to seek out and embrace those outside my personal circle of friends. Help me be willing to love one more person today. Amen.

February 9

Won't You Be My Neighbor?

The commandments . . . are all summed up in one word: You
must love your neighbor as yourself. *Love doesn't do anything
wrong to a neighbor; therefore love is what fulfills the Law.*
—Romans 13:9-10

If you grew up in a neighborhood, or you watched Mr. Rogers as
a kid, you might think that neighbors are those people who live
on your block. They're the people who watch out for your house
when you're out of town and the ones who stop by with a gift on
your birthday. They know you and love you.

But, these are not your only neighbors. You have neighbors
at work, people who have an office next to yours. Your newspaper
carrier and your hair dresser are also your neighbors and so is the
guy three states over who isn't on your Christmas card list.

Today's a good day to expand your definition of a neighbor.
Touch the life of someone you meet at the local coffee shop or
someone who sits by you on the subway. Take some groceries
to a shut-in. Your neighbors are everywhere, and they're only a
thought away.

When Jesus summed up the Ten Commandments with just
two, he was talking about love. Love your neighbor as yourself
and show God you know what it means to be neighborly.

In the Flow

*Lord, I am a good neighbor sometimes. I try to watch out for those
around me but I confess that I don't often think about the people I
pass by on the street. Help me see them too. Help me reach out in love
wherever you lead me. Amen.*

ANOTHER TO-DO LIST

People plan their path, but the LORD secures their steps.
—Proverbs 16:9

Are you a list maker? You know, you write out the things you'll do tomorrow, jotting notes to yourself about what you hope to achieve. You may not get all of it done, but at least it's on a list. Then you walk out the door and you forget to take the list. You strive to remember each thing you had so carefully noted, but somehow still arrive back home with the most important one of all left undone.

Setting goals and making plans are both good things. In fact, it's wise indeed to make plans for the things you anticipate. The Proverb here, though, reminds us of one important fact. Planning provides an invitation to pray. Only God can secure the way for you and create the opportunities that will bring the desired result.

What if you start your to-do list like this: Things I have to do tomorrow. No. 1: Pray. No. 2: Thank God for today because he created it for me. No. 3: Get some guidance about the things on my to-do list.

It's a new day and a new opportunity to makes some plans. Include your heavenly Father in your to-do list and it won't matter if you leave the house without your list. He knows what you need to get done.

IN THE FLOW

Lord, you know that I have a lot of things to accomplish today. I know that I can't do one of them without you. Please be with me today and help me get all my tasks done. Amen.

LOVE NOTES

If I speak in tongues of human beings and
of angels but I don't have love,
I'm a clanging gong or a clashing cymbal.
—1 Corinthians 13:1

Remember that crafty woman Delilah? She tried over and over again to sweet-talk Samson into telling her the secret of his strength. He finally succumbed to her wiles and ended up losing every ounce of strength he had, along with his hair. Delilah may have had the voice of an angel, but she didn't have love.

Adolph Hitler had a powerful voice too. He convinced millions of people that he wanted only their good and then turned the tables on them, showing his true face as one of the most evil men in history.

When we listen to politicians, theologians, teachers, and others who could cause us to follow them, we must listen with an ear for more than their words. We must seek to hear them from the heart, to discern the real music in their voices. Only then will we know if they speak from love or if they are driven by selfishness and loathing.

We need to speak with love to each other, as a gentle voice of harmonious notes. Let us be soothing and kind and most of all, speak from the heart to each other.

IN THE FLOW

Lord, it isn't always easy to know who to trust, to figure out the good guys from the bad ones, but you know who they are. Help us hear with our ears tuned to you so that we can know the ones who truly speak with love. Amen.

HOPE FOR A TROUBLED HEART

A joyful heart brightens one's face, but a
troubled heart breaks the spirit.
—Proverbs 15:13

A smile and a frown / Walk in the rain, / One with great joy— /
One just to complain. / The smile draws light / From the good
things about, / While the frown sees the shadows / That only
cast doubt. / They pause for a moment / On reaching the town,
/ The smile looks up / And the frown looks down.

—K. Moore

Whatever is happening inside the heart and mind steals across the
face and shows up wrapped in joy or sorrow. As you walk around
today, make it a point to study the faces of those who are near
you, looking for signs of what may be stirring in their hearts at
that moment. When you see a face with a great, bright smile,
thank God for the joy that person knows and was able to share
with you as they passed. When you see one with a broken spirit,
cast down by the burdens of life, ask God to strengthen and
renew that person.

Your ministry today is about standing on your feet, watching
out for others, and praying for their good. May this be a day
when your heart is not troubled, but smiles with the eyes of faith.

IN THE FLOW

Lord, help me notice the faces of those I meet today. Help me peer
inside their hearts and offer prayers of thanksgiving. You are the
great Source of all that brings real joy to our lives. Thank you for
giving us reasons to smile. Amen.

THE EYES OF FAITH

We live by faith and not by sight.
—2 Corinthians 5:7

Edward Teller is known for this wise saying . . . "When you get to the end of all the light you know and it's time to step into the darkness of the unknown, faith is knowing that one of two things will happen: either you will be given something solid to stand on, or you will be taught how to fly."

Sometimes your steps are uncertain. You feel like you're walking in the dark and waiting for God to give you a flashlight. Like a person in dense fog, you progress, get to the next spot, and notice that you can actually see just a little bit of the road ahead. You walk in the fog with faith.

When we're blinded by the fog that life can sometimes bring, it helps to remember these words from Helen Keller: "If the blind put their hand in God's, they find their way more surely than those who see but have not faith nor purpose."

God wants to walk with you and be your vision, your sight. He alone knows the path so well that he can keep your feet from stumbling. Today as you step into the world, ask him to come alongside you, to direct your steps and be your eyes. You can walk blindly, or you can walk with the eyes of faith, knowing that each step leads you where your Father would have you go.

IN THE FLOW

Lord, be with me today as I go about my business. Sometimes I think I know exactly where I'm going and sometimes I don't. Either way, I want to put my life in your hands, safe in faith. Amen.

JESUS WANTS YOU FOR A VALENTINE

*Now faith, hope, and love remain—these three
things—and the greatest of these is love.*
—1 Corinthians 13:13

Valentine's Day may have pagan origins, but its roots don't really
matter to those of us who understand and practice love. We know
it's important to spread love wherever we go in as many ways as we
can and to show the Ultimate Source of love to others.

As we exchange hearts and flowers thinking about the people
we love, let us remember why love exists in the world in any
form. It exists because our Creator is the author of all love and
he loved us first. He was the first Valentine.

You can define love for yourself with anything from a love of
chocolate to a love of the symphony. You can imagine it with the
love you feel for someone close to you. You experience it more
fully, though, when you go directly to your Father and plug in to
the love he has for you. With his love, you grow stronger. With
his love you can move mountains of insecurity and trouble and
leaven them behind. You then become all that he meant you to
be, a living, generous example of who he is today, tomorrow, and
always. Love is his motivation. Love is the result.

Jesus wants to spread his love and his heart of truth and joy
to everyone you meet. Go on, make some new Valentines. The
world needs a little more of his love.

IN THE FLOW

Lord, help me love others the way you love them. Amen.

What Motivates You to Do Good?

*Let's also think about how to motivate each
other to show love and to do good works.*
—Hebrews 10:24

Most of us want to do good things. We are interested in the
well-being of others and are motivated in that interest in a variety
of ways and for a host of reasons. For some, doing good comes
naturally. Compassion and empathy motivate our spirits. God's
love then pushes us to do even more.

For others, a sense of social activism drives the desire to take
on humanity and do good deeds. Some of us feel compelled
to do good things because of our social position or status in a
community. We do good, but our hearts are not necessarily in it.

What makes the difference? The key is to see if any of the
motivation for what we do comes from love. How much do
you have to think about the good things you do? How much
do you expect in return? How much publicity and ego-boosting
do you want about the things you do?

Let us choose to do good in any way that we can for those in
our midst today.

In the Flow

*Lord, there are people in real need all around me. Help me love
them enough to do what I can simply because you have made it
possible for me to act and because of my love for you. Amen.*

WHAT'D YOU SAY?

What fills the heart comes out of the mouth. Good people
bring out good things from their good treasure. But evil
people bring out evil things from their evil treasure.
—Matthew 12:34-35

Pascal remarked that "kind words do not cost much, yet they
accomplish much." What does it mean to you when someone
says the right thing at the right time? Words of encouragement
and support, words of love and caring are all part of what cause
us to thrive as human beings. The words that come from the
heart of a loving person offer healing.

It's not surprising then that what we speak to each other is so
important. What you say can stay in the mind and heart of another
person for all the years of their life. If you offer good words, kind
thoughts, and loving messages, then you add to the health and
positive growth of someone else. If you allow the harsh words, the
negative attitudes, and the cruel behaviors to come out, you can
crush the spirit and change the way that person embraces life.

What you say matters. If you speak from the heart, let it come
from a source of love. If you speak from anger or insecurity or
from some other depression of the mind, you may do great harm.

Today, you can choose how you will speak and what kind of
message you will deliver. Make it a great day for someone to hear
from you.

IN THE FLOW

Lord, help me speak kindly to others, to give what I can, and to share
my heart in truth and love. Amen.

IT'S NOISY OUT THERE!

*Peace I leave with you. My peace I give you. I give to you
not as the world gives. Don't be troubled or afraid.*
—John 14:27

Some days it's difficult to get your head above the noise. It might
be the literal noise of traffic or construction or the person on the
phone in the cubicle next to yours. It might simply be the noise
in your head of too many worries or too many things to do so
that you're feeling overwhelmed.

John reminds us in this passage that Jesus left us with a gift
when he ascended back into heaven. He left us something the
world cannot give us. He left us his peace.

We can tap into him at any time and he will show us how
to get back to him, how to feel the depth of spirit that brings
us peace again. He alone can provide that measure of peace, the
kind that stills the troubled waters of our minds.

IN THE FLOW

*Lord, thank you for providing a way for me to come back to you and
renew my strength and rest in peace. Grant me peace of mind and
soul and spirit today. Amen.*

LIVING OUT YOUR PURPOSE

Therefore, my loved ones, just as you always
obey me, not just when I am present
but now even more while I am away, carry out your own
salvation with fear and trembling. God is the one who enables
you both to want and to actually live out his good purposes.
—Philippians 2:12-13

When Rick Warren wrote his life-changing book, *The Purpose Driven Life*, he helped us develop an awareness of how important our relationship with God is.

God designed us intentionally, and he alone knows what he has called us to do. No amount of self-searching will get us to the answer.

You may still be hoping to discover your life purpose, feeling slightly off center, somewhat less than fulfilled in your current career. If something is nagging you, causing you to be uncomfortable, urging you to shift your attention in a new direction, then today is a good day to stop and listen. Today is the day to go back to your Father for clear guidance and direction.

As Albert Einstein once said, "The life of an individual only has meaning insofar as it aids in making the life of every living thing nobler and more beautiful. Life is sacred, that is to say, it is the supreme value to which all other values are subordinate."

IN THE FLOW

Lord, thank you for loving me so much and for designing me for a very real purpose. Help me keep coming back to you for guidance until the way is clear. Amen.

WHEN NOTHING FITS

Don't be conformed to the patterns of this world,
but be transformed by the renewing of your minds
so that you can figure out what God's will
is—what is good and pleasing and mature.
—Romans 12:2

Sometimes you may feel like a square peg in a round hole. No matter how much effort you put into getting in line with the thinking of the team at your office or the friends in your circle or the people in your Bible study, you're just not on the same page. Is it you or is it them?

It's probably both. It may be a good thing that you're struggling to fit, because the truth just may be that you DON'T. That's okay. Even if the group you're part of is doing wonderful things for the community, or building a new vision for the company or finding a new mission, they may not be a part of your unique calling. You don't fit for a reason. God created a little discomfort in you to get you moving again.

You're God's child and so you always fit with him. You fit into a great design that he constructed and only you can do the part he made you to do. Go out today and be purposeful about your choices. Give God every opportunity to shape you and mold you so you fit according to his will and purpose.

IN THE FLOW

Lord, help me see what you see. Help me be what you want me to be and give me the courage to be uniquely transformed by your loving hand. Amen.

WAS IT EVER ALL ABOUT YOU?

People whose lives are based on selfishness think about
selfish things, but people whose lives are based on the Spirit
think about things that are related to the Spirit.
—Romans 8:5

A few people in the world grow up with so much privilege that
they believe everything is about them.

Most of us realize there's another side to life, and that we're
not all there is, but we probably have days when we'd rather
think about ourselves first. It may be a temporary selfishness,
until we remember Jesus. We'd be hard pressed to think of a time
that he wasn't very aware of the people around him. Of course,
Jesus was a selfless giver.

In terms of things of the Spirit, we may need to check
in with ourselves to see how we're doing. How good are we
at putting others first? How conscious are we of the rest of
humanity?

Was it ever all about you? Yes. In fact, at one point in history
it was indeed about you. Jesus gave his life for one reason only,
selflessly, lovingly . . . why? Because it was all about you!

It's your day to show him what you have to give back. Let
his Spirit be your guide.

IN THE FLOW

Lord, you are so compassionate and giving. Remind me to lean in
to you and then open my heart and my hands to those who need me.
Amen.

THE STRENGTH OF TEN PEOPLE

Therefore, the LORD God, the holy one of Israel, says:
In return and rest you will be saved; quietness
and trust will be your strength.
—Isaiah 30:15

Are you good about lifting weights to strengthen your upper body or to give some tone to the rest of you? Do you meditate and pray to strengthen your soul and your spirit? Bravo for you if you do these things. But most of you only have friends who do these things.

Think about what you admire about a strong person. Some people you know have a kind of Samson strength where they can lift nearly anything, but they are still foolish about the way they conduct their lives. Some people have a deep resolve, an inner strength, that tells you not to mess with them at all because they know who they are and have unshakable faith.

You may not often feel like you have the strength of ten men, but God knows your potential. He knew how to build you and create a strength in you that is undeniable. It doesn't depend on you, it depends on him. Whenever you are weak, God is strong.

Show him your spiritual muscles today.

IN THE FLOW

Lord, thank you for the strength you continue to give me. Raise me
up past my weaknesses, to become stronger in you. Amen.

GOD'S COWORKERS

Each one had a role given to them by the Lord: I planted,
Apollos watered, but God made it grow. Because of this, neither
the one who plants nor the one who waters is anything, but
the only one who is anything is God who makes it grow.
—1 Corinthians 3:5-7

Thinking about your coworkers at the office or those who are part of your fellowship team is one thing. Thinking about having God sitting next to you, just down the aisle, one cubicle over, is another. The truth is, that's a good picture to keep in mind. You are meant to be part of God's team, working with him to accomplish his mission on earth. In fact, that's your main job. It's the one he brought you here to do.

In his love and mercy, he allows us to shine. Sometimes he lets us lead others right to him. Sometimes he lets us influence the lives of others so that they are changed in ways that please him. Whether we're a televangelist causing twenty million viewers to come to Christ or a church youth worker bringing one young teen into the fold, we're still nothing more than part of the team. We were given the opportunity to plant the seed or refresh the spirit of someone else, but only God has the role of opening the heart in such a way that the seed takes root and the spirit grows in faith. We each have a job to do.

Remember, in all that you do today, God is cheering you on.

IN THE FLOW

Lord, thank you for allowing me to play on your team. I know that
sometimes I get in there and make things happen by your love and
mercy. Help me create those moments today when someone else might
see you more clearly. Amen.

YOU HAVE AN INHERITANCE RIGHT NOW!

The Holy Spirit is the down payment on our inheritance,
which is applied toward our redemption as God's own
people, resulting in the honor of God's glory.
—Ephesians 1:14

The day you recognized that you were a child of a loving Father, when you chose to bear his name and his resemblance to the rest of the world, you were given an inheritance. He left you a portion to make your life a bit easier right now. He gave you a down payment in the form of the Holy Spirit.

What does it mean to have free access to God's Spirit? How does that help you right now? J. B. Phillips said, "Every time we say, 'I believe in the Holy Spirit,' we mean that we believe that there is a living God able and willing to enter a human personality and change it."

That's not the end of our inheritance, though. The Holy Spirit also dispenses gifts to us. They are gifts to help us live our lives in the best ways, able to accomplish the tasks at hand. He offers gifts like kindness and goodness and self-control. He directs our steps as long as we're willing to walk with him.

Spend your inheritance wisely and joyfully. It is the Father's gift to you today.

IN THE FLOW

Lord, you have freely loved and freely given so much to me. Please give me the wisdom to share my rich inheritance with others according to your will and purpose. Amen.

The Light and the Promise

Your word is a lamp before my feet and a light for my journey.
I have sworn, and I fully mean it: I will keep your righteous rules.
—Psalm 119:105-6

Did you ever find yourself in a situation where you felt utterly alone and in the dark? You were uncertain about the next steps and you wondered if you would end up in dismal failure or even if you might die? It's possible in that kind of situation that you might call out to God for help, asking him to light your path and guide your next steps. Along with that request is perhaps your bargaining position, your promise that if God does what you ask of him, you'll do something in return for him.

This psalm causes us to consider two important things. One is that you may encounter darkness at any time. You may find yourself holding on for dear life, gasping for fresh air. You may need more light for the journey at any time.

Once you're relaxed again, you need to be mindful of what happens to your thinking, what happens to your promises. You've been given a precious guide for all that happens to you through God's word, an opportunity to rest and smooth out the bumps life brings. When you rest in him, you also refuel and refresh yourself in a way that strengthens your path and allows you to carry on his work and fulfill your promises to him.

Today, it's your day to shine for him once again.

In the Flow

Lord, you are the oxygen, the air we breathe. Please help me shine
your light wherever I am today and not wait for rough air to do so,
but instead ensure the path is smooth for anyone I meet. Amen.

WHAT TO WEAR TODAY

Don't let loyalty and faithfulness leave you. Bind
them on your neck; write them on the tablet of your
heart. Then you will find favor and approval
in the eyes of God and humanity.
—Proverbs 3:3-4

As you go about the business of getting dressed and preparing
for the day, think about your outfit a bit more carefully. How
will you adorn yourself? One way is to add a great smile to your
choice for the day, another is to don a new necktie or perhaps a
new scarf around your throat. The writer of Proverbs suggests
that we remember to wear loyalty and faithfulness today.

Loyalty and *faithfulness* have almost become words of the
past. We certainly don't experience loyalty from the brands we
buy, the places where we've worked for twenty years, or even the
friends we've nurtured over time.

You can change that, though. You can choose to stick
your neck out and take a stand for loyalty. You can be loyal and
faithful yourself no matter what else the world may have to offer.
When you do, you'll be dressed for success. You'll be ready to
lead others and inspire them to shop for similar adornments.

As you get dressed today, put on loyalty and faithfulness.
You'll find favor in God's sight and he'll approve of your style.

IN THE FLOW

Lord, help me show my faithful heart to those around me. Keep me
dressed for your success as I stay loyal to you and the work you've put
me here to do. Amen.

THOUGHTS OF TRUST

Those with sound thoughts you will keep in peace, because they trust in you. Trust in the LORD forever, for the LORD is a rock for all ages.
—Isaiah 26:3-4

If there's anything missing in the world today, it's a sense of trust. Most of us feel an undefined concern about all aspects of life because it's hard to know what to trust, what to rely on. Your insurance carriers may want you to think of them as the "rock," the ones you can lean on when times are difficult. Yet, when you call, they may not be there as fully subscribed as they made things sound.

In order to live with a heart of peace and to have thoughts that are grounded and sound, you actually need to have a rock. You need to know there is a place for you to go that is unchanging, always available, and completely trustworthy. That describes only one being in this world and the next . . . Jesus. You have a foundation of trust in him that you can have in no other.

You're anchored to the Source of all life, and he will keep you safe. Yes, hardships will come, days will bring tumult and chaos, but nothing can shake the foundation of someone who trusts the rock of Heaven. Trust him. He'll give you the peace that passes all understanding right now.

IN THE FLOW

Lord, it is so crazy in my life sometimes that I don't know where to turn. Of course, that's when I need you the most and when I need to trust you the most. Please help me stand firmly on the foundation of your love and trust you for all I need. Amen.

February 27

Testing . . . 1, 2, 3!

All the ways of people are pure in their eyes, but the LORD tests the motives. Commit your work to the LORD, and your plans will succeed.
—Proverbs 16:2-3

When you set out to accomplish something new, do you ask yourself the questions, "Why am I doing this and who am I doing it for?" Most of us have a lot of sound reasons for the things we do. We are motivated by a desire to get ahead, to create more opportunities for ourselves and those around us. We're motivated by a passion for our work or a commitment to our families.

Proverbs 16 reminds us that commitment to ourselves and our families is important, but it's the commitment we make to the Lord that will offer us the biggest chance for success. Committing to him first makes great sense. After all, we want to do his work effectively and well and we want to make a difference.

You're right to make plans and you're right to go after fresh opportunities and promotions and those things that build a fruitful foundation for your family, but you have to check in now and then, actually daily, with the Lord. You have to commit your work to him so that your motivations are pure and sound.

God wants you to succeed. He wants your work to be blessed. He gave you the gifts you have to accomplish great things.

In the Flow
Lord, I'm off and running again, but before I go, remind me that I am working for you first and foremost. Inspire me and keep me motivated in ways that are healthy and that will serve you and my family well. Amen.

THE PLACE WHERE YOU STAND

Moses said, "I'm here." Then the LORD said, "Don't come any closer! Take off your sandals, because you are standing on holy ground."
—Exodus 3:4-5

How do we come into God's presence? How often do we recognize the place where we stand—when we talk to him, when we say our prayers, when we express our faith and our belief—as a holy space?

God's request was simple, yet it required one thing of Moses. It meant that he had to listen and obey. It meant that he had to understand that this was indeed an important moment in their relationship, for God was inviting Moses into his inner circle. It connected Moses most directly to the earth and perhaps gave him a way to feel God's presence even more.

We're not always inclined to remember God's holiness on a conscious level. We may not think of our conversations with him as taking place on holy ground, and yet that is where we stand every time we approach him with a humble heart, with a desire to get closer to him, with an understanding of our own humanity. God is holy.

IN THE FLOW

Lord, I thank you for loving me so much that you're willing to let me share your friendship and be part of your inner circle. Help me be worthy of your love today and be mindful of those places that are holy and set apart unto you. Amen.

February 29

Being Truly Happy

*The one whose wrongdoing is forgiven, whose sin is covered over,
is truly happy! The one the LORD doesn't consider guilty—in
whose spirit there is no dishonesty—that one is truly happy!*
—Psalm 32:1-2

Perhaps it is a good way to leave the month of February, the month where we at least give a passing thought to love and what it means to us, the month where we're reminded more fully of our connection to others, to look at what makes us truly happy.

The truth is we can only be truly happy when our hearts are right with God. We make them right by offering ourselves to him and to his service. He helps us get it right by forgiving our many blunders and unfortunate choices. God loves us, and that is truly reason to be light-hearted.

Today, we have a clean slate of options. We have a chance once again to come to our Father and ask him to show us the way to forgiveness. We can lay our burdens down, for his way leads to truth and light. Filled with his incredible light, our hearts become bigger. We're like the Grinch at Christmas while our hearts swell up five times beyond what they were. That's what makes us happy!

In the Flow

Lord, thank you for giving me the opportunity to be happy in you. Thank you for changing my blunders into chances to draw closer to you. Thanks for giving me a peaceful spirit and a light heart. Amen.

March

The LORD bless you and keep you.

The LORD make his face shine on you. . . .

The LORD lift up his face to you

and grant you peace.

Numbers 6:24-26

IT'S A GREAT DAY TO SHINE!

From the rising of the sun to where it sets, God, the
LORD God, speaks, calling out to the earth. From
Zion, perfect in beauty, God shines brightly.
—Psalm 50:1-2

Augustine of Hippo said, "Ask the earth and the sea, the plains and the mountains, the sky and the clouds, the stars and the sun, the fish and animals, and all of them will say, 'We are beautiful because God made us.' This beauty is their testimony to God."

What is our testimony to God? Do we see the beauty that he has so graciously bestowed on us in the landscapes that surround us and the skies that cover us? Do we see the beauty in others, within ourselves, and in God himself?

The psalmist reminds us that God is perfect in beauty and shines brightly. Perhaps today we can open our eyes to his gifts of beauty. Let's start by thanking God for doting on us like beloved children, making sure we have an environment where we can thrive, giving us everything we need to be nourished and strong. Thank him also for the beauty found in relationships that bless our homes and hearts.

God gave us life for one purpose, so we could share in a glorious relationship with him. Let's show him what we can do. Let's be his testimony!

IN THE FLOW

Lord, thank you for loving me so much that you allow me to be a light for you. Shine on me so that I can reflect you in all that I do. Amen.

WE'RE STILL IN TRAINING

*Our human parents disciplined us for a little while, as it
seemed best to them, but God does it for our benefit so that we
can share his holiness. No discipline is fun while it lasts, but it
seems painful at the time. Later, however, it yields the peaceful
fruit of righteousness for those who have been trained by it.*
—Hebrews 12:10-11

When we think of people in training, we may think of athletes
who consciously work to perfect the game of their choice or the
prima ballerina who spends hours literally on her toes.

Discipline feels better if we buy into its benefits somehow. As
we were growing up, being trained and nurtured by our parents,
we may not have appreciated disciplinary measures and yet, we
might honestly say, those actions helped shape who we are today.

God is our divine Parent, and in his love for us, he also
shapes and molds us. His discipline is meant to bring us closer to
him. The obedience he demands helps us become more than we
would be without him. As we learned to respect our parents and
teachers, those who stood in authority over us as kids, we learn
to respect our heavenly Father as well.

It's a good day to accept the beauty of discipline. Get out
and perfect your swing, set the bar higher, study the Word . . .
for God has a great desire to shape you into one of his own.

IN THE FLOW

*Lord, I'm not always happy to go through trials or work on the
things that are hard. Help me trust your hand in all that I face,
seeing your work perfected in me as much as possible. Thank you for
loving me so much. Amen.*

LIVING IN GRACE

*Therefore, once you have your minds ready for action and you
are thinking clearly, place your hope completely on the grace
that will be brought to you when Jesus Christ is revealed.*
—1 Peter 1:13

Dietrich Bonhoeffer wrote, "Cheap grace is grace without
discipleship, grace without the cross, grace without Jesus Christ,
living and incarnate. Costly grace is the treasure hidden in the
field; for the sake of it a man will gladly go and sell all that he has."

Most of us appreciate the sense that we live in God's grace.
We like knowing we can fall down and get up again without a big
penalty. We like knowing God takes us back again after we make
a mess of the life he's given us.

We're living right now in his incredible grace. We walk in
it, drink it in, and where we can, we direct it toward others. We
extend the hand of grace to friends and complete strangers. This
is the kind of action God wants us to take because of the hope
he has placed within us. Our hearts and minds are poised and
ready to be his voices, his hands, and his tireless feet. We have the
treasure of seeing God in everything, of realizing that his hand
alone brought all that we have into fruition.

Be gracious today to yourself and those you meet along the
way.

IN THE FLOW

*Lord, I am humbled by your grace, by your forgiveness, and your
tenderness toward me. Help me share those very same gifts with
everyone around me. Amen.*

THE POOL OF BLESSINGS

*The LORD bless you and keep you. The LORD make his
face shine on you and be gracious to you. The LORD
lift up his face to you and grant you peace.*
—Numbers 6:24-26

Charles Dickens commented that we should "Reflect upon our
present blessings—of which every man has many—not on our
past misfortunes, of which all men have some."

As human beings, it's sometimes too easy to slip into a
pattern of rewinding our past, telling old stories to the point
where most people could fill in the blanks for us and letting those
hardships become the face we bring to the world. We can slip
back to yesterday, but is it wise?

The Dickens quotation defines another option. It says we can
reflect on our blessings, those things that are good in our lives
and offer opportunities to speak of God's love and grace.

As we go forward today, let us reflect on all that God has
given us and count the blessings he has bestowed that are
without number. Splash your face with his morning light and
refresh your mind with the joy of all that he has done. You are
his workmanship, not carved from stone, but created by love to
enjoy the blessings of his handiwork. Live today in the present
light of his grace.

IN THE FLOW

*Lord, thank you for the blessings you have brought into my life. Let
me count the blessings without end you have given me today and
shine your light for others. Amen.*

March 5

Like a Watered Garden

The LORD will guide you continually and provide for you, even in parched places. He will rescue your bones. You will be like a watered garden, like a spring of water that won't run dry.
—Isaiah 58:11

Have you ever been really thirsty? You know the kind of thirst that chugging a big glass of water or slamming down a soda just won't cure? It's easy to take getting a glass of water to quench our thirst for granted, even though much of the world struggles to find good drinking water. Many people are thirsty. Many people are parched. Yet even in those places, God offers to be a spring of water that won't run dry.

He parted the waters of the Red Sea and brought his children safely across to dry land. He guided every step and refreshed their spirits with manna and birds. He opened up veins of water from solid rocks to relieve their thirst. God continues to guide and to refresh us wherever we are. He still offers to be our living water if we reach out to him.

If you're feeling a little dry today, needing a bigger splash of his love, then take your little cup and put it out to him. He'll fill it and then he'll keep filling every cup you are willing to put in his hand. Go and get refreshed and renewed in his love today.

In the Flow

Lord, I am thirsty. Sometimes I don't even realize that I've gotten away from you, but when I do, I know I want to leave the desert I've put myself in and draw from your wellspring of living waters. Renew my heart and my life in you today. Amen.

THE ONE AND ONLY MEDIATOR

*There is one God and one mediator between God
and humanity, the human Christ Jesus, who gave
himself as a payment to set all people free.*
—1 Timothy 2:5-6

Timothy tells us here that Christ himself is our mediator with God. He stepped in on our behalf to negotiate a place for us in Heaven. As John Calvin put it, "Christ's work as Mediator was unique: it was to restore us to divine favor and to make us sons [and daughters] of God, instead of sons of men. We became heirs to a heavenly kingdom."

So, okay, you may not stop to realize your life is on trial or that you need someone to go stand in the gaps, but the truth is you do, we all do, because God alone is Holy. We're on a finite path and only God himself could devise a way to bring us back home again from this journey. That's the work God did through our Mediator, Jesus.

Today, let's give thanks for our path and remember the one who gives us life . . . life eternal. Then, let's step out in faith and see what we can do to encourage a few more of God's children to step into the fold. Bring a little bit of heaven to everyone you meet today.

IN THE FLOW

Lord, I thank you for the great sacrifice you made on my behalf. I thank you for loving me before I was even born. Thank you for the great Mediator, our one and only way back to you . . . Jesus Christ. Amen.

THE LORD IS NEAR!

The Lord is near. Don't be anxious about anything; rather bring up all of your requests to God in your prayers and petitions, along with giving thanks. Then the peace of God that exceeds all understanding will keep your hearts and minds safe in Christ Jesus.
—Philippians 4:5-7

Do you remember a moment in your childhood, perhaps when there was a big thunder and lightning storm, and your daddy wasn't yet home? You may have cuddled up by your mom, just wishing your dad would return because somehow things would be okay then.

Since then, you've weathered a lot of the storms of life and you haven't always had someone by your side to hold you and help you through. Yet, we're reminded in this Scripture that the Lord is near. Because he's near, we don't have to worry. He'll calm the storms and lead the way. He'll bring us safely back to himself and he only asks us to do one thing.

Pray. Put everything that weighs on your heart into words. Without any concern for how those words get to him, simply tell him your story. Talk to him about your life, what you feel concerned about, what you think is missing. He will hear you because the Lord is near. He's always near. It's a new day. Draw near to the Lord and he will most assuredly draw near to you.

IN THE FLOW

Lord, thank you for being with me today. I believe that you have my life in your hands and that you know all the things that bring me stress or cause me to worry. I ask you to stand by me again and bring me your gift of peace. Amen.

Come Into the Light

Hence, I will also appoint you as light to the nations
so that my salvation may reach to the end of the earth.
—Isaiah 49:6

One frequent theme of the Bible is the effect of light and what it does to illuminate truth. God spoke the light into being, making it possible for us to see his world in the backdrop of the darkness. He made it possible for us to see him and to feel the light of his face upon us. Light then serves as an intentional metaphor for guidance and the gift of his presence.

So what happens when we slip into the shadows? Sometimes we step aside from the path, take the lead away from God and walk alone. We stubbornly hold independence as a valuable asset, perhaps the best asset we have. It is valuable, but it isn't everything, especially when we cease to be dependent on God, our source of light. We can only shine for him as we stand in his presence.

You've been given the flame. You are the light. In fact, you may be the only light of God's love that some people will ever see. Your work on this planet is to shine and to help others come into God's presence for themselves.

It's a great day to turn on your high beams.

In the Flow

Lord, I know that I sometimes hide the light you've given me. Help me shine in ways that please you and help others see you in a new way. Amen.

GETTING THE BEST TREATMENT

Therefore, you should treat people in the same way that you
want people to treat you; this is the Law and the Prophets.
—Matthew 7:12

You teach people how to treat you! Your behavior causes a similar
behavior in people around you. In other words, your presence,
your posture, your smile make a big difference in how any
encounter you have with someone will go. When you offer your
best self, show your best light, it returns to you in like manner . . .
usually.

Matthew is reminding us that we need to always be aware
of the other guy. We need to take responsibility for the way
our relationships turn out because we play a big part in their
construction. If we want kindness from someone else, we need to
bring kindness to the table. If we want friendship to evolve, we
need to offer the steady hand of friendship.

Most of us want to be treated kindly and well. We want
others to value our efforts and see us as good. We want to win
their respect and create trust. These are the things that make
relationships possible and valuable.

The best way to treat any other person in your life is to
simply remember the way you like to be treated. Look at the way
God is treating you.

IN THE FLOW

Lord, I know that I can do more to create stronger and more loving
relationships with some of the people in my life. Help me be kind and
giving, in the same way that you are to me. Amen.

GETTING TO ONE MORE BIRTHDAY

So you must carefully do exactly what the LORD your God commands you. Don't deviate even a bit! You must walk the precise path that the LORD your God indicates for you so that you will live, and so that things will go well for you, and so you will extend your time on the land that you will possess.
—Deuteronomy 5:32-33

We enjoy celebrating birthdays, especially if they are someone else's. We love the sweetness of traditions filled with ice cream and cake and little birthday songs. We can celebrate and bring the wishes, but only God can actually affect the length of days we get to participate in this dance of life.

How do we know the precise path, the one that will give us the opportunity to live fully and well? Perhaps your Bible doesn't feel exactly like a road map or even a guide sometimes, but it is. It is because it was written specifically with you in mind, all with the aim of keeping you on the path. Even more, God provided a ready interpreter in the form of the Holy Spirit. He is available all the time to take requests, to help you recall Scriptures that will guide your choices, to lead you to others that will bring you closer to where you're meant to be.

If you're feeling somewhat thrown off the track today, get back to the One who will lead you any time you ask for direction.

IN THE FLOW

Lord, I do get off the track and I'm pretty sure I don't follow your plan precisely. Please help me ask for direction for any step I take so I can live according to your plans for my life. Amen.

HOW NOT TO PLEASE GOD!

There are six things that the LORD hates, seven things detestable to him: snobbish eyes, a lying tongue, hands that spill innocent blood, a heart set on wicked plans, feet that run quickly to evil, a false witness who breathes lies, and one who causes conflicts among relatives.
—Proverbs 6:16-19

You probably prefer to please God in the manner by which you address life and the people you know. Well, this Proverb directs your attention to show what you can do to NOT please God. Of course, none of these apply to you, but let's look again at one and see if you note any shades of similarity.

It may not occur to you that you could be snobbish in any way, but anything that separates us from having compassion for another human being may well hit this chord. Like Jesus' disciples who argued over who could sit next to him when he came into his kingdom, you may unconsciously elevate yourself in ways that bring snobbish eyes into play.

We are all apt to NOT please God on any given day with the things we do or say. We're not so perfectly adjusted to this world that we know how to sidestep the evils no matter how little they might seem. Today, though, is a new day and a chance to offer God our best.

IN THE FLOW

Lord, I know that I'm as guilty as anyone of doing things that do not please you. Help me take quick note of those moments and realign myself with you and your love. Thank you for loving me just as I am. Amen.

MINDING YOUR OWN BUSINESS

*Aim to live quietly, mind your own business, and
earn your own living, just as I told you.*
—1 Thessalonians 4:11

It might sound a little harsh for you to be told to "mind your
own business," but it's also wise counsel. Living quietly, going
about your business, and earning your own living are certainly
worthy goals. So what's your business?

Your profession aside, the rest of your business has to do
with your spirit, your heart, and perfecting your soul to reflect
more of the divine Spirit. Your business is to keep growing, keep
watching and learning.

Thomas à Kempis offered us this thought. He said, "A pure,
simple, and steadfast spirit is not distracted by the number of
things to be done, because it performs them all to the honor of
God, and endeavors to be at rest from self-seeking."

Tend to becoming more of the person God meant you to be.

Your work is cut out for you and today is another gracious
opportunity to see what you can do to earn the kind of living
that pays off for others because you've grown in the spirit of
truth and have so much more to give.

Go about your business with joy.

IN THE FLOW

*Lord, thank you for being involved in my business and help me be
more about becoming all that you meant me to become. Help me live
quietly and joyfully in you. Amen.*

WHAT YOU SAY MATTERS!

I tell you that people will have to answer on Judgment Day
for every useless word they speak. By your words you will
be either judged innocent or condemned as guilty.
—Matthew 12:36-37

This has to be one of the scariest Scriptures in the Bible. After all, most of us do a lot of talking. This verse is a good reminder of the benefits of being brief and holding our tongues when the need arises.

What causes us to go on and on when we would be better served to remain silent? Jesus gave us an example of effective silence and limited commentary when he was in front of Pilate, being accused of things that simply weren't true.

Many of us have a tendency to either overexplain or demand detailed explanations from someone else, and before we know it anger erupts and caution is thrown to the wind. We spew things out of our mouths that if we choose to rewind the tape later and listen might cause us to wince.

Our lesson then is to be very aware of what we say. As we lean in on the Lord, we will have the grace and the kindness to treat others with respect and love. Words like that bless everyone, and apparently even bring blessing back to us.

Let's be kind today.

IN THE FLOW

Lord, help me remember that what I say to anyone is important. Let me speak only with forethought, with kindness, and with love. Amen.

WHAT IT MEANS TO BE TRULY HAPPY

The truly happy person doesn't follow wicked advice, doesn't stand on the road of sinners, and doesn't sit with the disrespectful. Instead of doing those things, these persons love the LORD's Instruction, and they recite God's Instruction day and night! They are like a tree replanted by streams of water, which bears fruit at just the right time and whose leaves don't fade. Whatever they do succeeds.

—Psalm 1:1-3

Imagine you're a blossoming and beautiful tree; your branches bring shade to those who need to rest, your fruit nurtures hungry souls. You're perfectly designed, standing tall, bringing life and breath and sustenance. Your days are calm and cool and your leaves never fade.

What a refreshing thought! What bliss! In this form, true happiness is fulfilling the purpose of a tree and is bringing the gifts of what you have to share to others. Yes, you're absolutely a breath of fresh air.

The psalmist wants us to take a stand. When we rise in the morning and choose to share our day with God, spending time in his Word, offering prayers for his response in love and mercy, we are firmly placed in a loving relationship. Not only that, but we give God the control over what we do and he then has every opportunity to cause us to succeed.

Success brings happiness when we get to fulfill the purpose for which we were designed. We want to lift our lives up to him to sustain us every day. When we do, we have every reason to smile.

IN THE FLOW

Lord, help me come to you first, dip my toes in the refreshing waters of your presence, and be washed anew every day. I know that then I'll be happy in you. Amen.

March 15

Sprinkled Clean

Therefore, let's draw near with a genuine heart with the certainty that our faith gives us, since our hearts are sprinkled clean from an evil conscience and our bodies are washed with pure water.
—Hebrews 10:22

It's always refreshing to come clean! Sometimes you're in a showering cascade of water that begins your day, other times you're getting the refreshment that comes from confessing your fears and sorrows at the feet of Jesus. Whatever way you do it you're always a little stronger, a little more ready to face whatever life brings next.

This wonderful reflection from Jane Truax helps illustrate the point. "Botanists say that trees need the powerful March winds to flex their trunks and main branches, so that the sap is drawn up to nourish the budding leaves. Perhaps, we need the gales of life in the same way, though we dislike enduring them. A blustery period in our fortunes is often the prelude to a new spring of life and health, success and happiness, when we keep steadfast in faith and look to the good in spite of appearances."

Work today to keep steadfast in your faith despite what appears.

In the Flow

Lord, you know that trials and sorrows come to all of us. When they come to me, help me remember that you are there, keeping me rooted in you and your love. Bless this day and help the winds of suffering cease to blow in the lives of everyone who seeks you today. Amen.

WHEN YOU SIGN UP WITH GOD

I'm convinced that nothing can separate us from God's
love in Christ Jesus our Lord: not death or life, not angels
or rulers, not present things or future things, not powers
or height or depth, or any other thing that is created.
—Romans 8:38

The good news about planting your feet squarely in God's
territory is that once you do, unless you put in a big request
to be removed from the space, you are connected to him
for all eternity. You're his child and you get the benefits of a
relationship that's like no other.

In fact, Paul says with great certainty that "nothing" can
separate you from the love of God. Those are big words. Those
are words to hold on to because they affect you today and
tomorrow and always. You are part of God's family, in his will for
the rest of eternity. You inherit all that he has for you.

When you discovered the faith in your heart, the faith that
desires to walk with Jesus, the faith that is tutored by the Holy
Spirit and led by the God of the universe, you signed up forever.
Not only that, but God signed up forever with you. It was a
mutual agreement.

Today, tomorrow, and always remember that you are never
far from the love of the One who bought you at a great price.

IN THE FLOW

Lord, thank you for being with me, not just today, but always.
Thank you for loving me even more than I really understand.
Amen.

DOES ANYTHING EVER STAY THE SAME?

Jesus Christ is the same yesterday, today, and forever! Don't be misled by the many strange teachings out there.
—Hebrews 13:8-9

It's more than a comforting thought to realize that Jesus isn't going to change his stripes or the way he thinks about us. He's not going to change his mind about redeeming us or about loving us. He's the same now as he was on his first visit to earth. His intent isn't skewed by what we go through or by what we do when we explore paths that aren't really good for us.

The good news about Jesus is that your quality of life can become more beautiful right now as you walk with him. It is up to you how much you allow him to guide your path. But the difference is that you can't create your own redemption. You can't lose the weight of sin without him. Only he can do that for you and since he has already done it, you're in. You're one of his favorite people, in fact.

So, you may not stay the same. You may gain some weight, or lose it. You may find a new job, build a new home, start a new path, but nothing you do will change the relationship you have with your Redeemer. He's the same today as he ever was and loves you always.

IN THE FLOW

Lord Jesus, thank you for loving me and keeping me near you. Thank you that I can totally count on you. Help me be someone you can count on too. Amen.

GOD WORKS WITHIN US

Glory to God, who is able to do far beyond all that we could ask or imagine by his power at work within us.
—Ephesians 3:20

We were born to do the work God called us to do. Sometimes, we aren't sure what the work is. Sometimes we are afraid to check in with God about our work for fear that the assignment will be too hard or perhaps seem too easy. We think about the way we work for God with the same energy we think about the work we do at the office, or the work we do at home. With God, the definition may be slightly different, though.

Look at what George McDonald shared about this idea. "Do you think the work God gives us to do is never easy? Jesus says His yoke is easy, His burden is light. People sometimes refuse to do God's work just because it is easy. This is sometimes because they cannot believe that easy work is His work."

In other words, don't assume that you aren't doing God's work simply because you're not building houses for Habitat, or teaching in a mission field. Your ministry may well be to offer hope and encouragement to one special person in your family or in your church. Your work may be to keep pointing the way to God in gentle and affirming ways.

Today, listen for his voice and seek to answer. Do his work with great joy!

IN THE FLOW

Lord, I don't always hear you speaking. I don't always listen. Today, help me work with you to bless the life of at least one other person. Amen.

HOW BIG IS YOUR BELIEF?

As Jesus departed, two blind men followed him, crying out, "Show us mercy, Son of David." When he came into the house, the blind men approached him. Jesus said to them, "Do you believe I can do this?" "Yes, Lord," they replied. Then Jesus touched their eyes and said, "It will happen for you just as you have believed."
—Matthew 9:27-29

We may tell ourselves that if our prayer isn't answered, it simply wasn't God's will or perhaps he has a better plan. However, this verse is asking more of us than that.

This Scripture puts the ability to believe in the desired result squarely on the ones who are seeking his help. The blind men may not have been able to see Jesus, but they had a vision for what they wanted. They knew that he was the key to changing their lives.

God is in the prayer-answering business. We know that sometimes he gives us exactly what we want. Other times we wait and wonder what to do next or why we don't have more direction. Sometimes we don't feel there was an answer at all. What part did our belief play in getting the answer?

Today, let's believe what we really want is exactly what God wants for us too. Let's imagine that and then go to him believing that he will indeed honor our requests. What an incredible day this could be.

IN THE FLOW

Lord, I know I need to work on my belief system. I have to trust that you love me so much that you will heal the blindness in any area of my life. I ask you to heal me today, trusting and believing in your willingness to do so. Amen.

CHILDLIKE WONDER

*"I assure you that whoever doesn't welcome God's
kingdom like a child will never enter it." Then
he hugged the children and blessed them.*

—Mark 10:15-16

One of the things most of us love about little children is their
approach to life. They see the best of life and believe that they are
totally surrounded by love and that they are always protected.

Perhaps in part, that is the kind of innocent love God wants
us to have. It's the simple faith that believes in the goodness and
the desire of God to want only our good. It's the kind of love
that too many adults have laid to rest with fairy tales.

God loves your work as an adult. He loves your maturity
and your willingness to take risks for him. He also loves the child
within you, the one who keeps going in spite of fears, that faces
challenges knowing that your Dad will bail you out if need be.

As you go about your work today, look for opportunities
to rediscover the awe of life, the little things that God gives you
to make you smile and bring you joy. God may have answered a
prayer before you could even ask, simply out of love and because
he's always looking out for you.

Be his child today and show him your smile of love.

IN THE FLOW

*Lord, I probably do get more serious in my thoughts of you, thinking
I have to be a responsible adult about everything, forgetting to
admire your handiwork all around me. Remind me today to simply
be your child in every good way. Amen.*

YOU'RE SO BRAVE!

God didn't give us a spirit that is timid but one
that is powerful, loving, and self-controlled.
—2 Timothy 1:7

The truth is that sometimes we're afraid we'll succeed. If we succeed at something we've been putting off and telling others for years we just couldn't do, then what happens? Our excuses are gone and we have to go about inventing some new ones.

We all have fears, and some of them are grounded and some aren't and it probably would do us good to figure out the differences. Some people fear God himself. Pascal noted that "there is a virtuous fear which is the effect of faith, and a vicious fear which is the product of doubt and distrust. Persons of the one character fear to lose God; those of the other character fear to find Him."

Whatever your fears are, God did not give you a spirit of timidity. He did not put you in the world to be a wall-flower hiding behind every shadowy tree wondering what might be lurking beyond. He made you a brave soul! He gave you strength and power and the ability to discern when to act and when to simply walk on.

Remember that you have not been left defenseless. You've been given the power to achieve your goals. Have no fear, God is with you.

IN THE FLOW

Lord, please remind me that I don't do anything ever without you
being part of it. Give me the strength I need to overcome the small
obstacles of fear that would keep me stuck. Amen.

FOREVER AGO TO FOREVER FROM NOW

The days of a human life are like grass: they bloom like a wildflower;
but when the wind blows through it, it's gone; even the ground
where it stood doesn't remember it. But the LORD's faithful love is
from forever ago to forever from now for those who honor him.
—Psalm 103:15-17

Perhaps this proverb from the Sanskrit says it best in regard to how we might live our lives day by day. It says, "Look to this day . . . In it lie all the realities and verities of existence, the bliss of growth, the splendor of action, the glory of power. For yesterday is but a dream and tomorrow is only a vision. But today, well lived, makes every yesterday a dream of happiness and every tomorrow a vision of hope."

It is always a good exercise for us to look at how we are spending our time. What are we doing to make this world a little better place? In what ways will we blossom and grow?

We have real, authentic, and important work to do. We have the power to develop those things and utilize those attributes for good any time we choose to do so.

No matter how we leave our mark here, one thing is certain. God is faithful and he remembers us from forever ago to forever from now. We are part of his bloodline, family members never to be forgotten. Live this day in a way that will make you both proud.

IN THE FLOW

Lord, keep me mindful of all that I can do to live well and to share
your Spirit in any way I can. Thank you for knowing me and
keeping me safe with your love. Amen.

March 23

From Winter to Spring

Here, the winter is past; the rains have come and gone. Blossoms have appeared in the land; the season of singing has arrived, and the sound of the turtledove is heard in our land. The green fruit is on the fig tree, and the grapevines in bloom are fragrant.
—Song of Songs 2:11-13

Those of us who live in regions where we can appreciate the four seasons are particularly fond of spring. The springtime brings with it the promise of Easter, the promise of new life and hope. It's inspiring to move past the winter landscapes at rest, and watch the earth blossom anew.

Our spiritual lives may well go through a similar process. We may find ourselves feeling as though we're simply existing, lying dormant, keeping the status quo of our faith. We're neither challenged by it nor drawn to it, we simply accept that it's there, somewhere tucked away until we're ready to find it again.

But then one day, something changes within us. Spring comes to our faith and awakens us again. As you wake up to the newness of what God has for you, remind yourself of his great love, his sacrifice, and his desire to know you better. It's a new day and a chance to grow, to blossom, to become more of what God created you to become.

In the Flow

Lord, as the earth renews itself and comes back to life, I ask that you would do the same for me, renewing me, strengthening me, and refreshing my spirit. In Jesus' name I pray. Amen.

GIVING THE SPIRIT THE BRUSH-OFF

*Rejoice always. Pray continually. Give thanks in every situation
because this is God's will for you in Christ Jesus. Don't suppress
the Spirit. Don't brush off Spirit-inspired messages, but
examine everything carefully and hang on to what is good.*
—1 Thessalonians 5:16-21

Of course, we don't mean to, but sometimes we simply ignore
the Holy Spirit, actually giving him the brush-off. We're too busy
with the work we have in front of us, too busy with parenting,
too busy with figuring out what to do tomorrow, to stop and
hear what the Spirit has to say.

If we do get a nudge that awakens our memory enough to
hear his voice, we may or may not choose to listen. God gave us
ears to hear his divine inspiration, to tune into the frequency of
his voice. Of course, really hearing it comes much more easily if
we actually tune in with frequency. The more we approach him,
the easier it gets.

Today is a new opportunity to tune in to your Creator.
Listen for his voice, rejoice in all that he has given you, and pray
continually. These are the things that really make a difference.

IN THE FLOW

*Lord, help me rejoice in whatever situations arise today and seek
your voice and see your hand in all I do. Thank you for your Holy
Spirit and all he does to help me walk more closely with you. Amen.*

KEEPING YOUR WORD

"Lord, why are you about to reveal yourself to us and not to the world?" Jesus answered, "Whoever loves me will keep my word. My Father will love them, and we will come to them and make our home with them. Whoever doesn't love me doesn't keep my words. The word that you hear isn't mine. It is the word of the Father who sent me."
—John 14:22-24

Did you ever make a promise and then have to go back on it for reasons not your own? Did you ever simply choose to not keep a promise? What does it mean then for us to love God so much that we would keep his word?

Part of keeping God's word means that we open our hearts to give him room to come in and share our lives. It means we are aware of him in all we do and that we seek his guidance above all else. He gave us the opportunity to keep his word with the Scriptures. Whatever translation you feel comfortable reading, the truth is still there.

God made many promises to us and we can be sure he will keep his word. We need to pay attention when we make promises. We have to be sure that we mean what we say and that we're ready to carry out any agreements we make.

Try today to be very aware of any promises you make and do your best to honor them. Remind yourself that there is no circumstance that will prevent God from keeping his word at the appointed time. It's a two-way proposition.

IN THE FLOW

Lord, help me remember all that you have promised me and all that I have promised you and those who are dear to me. Let me always be willing to keep your word. Amen.

Don't Pretend to Love

Love should be shown without pretending. Hate evil, and hold on to what is good. Love each other like the members of your family. Be the best at showing honor to each other.
—Romans 12:9-10

None of us likes to be patronized or scammed. When we've been duped into a false hope, or even a false love, it isn't much fun.

Do we ever pretend love, though? Sadly, even the best of us fall into that less-than-loving trap from time to time. We do it when we strive to accept strangers that we find off-putting, or to adjust to family members who are on a very different track than we are in the ways they handle life. We might pretend to love them more than actually loving them as Jesus would.

Our goal, though, is to love each other authentically, like family members that we adore. We want to honor and respect each other so much that we come together with a spirit of love and put wind in one another's sails. We want to give more than we receive and offer our hands and our hearts to act for the good of those around us.

We're not always aware of someone else's motives, but we are aware of our own. As much as possible, be ready to deliver the real thing. Love your neighbors as yourself.

In the Flow

Lord, help me always be real and operate with full integrity around others. Help me honor you in the ways that I act in any given situation. Amen.

DO YOU HAVE THE RIGHT EQUIPMENT?

*May the God of peace, who brought back the great shepherd
of the sheep, our Lord Jesus, from the dead by the blood
of the eternal covenant, equip you with every good thing
to do his will, by developing in us what pleases him
through Jesus Christ. To him be the glory forever and always.*
—Hebrews 13:20-21

Whenever you start a new task or a new job, it's always a good idea
to check to be sure you have what you need to get the job done.

Our work for God is somewhat similar. He calls us and then
he equips us to get the job done. We don't always know what
we'll need so we have to rely on him for the proper equipment.

You don't know where you'll be or who you might be with
when you suddenly realize a tool is missing, something that
might have helped you be more effective. Perhaps you need more
experience with a certain kind of person, so that you know how
to handle people like that in the future. It's all about learning.

As St. Augustine said, "Since you cannot do good to all, you
are to pay special regard to those who, by the accidents of time,
or place, or circumstances, are brought into closer connection
with you."

When those things happen, you need to be prepared. May
God continue to keep your tool box full.

IN THE FLOW

*Lord, only you know the people I'll meet and what kind of
information I'll need to be an effective witness for you. Please guide
me and equip me as only you can so I'm always ready to do good.
Amen.*

Going Against the Tide

But as for Noah, the Lord approved of him. These are Noah's descendants. In his generation, Noah was a moral and exemplary man; he walked with God.

—Genesis 6:8-9

This description of Noah is captivating. Noah was going against the tide of his own community. He was out of sync with his culture. In spite of what others did around him, he continued to do what he believed was right. He continued to behave in ways that were considered moral for his time and was a man of great integrity. He walked with God.

Not to be morbid, but that's quite an epitaph. What do you suppose Noah had that others of his day didn't understand? Why weren't more people on God's side?

We live in a world where it is easy to get drawn into the things that shut out the light, that deter us from following the path of good, that keep us numb, never realizing what we're giving up. We too could be corrupted, wasting away, losing God's favor and not really even know it was happening. We could, except God is watching out for us. He has given us the key to his approval, and it's to have faith in his only Son.

He's also made a promise to us, to be with us till the end of time. We have the opportunity even now to live moral and exemplary lives and walk with God. Walk with him today.

In the Flow

Lord, help me see your hand in all that I do. Let me walk with you in the light of your redeeming love. Amen.

JUST A LITTLE HUMBLE PIE

Humble yourselves before the Lord, and he will lift you up.
—James 4:10

Did you ever have to eat "humble pie"? Pride can be a tricky thing. It can slither into our hearts like a snake on its belly, giving us the illusion that we're okay. Eve may have needed to eat a little humble pie after listening to the snake in the garden. After all, didn't the snake simply appeal to her ego, her pride, when he seduced her into taking a bite of the forbidden fruit?

Chances are good that we've all had a taste of this bitter fruit and like it or not, it rears its head again before we realize it. We can even be drawn into its clutches very innocently.

Pride tells us that we are entitled to things. We have a right to be first or to sit at the best table. We have a right to be heard or to be given special consideration. So, how do we check in with ourselves to see what our egos really don't want us to see?

We humble ourselves before God. We come prostrate before him and ask him to search us and see what is in us that should be weeded out. We seek his guidance to shape and remold us so that we are more in line with his will and his work.

We have no need to put ourselves on a pedestal. Our Father in heaven will gladly raise us up when we seek him with a humble heart. Give God all your heart today.

IN THE FLOW

Lord, I know that I am guilty of letting my ego get in the way of things. Help me lay my ego at your feet and step away from a heart filled with pride. Let me only boast of you. Amen.

DRESSED FOR SUCCESS

*And everyone, clothe yourselves with humility toward each
other. God stands against the proud, but he gives favor
to the humble. Therefore, humble yourselves under God's
power so that he may raise you up in the last day. Throw
all your anxiety onto him, because he cares about you.*
—1 Peter 5:5-7

What do you wear when you clothe yourself in humility? The
One who cares for you and loves you every day will raise you up
any time you appear before him in humble style. He wants your
heart to be filled with his spirit and his love because that's what
makes you beautiful. He chose you to do the work you're doing
and he'll outfit you for every task.

St. Francis of Assisi said this about being humble: "To do the
wondrous work God had in mind to do, he chose me. For God
has chosen the foolish things of the world to confound the wise;
the mean, contemptible, feeble things of the world to confound
the noble and great; so that the grandeur of goodness should
proceed from God, and not from his creature; so that no flesh
should boast, but that God alone should be honored."

God knows exactly what he's doing. He wants your foolish
heart to be ready to serve him every day.

IN THE FLOW

*Lord, it's so tempting to want to dress up in ways that will make
people think I'm somebody special. Help me realize that I am
somebody special, not because of anything I've done, but only because
of what you've done. Amen.*

TEST PATTERNS

Don't be conformed to the patterns of this world, but be transformed by the renewing of your minds so that you can figure out what God's will is—what is good and pleasing and mature.
—Romans 12:2

When television was in its infancy, it would complete its daily broadcast by leaving a test pattern on the screen.

Sometimes, it brings a little nostalgic thought to some of us to remember those days when there seemed to be some control over what was sent across the airwaves. There was some real intention to offer programming that was wholesome.

We've lost that, and the noise has grown far beyond television, to computer screens and telephone apps, to endless streams of information that stimulates and even distorts our worldview. We have to work harder than ever to not be drawn in, to not conform to the standards this world sets, because the bar isn't set very high.

How do we keep renewing our minds then, so we can figure out what God wants for us and what he wants us to do? How do we stay aware of whether we're conforming to this world?

The best way is just to keep recognizing that we are influenced by all that we take in. The choice is always ours. God wants us to be careful not to lose our way in the patterns of the world.

IN THE FLOW

Lord, help me think for myself, align my heart and my thoughts with yours, and live in ways that please and serve you. I ask this in Jesus' name. Amen.

April

Let your light shine before people, so

they can see the good things you do and

praise your Father who is in heaven.

Matthew 5:16

Getting Closer to Your Daddy

Because you are sons and daughters, God sent the Spirit
of his Son into our hearts, crying, "Abba, Father!"
—Galatians 4:6

Sure, you're all grown-up now and may not really think about
God as your daddy. You may not even be convinced about what
it means to have God as your Father. Your heavenly Daddy is the
one who loves you so much he found a way to keep you safe and
keep you protected forever.

More than that, he also provided the good stuff for your
daily life while you're visiting here on earth, and then he tucked
in everything you need for your return trip home to heaven. He
has a great inheritance for you, a benefits package like no other.
He plans for you to inherit the kingdom, and it just can't get
better than that.

Any time you choose, your heavenly Father is there, ready
to listen and to offer comfort and to guide you. He never closes
his door, never gets too busy to hear you, and never judges you
without giving you a chance to be heard. He's your Father and
he wants the best for you that life can bring.

It's a great day to share your heart and your mind and draw
closer to him.

In the Flow

Dear Father, thank you for loving me so much that I can come
before you with anything that's on my mind. Thank you for helping
me become the person you want me to be. Amen.

TIME TO BLOSSOM AND BEAR FRUIT

*I am the vine; you are the branches. If you remain in me and I
in you, then you will produce much fruit. . . . If you remain in
me and my words remain in you, ask for whatever you want and
it will be done for you. My Father is glorified when you produce
much fruit and in this way prove that you are my disciples.*
—John 15:5-8

If you've ever had a garden, even a container garden on your city
patio, you recognize that it takes more than just a passing interest
in your plants to make sure they grow. Actually, it takes a fair
amount of attention from you to make sure the soil is properly
prepared and the right nutrients have been applied. You have
to check to see if your plant will thrive better in the sun or the
shade and then you're off to find the watering can. So far, you've
done a lot of work, but nothing has happened. You set the
groundwork, but the rest is out of your hand.

It's kind of that way with your faith too. Jesus is the vine
and when you came to faith in him, you became a branch on his
tree, rooted in his soil and ready to grow according to his will
and favor. Without him, you would wither up and die because
no matter what you do, you can't grow on your own. As with the
plant in your garden, attention needs to be paid in the right ways
for growth to happen.

Each time you seek the Son, you begin to stretch more
toward him, growing in his light and love.

IN THE FLOW

*Lord, thank you for nurturing me and guiding me so that I can
grow stronger in you. Amen.*

A SPLASH OF THE SPIRIT

*The Spirit and the bride say, "Come!" Let the one who
hears say, "Come!" And let the one who is thirsty come! Let
the one who wishes receive life-giving water as a gift.*
—Revelation 22:17

The invitations have been sent out. You're invited to come to a
fabulous party and it will be overflowing with fountains of joy,
refreshing spirits, and reasons to toast the host over and over
again. You're invited to a life-giving and life-changing bash and
you'll be splashed with the spirit of God.

Why were you invited? You asked if you could come. You
put your name on the roster the day you accepted the love of
Christ. You felt thirsty in your soul and parched in your spirit
and you fell in love. Everything suddenly made sense to you as
you learned more of what God's engraved invitation could mean.
What refreshment, what joy!

On days when you're parched, living in the desert of the
world's traps and confusion, you have a fountain, a place to come
to restore your soul. Visit often. Never go thirsty, because you
have an endless spring of living water ready to keep you strong
and nourished.

Come to the waters of God's love today and again
tomorrow. He'll be there waiting with a cool, refreshing taste of
all that is yet to come.

IN THE FLOW

*Lord, thank you for taking care of me even now. Thanks for giving
me a place to come and grow and be refreshed in you. Amen.*

RISKY BUSINESS

Send your bread out on the water because, in the
course of time, you may find it again.
—Ecclesiastes 11:1

God must be a risk taker. After all, he made this universe, saw
that everything was good, and then made human beings. He had
to have wondered just for a second whether that was one of his
better ideas. He took the risk so he could build a relationship
with a being who was more akin to himself.

His creative Spirit surely hoped for the best possible
outcome, yet, he also knew what would happen since he is God,
after all. He knew the whole scene, every being that would be
born, every century that would pass, and he knew it would
contain people who were absolutely worth the risk. He knew
what he was doing when he made you.

Sometimes, you have to cast your bread upon the waters too.
You have to put everything you've got out there and hope for
the best. You've got to take a chance on life and see if you win.
It's the only way to get the reward.

God risked his Son, his heart, and his love. He risked it all
for one reason . . . so you could have a home with him one day.
That's how much he wanted a relationship with you. Show him
in any way you can that you were definitely worth the risk.

IN THE FLOW

Lord, thanks for creating the universe, creating the life I have. Help
me be willing to step out in faith for you. Amen.

You're Such a Gift!

*Serve each other according to the gift each person has
received, as good managers of God's diverse gifts.*
—1 Peter 4:10

A gift is a wonderful thing. It is pleasant to receive, more
wonderful to give, and it is in the spirit of giving that we come to
serve each other. Unlike the packaged variety, our gifts can't be
used up, don't need to be dusted, and aren't likely to spoil. We
have gifts that are God-given and they last forever.

Our individual and collective gifts are meant to be a
contribution to help others live better and happier lives. We can
use our writing talents to share stories of God's love, to offer
insights and perspective that may be new, to make someone
laugh. We can use our analytical gifts to help someone organize,
prioritize, and balance laws of science, money, and investments.
We can use our creative talents in every way under the sun, and
we can teach and preach and reach people with our hope and our
optimism and our gifts of the Spirit.

In other words, we have no excuse, we each have gifts and
those gifts are needed for the good of others. We are meant to
use our gifts in any way we can for our good and the good of
those we meet along the way.

In the Flow

*Lord, remind me today that I have been given great gifts that I can
use for your glory to help others in your name. Amen.*

FLASHLIGHT, PLEASE!

Without guidance, a people will fall, but there
is victory with many counselors.
—Proverbs 11:14

When you have to walk down a dark street at night, it helps to
have a flashlight. It may not give a lot of light to the situation,
but it gives enough to keep you from falling into potholes.

Sometimes your flashlight comes in the form of other people.
They speak with a voice of authority that feels like God himself
must have put them directly onto your path. You may not have
expected them, but God knew your need and so they rushed in
and kept you on your feet. He knew adding their beam to yours
could make all the difference.

Take a look around today for people in your life with energy-
efficient "flashlights" who can help you move on to be victorious
over whatever is lurking in the shadows. With a little help, you'll
eventually move again into a faith that says, "Lord, I'm going
to walk today totally trusting you, and I don't even need a
flashlight."

Between his Word acting as a lamp to guide your feet and
your faith to keep you moving forward, you'll be on your way
rejoicing. It's going to be a great day!

IN THE FLOW

Lord, thank you for sending others to me to help guide my way.
Thanks for being the light of my life. Amen.

NOW YOU SEE IT, NOW YOU DON'T!

*Our temporary minor problems are producing an eternal
stockpile of glory for us that is beyond all comparison.
We don't focus on the things that can be seen but on the
things that can't be seen. The things that can be seen don't
last, but the things that can't be seen are eternal.*
—2 Corinthians 4:17-18

We're living in two different worlds. One of them belongs to the
here and now and appears to be real. The other one is invisible,
but belongs to the Spirit and is only slightly real to our senses.
We want to be about waking up to the world that contains the
invisible things, the ones that will actually have eternal significance.
We're figuring out where to stockpile our wealth for the kingdom
coming next more than the one we see before us now.

How are we doing that? We do it every time we overcome
one more obstacle, from illness to financial setbacks to job losses
and divorces. How we handle those things creates the eternal
stockpile. That's where our faith counts in a big way. That's
where we respond to God.

One writer said, "Every tomorrow has two handles. We
can take hold of it by the handle of anxiety, or by the handle of
faith." Whatever you have to handle today, let faith lead you on.

IN THE FLOW

*Lord, help me handle the days with faith and stockpile eternal joy.
Amen.*

Happy Birthday!

Even if our bodies are breaking down on the outside, the
person that we are on the inside is being renewed every day.
—2 Corinthians 4:16

Okay, so it may not be your literal birthday today, but every day
that you wake up refreshed in the spirit, ready to get going, you
experience a kind of rebirth. After all, our job on earth is about
waking up to what is real, waking up to our awareness of God
and the beauty of a spirit-filled life. Our bodies may well have
to deal with breaking down, but no matter how many candles
are on our cakes, we are building up for our trip home to the
embrace of our heavenly Parent.

So rise and shine, birthday person! It's your day to keep
growing and learning and becoming more of what God had in
mind for you. It's an exciting journey, and each day brings a
discovery of something you might not have realized before. You
have been kind of sleepy, you know, and it never hurts to stretch
a little so you can wake up more fully.

What will you do today to celebrate your birthday? What
light can you add to the world that will awaken the spirit of even
one other person? Go ahead, add a candle, sing a song of praise,
and get out there. The world needs you today to join in the
celebration.

In the Flow

Lord, help me wake up to you in every possible way. Lead me into the
paths of others who struggle to see you in a better and more consistent
light. Amen.

WHAT'S YOUR HEART'S DESIRE?

Instead, desire first and foremost God's kingdom and God's
righteousness, and all these things will be given to you as well.
—Matthew 6:33

"In the beginning was the Word and the Word was with God and
the Word was God." This Scripture from John 1:1 is one that
reminds us where to start each day. We start at the beginning. We
start with the Word.

Do you ever have a head full of worries and so you climb out
of bed, try to shake it all off in the shower, try to cover it over
with caffeine, and yet it still lingers? You tackle the problem, you
dig in deeper, and you only get deeper into the difficulty. You
work this way for hours, perhaps days, and why? Because you
forgot where to start! You forgot to go back to the beginning.

In our distress, we finally cry out to God, asking why he
didn't help us, only to be reminded that he would have, but we
didn't ask. We forgot to start with him. The breastplate of St.
Patrick is a magnificent prayer and may be a good one for you
to use to begin your day today. It reads, in part, "I rise today
with the power of God to guide me, the might of God to uphold
me, the wisdom of God to teach me, the eye of God to watch
over me, the ear of God to hear me, the word of God to give me
speech, the hand of God to protect me, the path of God to lie
before me, the shield of God to shelter me."

Let's rise today and start at the beginning, with God.

IN THE FLOW

Lord, thank you for loving me so much that you always give me a
place to start again. Be with me and those I love today. Amen.

MINDING YOUR BUSINESS TODAY

*Aim to live quietly, mind your own business, and
earn your own living, just as I told you.*
—1 Thessalonians 4:11

Do you sometimes fantasize about having a very quiet life?
Maybe you'd have a little house near a gently flowing riverbank.
You'd plant a garden where bunnies came to play and didn't eat
all your carrots. You'd simply be a happy camper and let the rest
of the world float by. It may seem like a fantasy, but in your own
way, you can create that life wherever you are. For one thing, you
have Jesus in your heart and as you follow him and learn to be a
better disciple of his, you also receive his peace, peace like a river.

If our strength comes in quietness and confidence, then
maybe it's a good day to shut out the noise of the universe. Shut
off the television set with its endless litany of dreadful news.
Shut out the "reality" TV which isn't ever based in any reality
at all. Don't read the paper, don't work on your laptop, just go
and get quiet and sit by the river, even if you can only see it in
meditation. You need time to be renewed and refreshed in the
Spirit. You need time to be quietly on your own.

Your quiet time will bring you back to the center, back to the
Source that helps you live more authentically. Sit with God and
let him help you get more clarity today.

IN THE FLOW

*Lord, I do want to sit with you today. Let's go to the river and rest.
Let's talk together about the things that really matter. Help me hear
you in my heart and mind and be at peace. Amen.*

A P R I L 1 1

Putting a Lid on Anger

Fools show all their anger, but the wise hold it back.
—Proverbs 29:11

Henry Drummond had some colorful insights to share about anger. He said, "No form of vice, not worldliness, not greed of gold, not drunkenness itself, does more to un-Christianize society than evil temper. For embittering life, for breaking up communities, for destroying the most sacred relationships, for devastating homes, for withering up men and women, for taking the bloom off childhood; in short, for sheer gratuitous misery-producing power, this influence stands alone."

There is, of course, a righteous anger, like the kind Jesus demonstrated in the Temple with the moneychangers. There is a time to stand up, perhaps in anger, when injustice rears its head in any form. On this side of things, Martin Luther said, "I never work better than when I am inspired by anger; for when I am angry, I can write, pray, and preach well, for then my whole temperament is quickened, my understanding sharpened, and all mundane vexations and temptations depart."

Just be aware of the things that trigger an angry response. Understand whether your motivation is to teach or destroy, to drive a point or to drive someone away. In any case, remember to not let the sun go down on your anger today.

In the Flow

Lord, help me use the emotion of anger only when it will help create positive change. Amen.

DON'T WORRY, BE HAPPY!

Don't be anxious about anything; rather bring up all of your requests to God in your prayers and petitions, along with giving thanks.
—Philippians 4:6

Do you remember that song from Bobby McFerrin that said, "Don't worry, be happy?" In his own way, Jesus told you the same thing. He asked if worrying would add a single hour to your life, or if God dressed the lilies and took care of the birds, why you don't believe he'll dress you and take care of you. Worry only makes you tell stories in your head that may never come true. So how do you stop worrying and be happy?

Henry Ford said, "I believe God is managing affairs and that He doesn't need any advice from me. With God in charge, I believe everything will work out for the best in the end. So what is there to worry about?"

Did you notice how his statement starts? He said, "I believe God." If you truly believe God is taking care of you, that he is totally in charge of the little things as surely as he is in charge of the big things, you have every reason to smile. You can be happy because you have put your troubles in the hands of the One who can actually do something about them.

IN THE FLOW

Lord, help me place my life in your hands. Thank you for loving me. Amen.

You're an Ambassador!

Instead, regard Christ as holy in your hearts. Whenever
anyone asks you to speak of your hope, be ready to defend it.
Yet do this with respectful humility, maintaining a good
conscience. Act in this way so that those who malign your good
lifestyle in Christ may be ashamed when they slander you.
—1 Peter 3:15-16

Did you know that you've been appointed as God's ambassador? You've been given the job to share your faith whenever you can with respectful humility. It's great to have zeal and fire for the Lord, but it's also tricky. The trick is to keep your enthusiasm without actually doing damage to those who might embrace the fold if they weren't rather scared that doing so will make them act like you.

As Christians, our actions speak louder than anything we can say. What we do is what really gets noticed. We don't have to stand in the pulpit, even if we have one at home; we don't have to make it our job to judge the world, or judge someone else's faith, or try to determine who is with the Lord and who isn't. Our job is to be an ambassador of good will . . . God's will. We want to invite others to come to the table, not force them to eat off our plates.

Your heart is in the right place, and your intentions are good. Now align them with God's grace and humility and you'll be an outstanding ambassador for the Lord!

In the Flow

Lord, I do want to share my faith with others. Help me plant seeds of
joy and grace wherever I am. Amen.

The Lamb of God and You

Like sheep we had all wandered away, each going its
own way, but the LORD let fall on him all our crimes.
He was oppressed and tormented, but didn't open his
mouth. Like a lamb being brought to slaughter, like a ewe
silent before her shearers, he didn't open his mouth.
—Isaiah 53:6-7

At this point on the calendar, you've either already celebrated the events of Easter or they are looming. This Scripture from Isaiah is so powerful because it foretells the events of Jesus' death. It reminds us of the conscious choice he made to lay down his life for us, to be a lamb taking our sins to the altar.

It is interesting to note that Jesus didn't try to explain things to his accusers. He didn't try to beg them to listen to him, to see things differently. He simply followed through with the plan, knowing it had an incredible outcome. He knew that you were coming down the road in the future, and he wanted to be sure you could get back to him, that you could be part of his flock.

What does it mean to you today to realize that your sins are forgiven? You wandered away and could easily have been lost out there, never to be found again, except for one thing. God loved you so much he couldn't let you go. He gave his Son just for you.

God loved you first. He loves you still. He wants you to always be part of his flock. He already provided the Shepherd.

In the Flow

Lord, thank you for loving me more than I can understand. Thank you for Jesus, the One who makes it possible for me to love you and live with you eternally. Amen.

THE ABCs OF ATTITUDE

*Happy are people who are downcast, because
the kingdom of heaven is theirs.*
—Matthew 5:3

It's hard to grasp the real beauty of the Beatitudes, but it's easy
to see that life carries one choice no matter what we're going
through. We can have an attitude of woe, or we can have an
attitude of joy based on belief that in due course, everything will
indeed be well again in the Lord.

If we look at this in an ABC style, we might think of A as
the *attitude* we will adopt. When we feel without hope, when
our dreams come falling down, when all the plans we've made
have not come to fruition, we still have reason to rejoice. We can
focus on what is ahead, knowing that God has every intention of
making sure we are smiling again soon.

Perhaps the B part of our attitude adjustment then is to
believe that God will indeed follow through with his plans to give
us the kingdom, to see us smile, and to grant us a more abundant
life on the earth. Believing is the key to it all.

Finally the C part of our attitude adjustment is *Christ*
himself. He is the reason we can have a positive attitude about
anything life hands us. It is because of his love for us, his sacrifice,
that we can call God our father. Today, let's adjust our attitudes
with great belief and great joy.

IN THE FLOW

*Lord, you always lift my spirits and remind me of your kindness
and your dreams for me, no matter what life brings. Help me keep
believing and trusting in you. Amen.*

MORE FAITH, PLEASE!

"If you can do anything, help us! Show us compassion!"
Jesus said to him, " 'If you can do anything'? All things
are possible for the one who has faith." At that the boy's
father cried out, "I have faith; help my lack of faith!"
—Mark 9:22-24

Faith is one of those concepts that grows with us. We may think we have faith when we're managing the world and all is well. We may think we have faith when we trust and believe in the hard times, but every now and then, our faith gets a little shaky. We're not as certain that God will come through and that all things are possible. Certainly, we can understand the cry of the man who would do anything to have his son healed. He knew Jesus was the answer, he just didn't know if he had enough faith.

Richard Greenham said, "The seat of faith is not in the brain, but in the heart, and the head is not the place to keep the promises of God, but the heart is the chest to lay them up in." Faith is not reasonable, but God is. We can reason with him from the heart and he will give us more faith to understand his will.

Today, set your reason aside. Set your perception of all you imagine faith to be aside too, and go ask for more. Ask the God of all that is possible to broaden your reach, widen your scope, and rescue you from your unbelief. When you do that, you may be surprised at how quickly your faith grows.

IN THE FLOW

Lord, some days, I have my fair share of faith and I live with it in my heart. Other days, I am not really awake to it. Please grant me a greater sense of what it really means to have faith in you. Amen.

GETTING THINGS RIGHT!

In those days there was no king in Israel; each
person did what they thought to be right.
—Judges 17:6

Now this is an interesting thought. What if we all just did what
feels right to us without any regard for what is right for someone
else? What happens when there are no rules?

When Moses left his people and went up on the mountain
to talk with God, they got bored waiting for him. When they
got bored, they started thinking maybe they knew best how to
handle things. Without any rules, they all just did what they
thought was right, and it didn't work out well. God sent Moses
back down the mountain with the rules, posthaste.

Most of us resist rules a little bit. Yet, the best thing for any
of us is to know the boundaries, to understand the limits. Moses
gave us the Ten Commandments and that helped establish how
God wanted things to be done. Jesus gave us the two rules of
love, love God and love your neighbor. When we follow God's
rules, we have a little better chance of getting things right.

IN THE FLOW

Lord, thank you for setting boundaries, reminding me of the
important things so that when I choose to make or break a rule, I
know I am measuring it against your rules that have everything to
do with love. Amen.

YOU'RE A KEEPER!

As the Father loved me, I too have loved you. Remain in my love.
If you keep my commandments, you will remain in my love, just
as I kept my Father's commandments and remain in his love.
—John 15:9-10

Love is kind of a slippery thing. It moves in, takes up a space in your heart, hangs its hat up, and then changes everything. The only problem is that love changes too and sometimes it moves on, packing up everything and leaving you empty again. It's difficult to understand the ins and outs, the subtle things that make it work or not work.

The good news for us is that God's love isn't fickle. It doesn't come in and then abruptly turn around and leave again. It doesn't choose to leave at all. It only leaves that option to us. We can remain, or we can go. Every moment that we choose God's love keeps us in the game. So why would we choose anything else?

God thinks you're a keeper. You're someone he wants to know more about, wants to have a personal relationship with. You're a work of art to him, a very special creation. It's not unlike that first day when new parents see the tiny little smile of their newborn infant. It's instant and forever love! That's what God has for you and he even knew you before you were born.

IN THE FLOW

Lord, thank you for loving me with all the spots and blemishes I bring with me. Thanks for being my forever love. Amen.

Now That's a Mouthful!

Your speech should always be gracious and sprinkled with insight so that you may know how to respond to every person.
—Colossians 4:6

You're speechless! Someone has just done something that surprised you and disappointed you so much, you hardly know what to say. Your first impulse is to charge in and make your appeal, let them know they crossed the line, totally messed things up, and yet . . . that isn't really the response God is looking for.

When you take a little time to breathe, to rethink the issue, you might be able to come up with a reasonable explanation for the incident, something that will give you a place to start in repairing the relationship before a major meltdown happens. You might be able to ease up on the resentments and see a glimpse of what God sees, even in this messy bit of drama. You can choose to be gracious, to take time to think through your response so that what you say can make a positive difference to the whole situation.

When you've been surprised by someone's actions or comments, it's not easy to do the right thing, and yet, God would have you try to do so. We're all still growing and all we can do is thank God that he gives us room to do so. Let's give each other that same space even when we're tempted to give out a mouthful.

In the Flow

Lord, you know it isn't easy to be quiet when my feelings are hurt. Please help me remember your incredible kindness to me when I'm tempted to say more than is gracious to someone else. Amen.

GETTING YOUR HEAD ABOVE THE CROWD

Now my head is higher than the enemies surrounding
me . . . LORD, listen to my voice when I cry out . . . !
—Psalm 27:6-7

Do you ever find yourself trying to calm the noise from the outside world, getting your head above the crowd so you can hear yourself think? This may not be exactly what David was thinking about here in this Psalm, but it's always good to step back and step aside when you can so you can get a broader perspective. We often just need time to think our own thoughts.

Goethe said it this way: "All truly wise thoughts have been thought already thousands of times; but to make them truly ours, we must think them over again honestly, till they take root in our personal experience." We may not be trying to reinvent the wheel or come up with a cure for cancer, but we still need some quiet moments to withdraw from the crowds and hear not only our own voice, but God's voice. It's difficult for him to reach us when our thoughts are crowded out by all that goes on around us. As you go about your business today, take a few moments to be silent somewhere. Then give God thanks for all that he has to share with you.

IN THE FLOW

Lord, sometimes I go for days without a break, doing everything that
needs to get done, running faster than my feet can keep up, and
certainly faster than my thoughts can take root. Be with me and
help me find the quiet time to hear your voice. Amen.

Is God Still in the Building?

Certainly the faithful love of the LORD hasn't ended;
certainly God's compassion isn't through! They are renewed
every morning. Great is your faithfulness. I think: The
LORD is my portion! Therefore, I'll wait for him.
—Lamentations 3:22-24

It's a struggle sometimes to remember that God hasn't left the building—that is, the building up of his people, the building of relationships, and the building of his church. He hasn't left us, and yet we may try to seek him the same way we'd do a celebrity sighting . . . hoping to catch a glimpse of him when we least expect.

The writer of this Scripture reminds us that God hasn't quit, hasn't walked away from his creation, and his acts of kindness aren't done. He begins them anew every morning. Think of that! God rises with fresh thoughts of love, not tainted by yesterday, not carried on as leftovers, but new and fresh and ready to be delivered to his children.

What does it mean that the Lord is our portion? If my portion is God, that means he's everything I get. He's my whole, my life, my breath and spirit. If I recall every morning with the rising of the sun that he is there, ready to feed me and renew me and shower me with grace, then I receive the portion he meant for me to have.

In the Flow

Lord, thank you for giving me your kindness and your goodness
every single day in fresh and loving ways. Help me take your love
with me wherever I go today. Amen.

HERE'S YOUR PROMOTION!

His master replied, "Excellent! You are a good and
faithful servant! You've been faithful over a little. I'll put
you in charge of much. Come, celebrate with me."
—Matthew 25:21

Most of us won't get an Academy Award for our performance in
this life. We may not even be up for the Best Supporting Actor.
We're most likely the ones who are always behind the scenes,
doing the little things to try to make a difference. We serve
others to help make their names greater, whether we serve our
bosses or our families or someone else who has a specific calling.

We serve God to make his name greater, too. We are good
and faithful servants when we willingly do the tasks God has
asked of us. We may not think he notices our efforts or that
anyone else does for that matter. We don't do it to win any
awards.

The truth is that God sees us and sees our work all the time.
Whatever role he has given us is never too small to be of service
to him. Now and then, he calls us out of that job and promotes
us to a new position. That's his way of rewarding us, promoting
us and putting us over even more of his projects. God needs you
to play the role he's given you and he will raise you up in his own
time. He loves what you do as his good and faithful servant.

IN THE FLOW

Lord, I don't know if my small contributions make a kingdom
difference or not, but I trust you'll let me know if you want me to do
something else. Thanks for being with me today. Amen.

ADMIT ONE!

Therefore, since we have been made righteous through his faithfulness combined with our faith, we have peace with God through our Lord Jesus Christ. We have access by faith into this grace in which we stand through him, and we boast in the hope of God's glory.
—Romans 5:1-2

Imagine what it means to have unlimited access to the God of the universe. That's right! You have direct access to God and he is never limited in his availability. He is never too tired to listen, too busy to pick up the phone, too stressed with the mess the world is in; he's there, all the time, every day.

How did you get so plugged in? You got there through his faithfulness, his willingness to be there for you all the time, and your faith. You got connected by his grace, and it really had nothing to do with you.

God gives you general admittance any time of day. He gives you the front row seat, the center stage, the attention of the universe. He's ready now, no delay, just your God waiting for you to call. It's a new day and a new chance to ask for his advice, seek his counsel for your life, thank him for the fine job he's doing with your family and friends. All you have to do is redeem your ticket.

IN THE FLOW

Lord, thank you for inviting me into your inner circle. I'm excited about spending more time with you this week. Amen.

Let's Call a Truce!

Put aside all bitterness, losing your temper, anger, shouting, and slander, along with every other evil. Be kind, compassionate, and forgiving to each other, in the same way God forgave you in Christ.
—Ephesians 4:31-32

Since we've recently celebrated Easter, it may be a good idea for us to reflect on the whole notion of forgiveness. After all, we've just experienced the death and resurrection of our Lord and Savior and we all know we couldn't get to heaven without him. Atonement happened because God initiated the possibility. He opened the door, making sure that we would find him again, that we could be redeemed.

Why do we accept that on one hand, yet find it so difficult to extend the hand of forgiveness to the people around us? Put aside bitterness, that thing that only serves to eat us up and spit us out, leaving us in utter darkness. With joy, come back to each other and be kind and compassionate. Remind each other of all that you have shared that is good. Speak words of forgiveness and charity. Forgive as you have been forgiven.

It's possible because you are redeemed, set free to love, to forgive, and to live according to a higher standard than the one the world sets. Let no bitterness or resentment take root in your life, open the door and let the Son shine in. You will experience the springtime in a whole new way.

In the Flow

Lord, you have loved me more than I understand. Help me forgive and love others and let go of any past heartaches. Amen.

YOU'VE GOT A FRIEND!

I don't call you servants any longer, because servants don't know what their master is doing. Instead, I call you friends, because everything I heard from my Father I have made known to you.
—John 15:15

You've got a lot of relationships. You've got family, co-workers, bosses perhaps, and church acquaintances, lots of people in your life. The best relationships, though, are the ones you attach to the word *friend*.

Authentic friendships are those you count on when life is going haywire, or those that bring you a laugh when you can't step outside your troubles long enough to find one on your own. These are the friends who will tell you when you're acting weird or who will love you when you're a bit crazy. They'll hold your hand in the middle of the night and walk with you through a scary surgery. These are your friends.

If we think about it, it's amazing that God would want to call us his friends. After all, that assumes a give-and-take relationship. That assumes we're there for him just like he's there for us. It also assumes trust and joy and depth of experience.

Today, think about your friendship with God. What do you have to give him? What do you think would make your friendship stronger? You and God are friends. You're on a first-name basis. Spend a little time with him. He'd love to hear from you.

IN THE FLOW

Lord, thank you for inviting me to be your friend. Help me be a better friend to you all the time. Amen.

FINDING JUST THE RIGHT RECIPE

*A person will harvest what they plant. Those who plant
only for their own benefit will harvest devastation from
their selfishness, but those who plant for the benefit of
the Spirit will harvest eternal life from the Spirit.*
—Galatians 6:7-8

Culturally, we're all about individuals. We honor self-indulgence, self-satisfaction, self-esteem. Of course, sometimes what we get back from those are things we're not so pleased with . . . self-loathing and self-righteousness come to mind. Though being a strong individual, one who can be counted on and respected, is a good thing, the call to most of us is about stepping aside from the self and looking out for the other person.

We've been planted on this earth for a reason, and part of that reason is about spreading the seeds of God's love, watering the tender plants someone else started, and helping to distribute the fruit of our labors. From there, we can create all kinds of recipes for good living.

Today, then, our job is to wave the self aside and discover what we can do to benefit at least one other person. You may not have the perfect recipe for doing good, but you have all the ingredients. You got them the day you signed up to live in God's garden. It's your day to bloom.

IN THE FLOW

*Lord, I get so caught up in what I'm doing, I sometimes forget that
you've put me in the midst of a lot of people who need to know you
better. Give me the wisdom to help in ways that please you. Amen.*

YOU'RE IN GOD'S WILL

Now I entrust you to God and the message of his
grace, which is able to build you up and give you an
inheritance among all whom God has made holy.
—Acts 20:32

You may not always be doing God's will, or you may not intentionally be seeking his will for each thing you do, but the truth is, you're in his will. He has an inheritance for everyone who accepts the message of his Son, everyone who lives in his grace.

You see, your Father is rich. That's right. He's a King. He's the ruler of the whole universe and that makes you the heir to his kingdom. It means that you're a bit of royalty yourself. Royalty always comes with privileges, and yours are many. For one thing, you'll receive a robe and a crown and you'll be part of a big celebration of all of his friends. You'll be happy forever. No more tears, no more sorrow, no more losses, no more worries, just joy and singing and love and laughter. The list of all the benefits is rather large, so you may have to check back and read the fine print, but there's time for that.

Today, just remember that you stand to inherit more than you ever thought possible and all you have to do is be willing to receive his Son, his blessing, and his gifts of great love.

IN THE FLOW

Lord, thank you for loving me so much that you've already provided
for my eternal well-being. Help me be worthy of your great love.
Amen.

PASS THE SALT, PLEASE!

*You are the salt of the earth. But if salt loses its
saltiness, how will it become salty again?*
—Matthew 5:13

Salt has always been a precious commodity. In ancient times, it
was a bit like gold because it was valuable for so many things. It
not only enhanced the flavor of food, it also was necessary for the
good health of the body. It helped preserve meat and other foods
from spoiling. In more contemporary times, even into the latter
twentieth century, salt was measured and given to royalty when
it was not available to anyone else. Kings and queens often had
lavish salt dishes to impress their guests.

Even though salt cannot actually lose its flavor, it can be
mixed with other things (as dishonest merchants did) and then
lose its effectiveness. Perhaps Jesus referred to that idea when he
spoke about salt in the passage shown here.

Today, you may be "the salt of the earth" if you're simply
a good person, but you're more apt to be the salt for God if
you're out to add richness and flavor to someone else's spirit. It's
important to watch what you mix with your saltiness, to protect
the effect you're able to have on others. If you create opportunities
and spread the joy of God's love, you act as the salt.

Be the salt for your heavenly father today.

IN THE FLOW

*Lord, help me enrich others, offering a way to taste your goodness
any chance I get. Thanks for passing your salt of joy to me. Amen.*

SHINING A LIGHT

In the same way, let your light shine before people, so they can see the good things you do and praise your Father who is in heaven.
—Matthew 5:16

You may not think of yourself as shining a light, giving off happy vibes, or sending out signals to the universe, but you are. You may not see that, but God does. Every time you do good things to bring nurture and sustenance, grace and joy to others, your own light gets a little brighter.

An old Chinese proverb says this about being a light in the world: "If there is light in the soul, there will be beauty in the person. If there is beauty in the person, there will be harmony in the house. If there is harmony in the house, there will be order in the nation. If there is order in the nation, there will be peace in the world."

Your light leads to peace. Your light stops the darkness from getting too close. Your light makes a difference. As you look at ways to shine your light today, pray that God will show you areas of darkness that may still reside in your heart. Ask him to heal you of the things that tend to hide your light under a bushel, keeping you from stepping out in even more ways to be the reflection of his love to others.

IN THE FLOW

Lord, please take from me any darkness that lurks in my thinking or in my heart. Help me be a joyful and ready light for you today. Amen.

When the Waters Stand Still

*The people marched out from their tents to cross over the Jordan. . . .
But at that moment the water of the Jordan coming downstream
stood still. . . . The water going down to the desert sea (that is, the
Dead Sea) was cut off completely. The people crossed opposite Jericho.
So the priests carrying the LORD's covenant chest stood
firmly on dry land in the middle of the Jordan.*
—Joshua 3:14-17

The people in biblical times might have gotten accustomed
to the idea of miracles, but then again, maybe not. When the
Israelites were walking in the desert, it didn't take long for them
to forget how God had parted the Red Sea so they could cross
on dry ground. They seemed to forget how he walked with them
in a cloud and in a pillar of fire. They glossed right over the fact
that he fed them with manna and birds. They had the miracles,
but it didn't mean they had the faith.

Later on, God made the Jordan River stand still. He not
only made it stand still, he folded it up so the priests carrying the
covenant chest could get across on dry ground. Rolling down the
river on a steamboat is one thing. Rolling up the river so people
can cross on dry ground is something else.

God is willing to create miracles if that's what we need. In
fact, everything about our existence is a miracle if we understand
it that way. Embrace the miracle of all God has done in your life
and give him thanks and praise today!

In the Flow

*Lord, you can stop rivers from flowing and keep the earth on its
course! Thank you today for the miracle of my life and all you do to
intervene for my good through your grace. Amen.*

May

Don't be anxious about anything

. . . the peace of God that exceeds all

understanding will keep your hearts

and minds safe in Christ Jesus.

Philippians 4:6-7

It's Okay to Be Happy

Be glad in the Lord always! Again I say, be glad! . . . The Lord is near. Don't be anxious about anything; rather bring up all of your requests to God in your prayers and petitions, along with giving thanks. Then the peace of God that exceeds all understanding will keep your hearts and minds safe in Christ Jesus.
—Philippians 4:4-7

We can get so caught up in the troubles of the world that we almost forget to be happy. When you find every news headline bombarding your senses and every talk show bringing you down, you might want to stop the presses, get off the negative news network, and remember that the Lord is near.

If God is near, you have no real reason to be anxious. You have every reason to be happy. In fact, it's more than okay to be happy, it's a way of showing God how much you trust him. It's a way of thanking him. Don't parents always feel better when they see their kids smile? Your heavenly Father likes to see you smile too.

The first day of May brings another opportunity to rejoice that spring has come and see that flowers still bloom. You can hope in the Lord and carry your burdens to him. Give thanks for all he has done and what he is yet to do to help you grow, to help you be at peace, and to give you wings to fly. Believe him and trust him. He will keep you safe beneath his wings of love.

In the Flow

Lord, thank you for taking my cares and concerns today and delivering me from the burdens they put on my heart. Bless all that I am and all that I can be with your love. Amen.

Jesus Christ Isn't a Swear Word!

*Don't let any foul words come out of your
mouth. Only say what is helpful.*
—Ephesians 4:29

A small sports car suddenly weaves in front of you and gives you a momentary scare. A friend gives you some startling news. Some people greet incidents like these by jumping up and shouting, "Jesus Christ!" Of course, they aren't actually hoping to invoke the Lord's attention and they haven't just encountered him in a spiritual way, in fact they aren't even thinking of the Lord himself.

A swear word never serves to build up and bring benefit to others. Perhaps you aren't prone to foul words in the way we're addressing it here, but "foul words" may simply mean those words you used to brush someone off in conversation, to be a judge when it wasn't really your job to do so. Foul words stink! They don't bring good to others.

Your job is to be aware of what you say and note the impact of your words, for you can either injure or build up. You can bless or curse. As Mother Teresa said, "Words which do not give the light of Christ increase the darkness."

A word to the wise!

In the Flow

Lord, help me never to use your name in vain and also help me to be much more aware of any words I speak so that I bring blessing and kindness to others the way you do to me. Amen.

ANGELS ON THE HEAD OF A PIN?

Avoid stupid controversies, genealogies, and fights about the Law, because they are useless and worthless.
—Titus 3:9

Religious scholars can get caught in seemingly meaningless debates as well. They question how many angels can dance on the head of a pin, which religion is the true one, or what is the absolute way to get to God.

The good news is that God in his infinite wisdom chose to keep us slightly confused. He knew that if we could figure out every detail, figure out how to reinvent him, we would. He also knew we wouldn't come up with the exact right answer and so we would have to give him credit for being, well, God.

You may remember the story of Jesus' disciples who wanted to know who would sit on his right and left when he came into his kingdom. They weren't thinking then of how to serve God. They wanted to sit at his right hand because they believed they had earned that right. It was all about them!

If you grab your ego and bind it up long enough to see what motivates you, you may find that most of the battles you've engaged in weren't necessary at all. There won't be any need to try to figure out how many angels can dance on the head of a pin.

IN THE FLOW

Lord, it's the little arguments that come up, those frustrations that happen almost unexpectedly, that eat up my spirit. Let me hold on to you and only fight when you call me into the battle. Amen.

DON'T LOOK BACK!

After getting them out, the men said, "Save your lives!
Don't look back! And don't stay in the valley. Escape to
the mountains so that you are not swept away." ... *When*
Lot's wife looked back, she turned into a pillar of salt.
—Genesis 19:17, 26

Warning! Danger ahead! Do you ever wish you had some
warning signs posted all around you when you're about to
do something really stupid? You may have been given ample
explanation for why you must follow the rules to the letter, but
you're still tempted to bend the rules a little bit.

Unfortunately for Lot's wife, trying to bend the rules was
a deal-breaker. God no longer protected her, and the harsh
destruction of Sodom and Gomorrah fell on her like acid rain.
She had been warned not to look back, but she couldn't resist
the temptation to turn around and see what was happening. She
became a standing pillar of salt.

Lot's wife isn't the only one tempted to look back. We hold
on to old hurts, old stories, or people who betrayed us. We
keep looking back, revisiting the storms and destruction we've
been through, acting like maybe God didn't really forgive us, or
wondering if the story is still good for a little sympathy.

Your marching orders are only about living in the present
and moving into the future. Don't look back. Look to today and
listen for God's voice.

IN THE FLOW

Lord, help me keep in the flow of life, doing what you would have me
do to live fully and well without looking back. Amen.

GOD IS OUR HELP!

Lord, you have been our help, generation after generation.
Before the mountains were born, before you birthed
the earth and the inhabited world—from forever in
the past to forever in the future, you are God.

—Psalm 90:1-2

Time is a relative thing and may not seem like an issue. You may not even have a good sense of what it means for something to be permanent since so few things are. Perhaps that is why we don't quite understand our God, who is the same yesterday, today, and forever. We try to grasp what *forever* means, but it's beyond our time zone.

This psalm reminds us that God is still our help. Fortunately for us, he has not grown weary of watching over us or taking care of us. Norman Vincent Peale offers us an idea of how to embrace God's help. He says, "This is one of the simplest teachings in religion, namely, that Almighty God will be your companion, will stand by you, help you, and see you through. No other idea is so powerful in developing self-confidence as this simple belief when practiced. To practice it simply affirm, 'God is with me; God is helping me; God is guiding me.' Spend several minutes each day visualizing his presence. Then practice believing that affirmation."

God is your help. Ask him for his help and he'll be there. That's a promise!

IN THE FLOW

Lord, thank you for helping me and watching over the details of my life. I love you. Amen.

DON'T GET HOOKED!

*A sensitive answer turns back wrath, but an offensive
word stirs up anger. The tongue of the wise enhances
knowledge, but the mouth of a fool gushes with stupidity.*
—Proverbs 15:1-2

An old adage reminds us that a fish only gets caught when its
mouth is open. The same might be said of us. Sometimes the
best thing we can do is keep our mouths shut. Not as easy as it
sounds, is it?

It's one thing to give advice when someone asks us for it, or
to give a response when a question has been directed our way,
but sometimes we jump into an opportunity to give our not-so-
humble opinion before a request was made. When we do that,
we may give valuable advice, but many times we have our own
agenda for the response we give and so we're not really much
help.

A rule of thumb might be this. Don't give advice unless
someone asks you directly for it. Then don't give advice unless
the two of you have spent some time in prayer, taking the
situation to your heavenly Father so that what you then discuss
is part of his design, removing personal agendas and bringing
clarity to the situation. Today and every day, seek God's advice
first, seek his heart before you choose to share yours.

IN THE FLOW

*Lord, I admit that I get caught in other people's drama. I try to fix
things that aren't mine to fix. Please help me always seek wisdom
from you before I offer my thoughts to anyone else. Amen.*

THE MESSAGE OF ANGELS

All of God's angels must worship him. *He talks about
the angels:* He's the one who uses the spirits for his
messengers and who uses flames of fire as ministers.
—Hebrews 1:6-7

If angels are messengers and still making visits to the earth today,
God is still actively doing all he can to help us get the message.
He may use an angel to remind us that he's there, and when he
does we can be sure it's serious business.

The angel stories recorded in the Bible range from the
angel Gabriel's announcement to Mary about the plan of God
to redeem the world through his infant son, the singing angels
at the birth of the baby Jesus, and the angels who helped Peter
escape prison. From the Old Testament, we're told of the angels
who went out to destroy Sodom and Gomorrah and the angels
who killed 185,000 of Sennacherib's army in a single night.
Safe to say, angels have been busy throughout earth's history,
bringing messages to God's people who are willing to hear them.

God does that because you are of even more value to him
than the angels. You were redeemed by his Son and that makes
you very special indeed.

Bless your angels, thank them for watching over you, and
listen for their messages in your own life. God is always ready to
speak with you in any way he can.

IN THE FLOW

*Lord, bless my life today and guard me through the loving spirits of
your divine angels. Grant me wisdom in all I do and peace in my
soul. Amen.*

May 8

When Justice Prevails

The LORD—he is our God. His justice is everywhere throughout
the whole world. God remembers his covenant forever, the
word he commanded to a thousand generations.
—Psalm 105:7-8

Justice may defy real definition. We tend to attach our own view
of what justice is, based on where we live or the way we were
raised or the faith we express. Most of us struggle with what
fairness actually is and can debate our views.

The psalmist got it right though. He says that God has
placed his justice "everywhere throughout the whole world." In
other words, we have no excuse. We know what is just and what
isn't. Carl Rowan said, "It is often easier to become outraged
by injustice half a world away than by the oppression and
discrimination half a block from home." Perhaps this is why God
said it isn't our place to judge one another.

We think God set boundaries, but nothing has gagged and
tied us like our own rules, all in the struggle to figure out what is
just. Jesus even took us further when he explained that the most
important rules were about loving God and loving one another.
If we just got those two right, we would be in good shape.

As you walk with your neighbors today, offer them the kind
of love that desires nothing but a just and joyous day.

In the Flow

Lord, thank you for being a just God. Thank you that I don't have
to decide what is right and fair for the whole world. Help me stand
up for justice when and where I can. Amen.

TALK ABOUT WEIGHT LIFTING!

*But me? I will sing of your strength! In the morning
I will shout out loud about your faithful love
because you have been my stronghold,
my shelter when I was distraught. I will
sing praises to you, my strength, because
God is my stronghold, my loving God.*
—Psalm 59:16-17

Strength training has increased in popularity over the years.
We've discovered the benefits of stretching and working out and
getting better tone in our muscles. With the right training, a
person can lift weights that are hundreds of pounds.

Of course, lifting weights means we're taking our weak
bodies and practicing and flexing and becoming stronger on our
own. Lifting God up and raising our spiritual muscles actually
means we become weaker, that is, our ego becomes weaker.
God's work in us is perfected in our weakness. He can only
become stronger if we give him room to work in our hearts and
minds and take over that stronghold known as the ego.

Surrender all that you are and all that you hope for so that
he can lift you up in his way and give you the strength you need
to carry on. Remember the words from Philippians 4:13, which
says, "I can endure all these things through the power of the one
who gives me strength."

Be strong in the Lord today!

IN THE FLOW

*Lord, thank you for giving me your continued strength and love.
Thank you for taking so many weights off my shoulders. Amen.*

READY FOR ANOTHER ROUND?

But we have this treasure in clay pots so that the awesome power belongs to God and doesn't come from us. We are experiencing all kinds of trouble, but we aren't crushed. We are confused, but we aren't depressed. We are harassed, but we aren't abandoned. We are knocked down, but we aren't knocked out.
—2 Corinthians 4:7-9

If you've ever watched a boxing match, you might relate to the idea that the fighters are in it to win it. They come back for another round after the bell rings, after they've had a little water and gotten their eyelids reshaped so they can see again. They keep at it because they have just one goal, to win!

We may not get into the ring waiting for the final bell, but we are out there every day fighting. We're fighting for better health or we're fighting to save a marriage or we're fighting to get our kids on the right track. We're trying to be the last one standing and the first one smiling.

We may get confused or even crushed temporarily as we receive a blow we didn't expect, but the good news is that with God's help, we may get knocked down, but we won't get knocked out. He is there, fighting with us, advising us and shaping the way things go. He is there to help us win, to fight the good fight.

Whatever you're facing, whatever is going on in the ring around you, remember that you're not alone. Your God has already won and you're on his team. You two have some good sparring to do with your opponents and it's going to turn out great.

IN THE FLOW

Lord, thank you for jumping into the ring with me, helping me stand when I feel faint. I know I can't do it without you. Amen.

GOD CHOSE YOU!

Therefore, as God's choice, holy and loved, put on compassion, kindness, humility, gentleness, and patience. Be tolerant with each other and, if someone has a complaint against anyone, forgive each other. As the Lord forgave you, so also forgive each other. And over all these things put on love, which is the perfect bond of unity.
—Colossians 3:12-14

Sure, God could have passed you by. He could have decided that you had too many issues, too much ego, too many sins to deal with. He could have thought you were just too much trouble. He could have. But he didn't.

In fact, he looked at you with the eyes of compassion and thought how wonderful it would be if you could see yourself as the whole and beautiful person he sees when he looks at you. He thought about your willingness to be tender at just the right moments and your ability to tolerate those who aren't quite like you. He saw you in a way that raised you up above the turmoil and the mess that life can be and he determined that everything about you was good. He chose you.

Today, he wants you to go out and walk in love, share your heart, and do whatever you can to bring peace and kindness to just one other person. You have been forgiven, loved, and entrusted with this one job. You have been chosen. Show him what you're doing with his unending love for you. Make him proud!

IN THE FLOW

Lord, thank you for taking me in, choosing me, and forgiving me. Help me put on love and share it everywhere I am today. Amen.

May 12

You're Not Alone Anymore!

The Lord looks down from heaven; he sees every human being. From his dwelling place God observes all who live on earth. God is the one who made all their hearts, the one who knows everything they do.
—Psalm 33:13-15

Many of us suffer from loneliness. We feel invisible and wonder if anyone really wants to know us, or see us for who we are. We just don't seem to get plugged in and we can't figure out why. Some days we aren't even sure there's a reason to keep trying.

The good news is that with God, you don't have to wonder. You don't have to feel invisible because he sees you right where you are. In fact, he's ready to embrace you and share more of life with you any time you're ready. You're not alone anymore.

When those feelings of loneliness creep in, when you feel homeless even in your living room, take some time to reconnect to the God of your heart. Take time to plug into all that he wants for you and all that he sees you can be. Spend some time in his Word and discover the richness of life he meant for you to enjoy. You're his child, his beloved, and he wants you to find fulfillment and peace and abundance in this world. He's there 24/7.

Today, invite him in. Ask him to share his thoughts with you in prayer or in his Word or to help you through a conversation with someone you may not be expecting to talk to. He's in and waiting to connect with your call.

In the Flow

Lord, I am so thankful that you see me and that you know me so well. Thanks for loving me beyond measure and reminding me I'm not alone anymore. Amen.

Fish and Chips, Anyone?

Philip replied, "More than a half year's salary worth of food wouldn't be enough for each person to have even a little bit." One of his disciples, Andrew, Simon Peter's brother, said, "A youth here has five barley loaves and two fish. But what good is that for a crowd like this?" Jesus said, "Have the people sit down." There was plenty of grass there. They sat down, about five thousand of them. Then Jesus took the bread. When he had given thanks, he distributed it to those who were sitting there. He did the same with the fish, each getting as much as they wanted.
—John 6:7-11

It's one thing to try to come up with a meal for your family. It's another thing to feed a couple hundred guests at a wedding reception, but imagine trying to feed five thousand people at an outdoor picnic without a caterer.

Beyond the miracle of feeding five thousand people with five loaves of bread and two fish is the story of Jesus' compassion. The crowd had been with him all day, soaking in his sermons and trying to understand how God wanted them to act. They were exhausted, hungry and thirsty, and yet nobody wanted to leave. Nobody wanted to miss a word Jesus had to say.

God opened the heart of one child and with that child's one unselfish move, he was able to create a miracle. Imagine if we could do one unselfish thing today, what he might do to feed those around us.

In the Flow

Lord, you have created miracles that I will never understand, and the greatest of those is your love for me. Open my heart to always be willing to do what you would ask of me. Amen.

MEAN PEOPLE NEED NOT APPLY

There are six things that the Lord hates, seven things detestable to
him: snobbish eyes, a lying tongue, hands that spill innocent blood, a
heart set on wicked plans, feet that run quickly to evil, a false witness
who breathes lies, and one who causes conflicts among relatives.
—Proverbs 6:16-19

If this Proverb was a job description, we'd know who not to hire.
One haughty expression would send the first candidate out the
door. One scheme to take over the company would get rid of
another. A gossip would be gone in a heartbeat, and the person
who just couldn't understand this was a family business probably
wouldn't survive.

Today, take a look at this list and see if you'd have any
trouble applying for a job in God's kingdom. He's always looking
for good people and enlists all those who come to him ready
and willing to work. You don't need to be skilled at cooking or
creating revenue streams or healing, but he appreciates those gifts
too. In fact, he gave you the gifts you have so that you could
apply anytime to work with him.

Is there anything you might have to clean up, any area where
you might need some retraining or further education before you
can sign up for his job? He's waiting for you and has all kinds
of wonderful things planned. The good news is he has so much
work, you'll never be unemployed again.

IN THE FLOW

Lord, help me be everything you want me to be. Forgive me if I have
any dark corners still lurking in my heart that need to be refreshed
and renewed by you. I'm ready to get to work for you today. Amen.

WHAT'S COOKING?

And don't let something you consider to be good be criticized as wrong. God's kingdom isn't about eating food and drinking but about righteousness, peace, and joy in the Holy Spirit. Whoever serves Christ this way pleases God and gets human approval.

—Romans 14:16-18

One old adage says, "You are what you eat." In some places, people eat a lot of rice, others eat a lot of rice and beans, and others just eat anything they can put their hands on. In spiritual terms, you're pretty much free to eat anything as long as it serves your body and gives you the strength to serve the world.

Paul delivered this message to the people of his day because they were getting more legalistic about what someone ate or didn't eat than they were focused on opening their hearts to the things that would please God.

The relevant message, though, is that you can get out your cookbook and create any masterpiece of culinary delight that you wish. God wants your heart and your mind and your body to be at peace, to be in union with him, and so what you eat or drink only matters if it limits your ability to be present with him.

Today, whatever you eat and wherever you enjoy a meal, ask God to bless the meal and keep you strong and healthy in him. If you do, no matter what you're eating, it will be a feast.

IN THE FLOW

Lord, thank you for the food that sustains me and the variety of tasty things I get to prepare and enjoy. Strengthen me always in you. Amen.

A SALUTE TO MOTHERS

When a woman gives birth, she has pain because her time has come. But when the child is born, she no longer remembers her distress because of her joy that a child has been born into the world.
—John 16:21

Since we just recently celebrated Mother's Day, it might be a good idea to give God extra thanks for the woman who brought you into the world. She may not have been perfect in every way, but she brought you here and that's reason enough to honor her.

Mothers across the globe are more similar than they are different. They all hope and pray for their children. They all love with every fiber of their being, and they all look to the God of their hearts to help make a difference in their child's life. They do what they can to guide and teach, and when they can't, they find another way to get the job done. Mother's are God's helpers, his arms and legs, his hugs and kisses.

Today, whatever else you do, think about your mother and whisper a prayer in her honor, asking God to watch out for her, to embrace her, and then thank him for his wisdom in putting such a wonderful woman in your life.

We all recognize the truth in the saying, "God could not be everywhere and so he created mothers." Love your mom with all your heart.

IN THE FLOW

Lord, thank you for my mother. Thank you for her gifts of love and her efforts to help me grow to be the person I am today. Amen.

PRAYER ATTITUDES

But when you pray, go to your room, shut the door, and pray to your Father who is present in that secret place. Your Father who sees what you do in secret will reward you.

—Matthew 6:6

The what, where, when, and how of prayer probably have as many definitions as there are people to offer a point of view. Whether you go in your room and shut the door or sit on your front porch and pray for the people who pass by on the street, God hears your prayer. The truth is that sometimes, praying in private may be the exact thing you need. Other times, you may be more in the "pray without ceasing" mode where you offer up short prayers for everything that crosses your mind.

Your attitude about prayer time mostly makes a difference to you because like most things, you'll get back in some measure what you put into it. If you are seeking God's help with all your heart and you pray with all your heart, then you can be sure God hears you. If you do a half-hearted prayer, it may not serve you as well.

Whatever way you define prayer, be sure to pray. Pray when you're happy, when you're in need, when you're lost, when you're rejoicing, and when you simply need to sit hand in hand with the God of the universe. He's ready to talk with you any time at all.

IN THE FLOW

Dear Father, thank you for hearing my prayers and creating a way for me to talk with you, because I need you all the time. Amen.

MAY 18

WISE, SMART, . . . OR JUST DUMB LUCK?

So be careful to live your life wisely, not foolishly. Take
advantage of every opportunity because these are evil times.
—Ephesians 5:15-16

A hundred times a day, we make choices. Those choices range
from the ones that have little consequence to those that are life
changing. Sometimes we choose wisely, sometimes we don't.
Sometimes we have all our wits about us. We pray about a
potential choice, look at all sides of it, talk to others and get
advice, and we're ready to go. Whatever happens, we're sure
we've done all we can.

Sometimes we try something that takes a bit of risk and we
take all the right steps to see it through only to have it blow up.
The good news is we're taught wisdom by the things that we do
right and also by the things we do wrong. Whatever the outcome
of our decisions, we can always learn from the results and that is
where wisdom lives.

When we come to God with our choices, asking for his Holy
Spirit to help guide us, we can be sure we've done what we can
to be wise. God knows we need his help, and as long as we know
it too, we'll stay on the right track. He knows we're smart, but
he wants us to be wise.

IN THE FLOW

Lord, thank you for teaching me to be wise. Help me seek your
guidance in the things I do so I can avoid acting in foolish ways.
Amen.

AUTHORIZATION CODE, PLEASE!

A huge storm arose on the lake so that waves were sloshing over the boat. But Jesus was asleep. They came and woke him, saying, "Lord, rescue us! We're going to drown!" He said to them, "Why are you afraid, you people of weak faith?" Then he got up and gave orders to the winds and the lake, and there was a great calm.

—Matthew 8:24-26

We've become pretty skeptical about any voice of authority because those who have that voice often abuse their power. So what about Jesus? What shall we say in this day and age about his authority?

Matthew 28:18 quotes Jesus as saying, "I've received all authority in heaven and on earth." That's why we can believe that even now, he can speak to and for us. We can trust in his authority.

We all have days when we feel like we're drowning. We're drowning in paperwork or caving in to worry or overwhelmed by grief. We have something that sends the winds and waves crashing over us just as surely as if we were in a rocky boat. We can't calm things down on our own. We need someone who can find the right code to address our problem and authorize a change. That is why we need Jesus!

As you walk through today, whether you stand firm or have shaky knees, remember that you have a solid place to stand because you live and breathe and stand on the authority of God's only Son!

IN THE FLOW

Lord, thank you for taking the guesswork out of my hands. Thank you for being the One I can turn to for anything I need. Amen.

GRACIOUS HOSPITALITY!

*Keep loving each other like family. Don't neglect to
open up your homes to guests, because by doing this some
have been hosts to angels without knowing it.*
—Hebrews 13:1-2

Nobody has the gift for putting a home together like you do! You always know exactly the right touch to make every little nook and cranny more inviting and more homey. You have a style all your own, and it's one of the things God loves so much about you.

In Bible times, there weren't hotels on every other corner, just people who would put travelers up in their homes and catch up on the news. It was usually a good experience for the travelers and for the hosts as well.

Today, we still may be asked to house exchange students who visit our communities from other towns and other countries, or missionaries as they pass through the area on a fund-raising tour. Whatever the opportunity is to invite others into our homes, the idea is to treat them like family. In fact, we're to love them like family.

If we think about it, we're all travelers here on planet earth. We're all here at the invitation of our Creator and we're just passing through. Today, let's remember that every person we meet is God's child, and since we have the same Father, we're all family! Who knows, one of them just may be an angel!

IN THE FLOW

*Lord, you have given me so much and I am truly grateful. Help
me open my heart to others and embrace each one I meet as family.
Amen.*

BRAGGING RIGHTS!

Who says that you are better than anyone else? What do
you have that you didn't receive? And if you received it,
then why are you bragging as if you didn't receive it?
You've been filled already! You've become rich already!

—1 Corinthians 4:7-8

Most of us are somewhat competitive. We like that we were the
best at something. At least, we think so! With that little bit of
power comes the great desire to also brag about what we can do.
It's all okay to a point, but then some of us don't let it go there.

The giant Goliath bragged that he could fight a whole army
and certainly that he could take on the biggest, strongest, bravest
soldier in Israel. As is often the case when you're around a
boastful and arrogant person, it doesn't take too long to get tired
of hearing the banter.

That's where David came in. David didn't care how big
the giant was; he just believed one thing: with God on his side,
he had an invisible force field, a shield that nothing could get
through. He knew he would win!

When you're tempted to brag a little, remember that you
were given all the power, all the intelligence, all the skill, all the
grace, all the possibility to do what you do by the One who loves
you. If you're really going to boast, then, tell the whole world
what he has done using a little vessel like you. God will give you
real bragging rights if you do that.

IN THE FLOW

Lord, forgive me when I get just a little too full of myself. I know
that I have nothing that I did not receive from your loving hands.
Amen.

THE RUBY SANDALS

While he was still a long way off, his father saw him and was moved with compassion. His father ran to him, hugged him, and kissed him. Then his son said, "Father, I have sinned against heaven and against you. I no longer deserve to be called your son." But the father said to his servants, . . . "We must celebrate with feasting because this son of mine was dead and has come back to life!"
—Luke 15:20-24

The character of Dorothy in the movie *The Wizard of Oz* goes off on a remarkable journey, facing fears, finding her true self, and ultimately discovering that she always had the way home. All she had to do was tap the ruby slippers on her feet.

The prodigal son was a bit like that. He had the way home all the time. When he finally figured it out he took the long journey home again with his heart in his hand. His father was waiting with open arms and forgiveness.

All of us take this same journey. We identify a place as home, even if we have never really understood what it means to us, and then we wander away from it. We go because we have to discover for ourselves who we really are. We have to know the truth of what our Father means to us.

Today, be grateful to your Father for loving you so much that he waits for you. The good news is that now and forever he offers you a way to come home.

IN THE FLOW

Lord, thank you for taking me into your family and for loving me even when I stubbornly go my own way. Thank you for bringing me safely back to you every time. Amen.

Hide and Seek!

Those whose way is blameless—who walk in the Lord's Instruction—are truly happy! Those who guard God's laws are truly happy! They seek God with all their hearts. They don't even do anything wrong! They walk in God's ways.

—Psalm 119:1-3

This psalm is such a beautiful reminder of what life is like when we don't play hide and seek with God. When we walk in his ways and say our prayers and come to him for advice, our spirits soar and our hearts are truly happy. In fact, when we're in that space, we can't even imagine leaving it again. We can truly do no wrong and life is good!

As a loving Father, God has blessed us with all the opportunities we need to know more of him and more about ourselves. He is a great teacher and reaches out to each of us every moment, bidding us to come to him or to try something new. He watches us proudly when we do well and find more joy in our relationship with him and turns his head slightly when he knows we've gotten ourselves in a bit of a fix.

We don't need to play hide and seek with God. We need to come out of hiding and just seek him. Seek his advice, his kindness, his permission to move and grow and learn, and seek his love, his incredible never-ending love. Seek him today and you'll realize that being near him is what really makes you happy.

In the Flow

Lord, I want to draw near you today no matter what I do. Please walk with me and keep me safe in your tender care. Amen.

May 24

Thinking Practice!

*From now on, brothers and sisters, if anything is excellent
and if anything is admirable, focus your thoughts on these
things: all that is true, all that is holy, all that is just, all
that is pure, all that is lovely, and all that is worthy of praise.
Practice these things. . . . The God of peace will be with you.*
—Philippians 4:8-9

Okay, stop right now and take inventory about what you allowed
to go through your brain. Was it in the category of the things
that are excellent, or perhaps admirable? Were you thinking
happy thoughts of things that are pure and lovely and worthy of
praise? Chances are your thoughts were on some issue of the day,
some problem you're trying to address at home, some deficit in
your bank account, thoughts that bring you anything but peace.

So maybe you need practice thinking about the good things.
Take three deep breaths and let out all the stressful, noisy, fearful
stuff that takes more space in your head than you want anyway.
Then, look up or out or over and focus on the One who loves
you. Make a list if you must of all that is holy and just and bright
in your life. Read the list and think about each thing on it at least
three times a day.

If you practice thinking about all that God has done to make
your life joyful, you'll find your heart and mind are ready for his
peace. Be at peace today.

In the Flow

*Lord, it is so hard to drown out the noise of life. Help me be
intentional about thinking thoughts of joy and love. Let me praise
you with my whole heart. Amen.*

THE PLACE OF SACRIFICE

*All have sinned and fall short of God's glory, but all are treated
as righteous freely by his grace because of a ransom that was paid
by Christ Jesus. Through his faithfulness, God displayed Jesus as
the place of sacrifice where mercy is found by means of his blood.*
—Romans 3:23-25

What if getting into heaven was your job? According to this
Scripture, all have sinned and have fallen short of God's glory.
That means none of us would have a free pass.

That does present a dilemma, because we like to think that
we're clever enough or smart enough, or maybe even religious
enough, that we could at least get up to the door. Unfortunately,
even if we got to the door, we might find a sign that said, "sorry,
no room at the inn."

God didn't make the way back home quite that perilous. The
truth is, the way back has been taken care of and your ticket has
been purchased. All you have to do is redeem it.

God alone made the sacrifice, the pure, loving, all-for-one,
one-for-all sacrifice and so we all have a way home again. Today,
as you use your skills and talents to do the work you do, keep in
mind this one thing, you're free. You're free to be everything you
can be because you have a ticket to get back home. All you have
to do is pick it up and thank your Redeemer.

IN THE FLOW

*Lord, thank you for not leaving the ride home up to me. I know I'd
never find a way to get there. Thank you for your grace and your
mercy. Amen.*

BECAUSE GOD KNOWS YOUR NAME

But now, says the LORD—the one who created you, Jacob,
the one who formed you, Israel: Don't fear, for I have
redeemed you; I have called you by name; you are mine.
When you pass through the waters, I will be with you;
when through the rivers, they won't sweep over you.
—Isaiah 43:1-2

God always remembers your name. Sure, he has millions and millions of people on his roster, but somehow when it comes to you, he knows you right away. He doesn't have to slip quietly to the side and ask someone else to remind him who you are. Why? Because you are his!

When someone knows you well and has a relationship with you that is that familiar, they do their best to help you in the hard times and be with you when you might feel alone. God does that too, only he is always with you, always at your side and won't leave you alone. He wants you to hear him call your name as he puts out the welcome mat.

Scary things will come up. Hard times will hit you. You won't know what to do every time. The good news is this: God put your name in before you got there, so he made a reservation for you to walk right up to him and let him know what is going on.

Just call on him any time you need his help.

IN THE FLOW

Lord, wherever I am today, I pray that you will be near me, guiding
and guarding me. Thank you for knowing my name. Amen.

GOD'S NOURISHMENT!

The LORD's Instruction is perfect, reviving one's very being.
The LORD's laws are faithful, making naive people wise. The
LORD's regulations are right, gladdening the heart. The LORD's
commands are pure, giving light to the eyes. Honoring the LORD
is correct, lasting forever. The LORD's judgments are true.
—Psalm 19:7-9

If you're into energy drinks, you probably like that you can
mix a sprinkle of this and a smidge of that, blend it with some
yogurt and bananas and strawberries, and off you go for the day,
fortified and energized. You have been revived.

God nourishes you in a similar way in that he is the One
Source that you can go to for all your needs. When you want
to learn from him, when you're ready to listen, he's there with
amazing insights and new ideas. He's ready to pour out his Spirit
in your direction, guiding you and giving you a new perspective.
He's interested in making you brilliant so that you can be proud
of your choices and become wiser in the things you do.

Honor him and praise him. Give him a chance to renew your
enthusiasm so you can fulfill the life purpose he designed for you.
He wants you to succeed and he will make sure you have all you
need to make that happen. Only he can truly nourish your soul!

IN THE FLOW

Lord, thank you for teaching me and revitalizing me today. Help
me keep my eyes open to all that you have for me and let me shine my
light for you. Amen.

GETTING THROUGH THE SATs!

Dear friends, don't be surprised about the fiery trials that have come among you to test you. These are not strange happenings. Instead, rejoice as you share Christ's suffering. You share his suffering now so that you may also have overwhelming joy when his glory is revealed.
—1 Peter 4:12-13

Remember when you were getting ready to leave high school and you had to take the SATs? That was the big test that colleges would use to get a sense of your readiness to perform well in college. It was also a screening tool that they could use to advise you about what the best direction might be for your life.

Welcome to life's SATs! You're always going to have more tests to take no matter how far away from school you get. We might call the ones you're going through now Suffering and Training—at least that's how some of those tests feel. We might call them Spiritual Activity Training. Those would be the ones that remind you to plug in a little more often to the One who made you. He brought you here and he sticks with you till you get back to him, so a little training helps you both gauge how things are going.

Whatever is going on, know that in faith you already passed with flying colors and one day you'll be overwhelmed with joy as you see your Father standing ready to applaud your hard work and give you a diploma.

IN THE FLOW

Lord, sometimes I do feel like I'm still being tested. I guess you're working with me to help me graduate with flying colors. Thanks for being there through every test I have to take. Amen.

ANOTHER SHOT OF CAFFEINE!

*Stay awake, stand firm in your faith, be brave, be
strong. Everything should be done in love.*
—1 Corinthians 16:13-14

Some mornings, no matter how much coffee you pour into
your veins, you can't quite wake up. It's like you're in a sleep
hangover and no matter what you do, you're just slightly off
center. You're somewhere between that sleepy dream state and
that wakeful, jump-back-into-the-world state.

No amount of caffeine will be able to wake you up enough
to get your spirit's motor running. Only God can do that. He
does it through turning up the light of your faith. It's through
faith that he can strengthen you, firm up your direction and your
resolve to get you going again. Faith then is the thing you have
to drink in and feed upon. It alone can starve your doubts.

As you wake up to the people God has put into your life, all
for his great purpose, be sure to meet them with joy and with
love. So remember today that God is not looking for you to seek
him with your mind and your feelings, things that a little caffeine
may help you with. He's looking for you to experience him today
through faith and love.

IN THE FLOW

*Lord, I know I'm not always awake to the things you have for me,
the love you give me and the mercy you offer me. Grant me the faith
and the love to see those things in you and share them with those
around me. Amen.*

WITH WINGS TO FLY!

The Lord is the Spirit, and where the Lord's Spirit is, there is freedom. All of us are looking with unveiled faces at the glory of the Lord as if we were looking in a mirror. We are being transformed into that same image from one degree of glory to the next degree of glory. This comes from the Lord, who is the Spirit.
—2 Corinthians 3:17-18

Some of us came into this world and we hit the ground running. We had a lot of life to live and only a short timeframe to get things done and so we weren't going to let any grass grow under our feet. We were free spirits right from the starting gate.

Others of us weren't really ready to fly from the outset. We needed a little more time to be nurtured and loved, protected in the nest with the rest of our family before we had to be literally pushed out. At that point, we hoped we had developed wings and that they actually would work so we could fly.

God is working in each of us to bring us a certain kind of freedom, the kind that will allow us to one day be reflections of his Spirit, images of him in the things we do and the ways we act. He gives us that freedom whenever we're ready to embrace it.

Our truth comes from the Spirit of grace and love. Our freedom is reflected in all we do to project his image onto the world. We are free to share his truth with others and to shine a light on his amazing Spirit. With his arms, he will bear us up and give us wings to fly.

IN THE FLOW

Lord, I know that with you, I am free to be myself and to be all that you would have me be in this life. Amen.

ARE YOU WITHIN EARSHOT?

I am the good shepherd. I know my own sheep and they know
me, just as the Father knows me and I know the Father. I give
up my life for the sheep. I have other sheep that don't belong
to this sheep pen. I must lead them too. They will listen to
my voice and there will be one flock, with one shepherd.
—John 10:14-16

A popular cell phone company has a great advertising slogan
in their "Can you hear me now?" campaign. They place their
spokesman in a variety of situations, inside tall buildings, up in
mountain camps, and at other remote sites to make sure that
wherever a customer is using their phone, they will be well
connected to their party and be heard.

It's easy to imagine God asking us the same thing. No matter
where he has placed us on this planet, he really has one question.
"Can you hear me now?" Jesus used to use the phrase, "let the
one who has ears to hear, hear these words." Well, we have ears
to hear, but are we really listening? Are we really within earshot
so that we can respond to his voice?

Jesus has been leading us to become part of his fold and
though he has other sheep, other people that he plans to call,
he only needs us to be concerned with that moment when he
calls out to us individually, when he asks us to listen to his voice.
Today, let's give him the ears of our hearts and listen to his voice.

IN THE FLOW

Lord, help me hear you and be ready to receive your words and your
instruction for the things I do today. I'm ready to hear you now.
Amen.

June

I know the plans I have in mind

for you, declares the LORD; they are

plans for peace, not disaster, to give

you a future filled with hope.

Jeremiah 29:11

LIONS AND TIGERS AND BEARS, OH MY!

*Along the roads animals will graze; their
pasture will be on every treeless hilltop.
They won't hunger or thirst; the burning heat and sun
won't strike them, because one who has compassion for them
will lead them and will guide them by springs of water.*
—Isaiah 49:9-10

God has compassion on all that he made and those of us who appreciate and love the animals on this planet will be pleased to know he works to take care of them as well. He guides them and leads them to places where they can be fed and nourished, and when he needs our help, he sends us to aid them.

God designed the earth with a great sense of efficiency and order. All things work together for good, and we're intricately woven and connected. The sense of awe we feel when we see the vista of an incredible landscape from a mountaintop or from a beautiful valley speaks to that part of our spirits.

Nature's balance is indeed important to us and to the world we serve. Our willingness to also protect it and keep it healthy in ways that serve others and please God is part of our mission on earth. We were called to protect and keep the planet in good shape.

IN THE FLOW

Lord, help us always to be good stewards of your resources. Let us care for the animals and the plants and the aspects of our environment that keep everyone safe and well. Amen.

MILLION-DOLLAR QUESTIONS

*What are human beings, that you exalt them, that you take note
of them, visit them each morning, test them every moment?*
—Job 7:17

When we're passing through trials and tribulations, or even
rejoicing over incredible good fortune, we're tempted to ask God
why. Why indeed does he care about us so much?

We must each answer the question for ourselves, but the
facts remain clear that we are important to him. He's been taking
note of every detail of our lives since the day we came into being.
We're his and there's no mistake about that.

What do human beings, then, want from God? Maybe that's
another million-dollar question. Maybe we need to stop and ask
ourselves what we get that we wouldn't have without him.

Of course, eternal life pops into our minds pretty quickly,
but what about all the other things? To name a very few, we have
someone to turn to in prayer, someone we can talk to any time
at all. We have someone who sees us and validates our existence
and helps establish our purpose. In fact, without God, we have
nothing at all.

Today, whatever you're doing, give thanks to God for
greeting you with each morning sunrise and for desiring a
relationship in every possible way with you. Give him thanks and
praise!

IN THE FLOW

*Lord, I am in awe of your willingness to create a personal relationship
with me. Let me be all that I can be for you today. Amen.*

A Match Made in Heaven

The Lord God proclaims: I myself will search for my flock and seek them out. . . . I will rescue them from all the places where they were scattered during the time of clouds and thick darkness.

—Ezekiel 34:11-12

If God went on a version of a dating site to try to find you, chances are he would be intrigued by your profile. He's here because you have definitely attracted his attention. Looking at your profile further, he's especially interested in your post, "Spiritual, but not religious." He can't help smiling at that because you are indeed a spiritual being, a body wrapped around a spirit as it turns out, so this one makes him wonder. What do you mean by that?

What is *religious*? Does that mean you go to church every Sunday? Does it mean you do something religiously, like drinking coffee every morning at eight? You're definitely spiritual and God is Spirit, so this one sounds like a match made in heaven.

Since you're posted on God's version of Match.com, he can assume you're searching for a relationship too. You may not know exactly what you're looking for, but you know you need something more solid and more intentional in your life. Yes, you are both searching for each other.

Today is a good day to respond to the One who searches for you wherever you are.

In the Flow

Lord, thank you for being willing to search for me wherever I am. Help me recognize your voice when you call. Let me always match my heart with yours. Amen.

JUNE 4

THE SPIRIT OF TRUTH

*If you love me, you will keep my commandments. I will ask the
Father, and he will send another Companion, who will be with
you forever. This Companion is the Spirit of Truth, whom the
world can't receive because it neither sees him nor recognizes him.
You know him, because he lives with you and will be with you.*
—John 14:15-17

Truth, nothing but the truth, so help me God. That thing we swear
in courtrooms is an elusive notion. Your truth may not be the
same as someone else's. It doesn't mean one of you is right and
one is wrong, it means there may well be separate truths.

When Jesus sent us the "Companion," who is the Spirit of
Truth, he did so that we might know truth and be set free from
the little prisons we slip into in our own minds. He didn't just
lend us the Spirit of Truth, he gave us a lifelong companion who
would live with us forever. You know him and you recognize him
because you received Jesus.

We live with the Spirit of Truth. We may or may not wish to
always know the truth, because we sometimes prefer to bend it
or shape it to fit what works best for us, but we have the option
of seeking real truth. We have the opportunity always to replace
our own thoughts with those that line up more precisely with the
One who shares life with us all the time and knows us better than
we know ourselves. May truth prevail in all that you do today.

IN THE FLOW

*Lord, thank you for your precious Spirit of Truth. Thank you for
giving me the freedom to always tell the truth as your Spirit guides
me. Amen.*

FROM THE INSIDE OUT

I won't leave you as orphans. I will come to you. Soon the world will no longer see me, but you will see me. Because I live, you will live too. On that day you will know that I am in my Father, you are in me, and I am in you.

—John 14:18-20

If you have a favorite sports team and you watch the game from your armchair view, you'll be involved, kind of, in the game, but you're only looking in from the outside. We do a lot of things by observing them, staying enough removed that we don't actually have to make a commitment or get involved, but keeping a safe distance.

Jesus is committed to you. As he lives in the Father, so he lives in you and you live in him. You're no longer standing on the outside looking in. You're in the game; you're a player on God's team. You really can count on the fact that he won't let anything happen to you today that the two of you won't handle together.

You're not separate, you're together as one. It's a tricky concept, and you may not always know exactly what it means to you, but imagine that you're not looking into God's window today, you're sitting in the big easy chair in his living room. You're both wonderfully and mysteriously connected.

IN THE FLOW

Lord, it's hard for me to actually understand how we're connected sometimes, but I recognize that you're in my heart and that's enough for me. Thank you for loving me so much. Amen.

JUNE 6

KEEP WORKING ON YOURSELF

Focus on working on your own development and on what you teach.
If you do this, you will save yourself and those who hear you.
—1 Timothy 4:16

God wants you to make it your business to develop who and what you are. He wants you to understand your role in being his child and to do what you can to reach and teach others.

Getting to know yourself sounds easy on a superficial level. You may like the person you try to project to the world. If you dig down a little further, though, you'll come to that layer just under the skin where you hide the things you aren't sure about. That part of you is not as often revealed to others. Then, somewhere buried inside yourself too is the you who truly wants to understand the mysteries of life, the you who wonders about purpose and about God's plans and what part you really are to play in those plans.

God wants you to keep working on yourself, tossing out the stuff that doesn't serve you or him well and looking for the things that resonate with your heart and excite your spirit. The closer you get to that person, the more you'll be able to work for your heavenly Father. He likes the skin you're in, but he wants you to get comfortable with the places deep in your heart. You're not thin-skinned or thick-skinned. You're absolutely perfect in God's sight because he has you under his skin.

IN THE FLOW

Lord, I'm still learning and there's no doubt about that. Help me develop every aspect of my character in ways that please you. Amen.

GOD'S GOOD PURPOSE FOR YOU

*God is the one who enables you both to want and
to actually live out his good purposes.*
—Philippians 2:13

You live and breathe and work and dance for only one reason: because you have a purpose in this life. You were born to carry out a particular job for God and he invites you every day to keep seeking that purpose. You may identify it in some way through the things you feel passionate about since God inspires your passions. You may see it through the eyes of compassion, the tears you shed on behalf of others who are in pain.

Whatever calls you, whatever rings truth in your ears so loudly it won't go away, is more than likely a piece of the puzzle, a piece of the mission and the thing you can define as your purpose. You are the only one who can actually fulfill it, the only one given that particular assignment. Oh sure, God will reassign your task if he has to, if for some reason you don't choose to complete it, but when you return home, he won't ask how many church services you attended, he'll ask how often you attended to the needs of those around you and how many ways you found to serve others. He cheers you on even now as you seek to fulfill his incredible purpose in your life. He knows you can do it.

IN THE FLOW

*Lord, I don't always know for sure if I'm on the right track, but
I look forward to fulfilling my mission for you. Thank you for
believing in me and trusting me to get it done. Amen.*

UNDER CONSTANT CONSTRUCTION

Every house is built by someone, but God is the builder of everything.
—Hebrews 3:4

If you stand in front of the Taj Mahal or Buckingham Palace or even the White House, it's easy to be awed by the architecture and the intricate design. It's awesome to imagine the one who conceived that design, created the blueprints, and made it come to life. It's an amazing and awesome work of art.

When you reflect on the joy you get from the home you've chosen to live in or perhaps the dream home you hope one day to have, remember that whoever designed the house was inspired by the same Source that inspires everything you do each day. There is only one builder of all things and that is God. He sees what you need and he constructs the best possible way for it to work out. He creates all the blueprints and someone else builds on his design.

As you stand in front of your own front door, your own little "White House," remember the builder. Remember the one who wants to be the head of your house, the one who built in some very special options just for you. It may well be under construction, but that's okay. God is willing to redesign as you understand more fully what making a home with him is all about.

IN THE FLOW

Lord, thank you for building a house that is so warm and inviting. Thanks for working on it with me to create it in a way that fulfills your purpose for my life. Amen.

IN CELEBRATION OF FATHERS

*As for children, obey your parents in the Lord, because it is
right. The commandment* Honor your father and mother *is
the first one with a promise attached:* so that things will go
well for you, and you will live for a long time in the land.

—Ephesians 6:1-3

The Scripture reminds us that it's good to honor our fathers and
listen to them and obey them and love them, and in doing so we
receive the opportunity of a promise from God. When we pay
due respect and give honor to our dads, we receive the gift of
living a long life and having things go well for us.

Alexandre Dumas said, "Without respect, love cannot go far
or rise high: it is an angel with but one wing." Loving our dads
may have amazing moments of joy and crashing moments of
bewilderment, and yet, we cannot grasp our connection without
respect.

Wherever your dad is today, think of him fondly, send him
warmth and love, and if he's still near you, give him a call and let
him know all that he means to you. He'll enjoy the call and you'll
be assured that you're doing things right.

IN THE FLOW

*Lord, thank you for my dad. I can't say I always understand him,
but I always love him and I'm grateful for all he did to help me
become the person I am today. Amen.*

THE RUNNING STREAM AND THE ROCK

Don't you know that all the runners in the stadium
run, but only one gets the prize? So run to win. Everyone
who competes practices self-discipline in everything. The
runners do this to get a crown of leaves that shrivel up and
die, but we do it to receive a crown that never dies.
—1 Corinthians 9:24-25

In a confrontation between a stream and a rock, the stream always wins. It doesn't win through strength or might, it simply wins because it perseveres. Perhaps if we take this thought a bit further, we might see that even though the rock is solid and holding its own, it's also standing still. We might assume the rock would win simply because it looks more intimidating. But that isn't so. Sometimes in life, we're like the rock. Other times, we're the stream.

We spend our days trying to win at something. It's good to set goals, even if there's only one prize. Like the stream, we keep moving, being a part of the process, and flowing past the obstacles to create fresh opportunities. When we do that, regardless of where we come into the flow, or who notices our achievement, we win. God sees our efforts and rewards our self-discipline. He serves as our Rock, our steadfast and worthy prize, and he gives us the stream of grace to keep getting closer to his throne.

IN THE FLOW

Lord, I know that I am not always willing to move to get things
done. Sometimes I'm more like the rock and I just let things pass me
by. Help me move today like a persistent stream so I get a little closer
to the goals you've set for me. Amen.

Love, Prayers, and Enemies!

You have heard that it was said, You should love your neighbor and hate your enemy. But I say to you, love your enemies and pray for those who harass you so that you will be acting as children of your Father who is in heaven.
—Matthew 5:43-45

There are days when we might wonder why the "bad guys" seem to keep finding a way to succeed in the world, while we hang on for dear life. Then, along comes this Scripture from Jesus telling us to pray for those "bad guys" and even love them because that's what God wants from us. God makes it bright and cheery for everyone regardless of how he is treated, and he expects us to do the same.

Wow! There's a little show-stopping thought! Why does God treat everyone the same? Ah, perhaps it is that he can only do good. He only knows how to love so that's what he offers.

How about us? What if we didn't have an ounce of hate or jealousy or unkindness in our bodies? We'd probably be a little closer to our Father because then we'd pray and love and offer our hearts to everyone, friends and enemies alike. All who see us would see his face for exactly what it is—the face of love.

Let's pray for those who annoy us, challenge us, and most of all need us to help them find the God of love today.

In the Flow

Lord, I have to admit I don't always understand how life works, or even how to tell the bad guys from the good guys. Help me be on the side of good, though, according to your will and purpose. Amen.

Is That a Gray Hair?

I am the one, and until you turn gray I will support you.
I have done it, and I will continue to bear it;
I will support and I will rescue.
—Isaiah 46:4

If you're of a certain age, you probably remember the first gray hair. You were startled, annoyed at its presence, ready to immediately pull it out. After all, you're far too young for that.

If the hair-dye manufacturers have their way, you won't have to worry about those telling gray hairs. You can cover them up and no one will know. Okay, God will know.

This brings the realization that God has been with you since before you were born, watched over you relentlessly like a mother hen, and will never see you as anything but his child to care for and support. He will keep his end of the bargain until he has you safely tucked back into his arms.

Today, whatever you might be doing, stop and really think about what it means that God sees you right now. The God who created the whole universe, set the stars in motion, and made the mountains and the ocean, that same God sees you right where you stand. Reach out to him and thank him for all he has done to keep you safe and to let his face shine upon you. Remember too that he knows every hair on your head, the gray ones too, and even if you had no hair at all, he'd still see you as his beloved child.

In the Flow

Lord, thanks for knowing all that I will be going through today.
Bless my work and my family and those I love in Jesus' name. Amen.

HAVING THE MOST TOYS

*Why would people gain the whole world but lose their lives? . . .
Whoever is ashamed of me and my words in this unfaithful and
sinful generation, the Human One will be ashamed of that
person when he comes in the Father's glory with the holy angels.*
—Mark 8:36-38

There's a saying that goes, "The one with the most toys, wins."
Thankfully, many of us are a little more in touch with our
humanity. Jesus told the disciples once that the poor would
always be around and so we might assume that means the rich
will always be around as well. Politically, religiously, humanely,
we try to come up with answers for the imbalance, and yet greed
persists and rears its ugly face so that the division just becomes
greater, in spite of the obvious generosity of many.

Perhaps it is truly a matter of the heart and an individual
decision. You either have a generous spirit or you have a greedy
spirit.

What we will exchange for our lives is a good question for
any of us to contemplate. We can be generous with our money,
our time, our talents, our dreams, our friendships, and any
opportunity to give that presents itself, or we can close our hands
and make a fist and hit hard, because someone who didn't receive
from us just got knocked down. It's worth considering every day.
Perhaps the one with the most heart wins!

IN THE FLOW

*Lord, help me remember to be generous in those areas where I might
not think to be. Help me give more time to others in ways that will
bring relief and joy. Amen.*

EAT, DRINK, AND BE MERRY!

*All of you who are thirsty, come to the water! Whoever
has no money, come, buy food and eat!*
—Isaiah 55:1

If you were invited to a fancy five-star restaurant, free of charge,
no strings attached, would you go? You're not going to be
pressured to buy a time-share or form a co-op, you're simply
going to mingle with others and have some fabulous food and
your host will take care of it all. Well, the invitation is an open
one and you're invited every day to come to the feast. It's a
standing invitation and allows you to bring friends along too if
you'd like. All you have to be is a little bit thirsty.

One writer said, "I was dying of thirst. When my spiritual
eyes were opened I saw the rivers of living water flowing from his
pierced side. I drank of it and was satisfied. Thirst was no more.
Ever since I have always drunk of that water of life, and have
never been athirst in the sandy desert of this world."

God never wants you to thirst. He alone knows the way to
the living waters, the place that will make your soul come alive
and open the eyes of your heart. He invites you with each sunrise
to come to his table, to start your day with him so that you
will not thirst in the desert of this world. It's a good day to be
refreshed and renewed in him. Come to the feast!

IN THE FLOW

*Lord, thank you for always inviting me to your table. I come with
great joy and gratitude today. Amen.*

SAFE WITHIN GOD'S HEART

I will gather them from all the countries where I have scattered them in my fierce anger and rage. I will bring them back to this place to live securely. They will be my people, and I will be their God.
—Jeremiah 32:37-38

It's scary to watch the news these days. Everywhere you look, chaos seems to reign, and people are impoverished, starving, wandering like lost children in a desert. Sometimes it appears that humanity has gone crazy.

It's helpful then to resort to God's promises like the one we have here. God is still granting us the grace to live in this land, to find our home here on earth, and he has called us to be part of his family. He wants to be our God and promises to never stop treating us well and with love.

What wonderful news! We may or may not be able to do something about the troubles of the world, or even the troubles in our own neighborhoods or families, but whether we can or can't, we have an advocate. We have One who has set himself over us, who is bigger than any dictator, any self-made prophet, any destroyer that the world may discover. We already know who wins, and as members of his team, as his people, we win too.

Today, remember that you're safe in God's hands. He will lift you up and keep you protected by his grace and love.

IN THE FLOW

Lord, this world comes to nothing without you. I am nothing without you and so I am grateful for your loving and generous spirit and all you do to watch over my life. Amen.

GOD'S PLANS FOR YOUR GOOD

I know the plans I have in mind for you, declares the LORD;
they are plans for peace, not disaster, to give you a future
filled with hope. When you call me and come and pray
to me, I will listen to you. When you search for me, yes,
search for me with all your heart, you will find me.
—Jeremiah 29:11-13

When you've made your plans and filled in your to-do list, but all you accomplish is the right to watch your plans go up in smoke, or you check off just one thing on a list, it might be good to go back and remember whose you are. Go back to your Source of all that is good, get on your knees, and let him know that you've been wandering a bit too long on your own and you really need his help. Search for him!

If you do that, God promises to answer, to share the things he has in mind for you and to give you what you need. All things are possible with God and most things are slippery slopes without him. He doesn't want you to live in fear, or challenge you with one disaster after another, he simply wants you to give him your heart. He'll provide all you need from that point on.

Hang this thought on the mirror of your heart today, and reflect the joy only God can give you.

IN THE FLOW

Lord, thank you for bringing me back to you and for giving me
hope. I look forward to all that you have planned for my life and
I'm grateful. Amen.

IN THE FOOTPRINT OF LEADERS

*Jesus knew the Father had given everything into his hands and
that he had come from God and was returning to God. So he
got up from the table and took off his robes. Picking up a linen
towel, he tied it around his waist. Then he poured water into
a washbasin and began to wash the disciples' feet, drying them
with the towel he was wearing. When Jesus came to Simon Peter,
Peter said to him, "Lord, are you going to wash my feet?"*
—John 13:3-6

The idea of servant leadership starts with this Scripture. This
is the moment when we see that to lead others, we have to be
motivated by our willingness to serve them. We have to set their
needs before our own and create opportunities for them to stand
firmly on their own two feet.

In serving others, we want not only to be willing to do
whatever it takes to get the job done but also to be willing to
guide and teach and assist their walk with God in numerous
ways. In Bible times, washing the feet of guests was considered
a way to honor them because the streets were dusty and most
people walked a long way in their sandals. You can imagine how
inviting it would be to have your feet washed and cleansed and
refreshed. Imagine Jesus washing your feet with great love today,
preparing you to step out in greater faith to get your work done.

IN THE FLOW

*Lord, only you can really wash me clean, so I thank you for renewing
my spirit in you and staying with me every step of the way. Amen.*

THAT'S NOT MY JOB!

If I, your Lord and teacher, have washed your feet, you too must wash each other's feet. I have given you an example: just as I have done, you also must do. I assure you, servants aren't greater than their master, nor are those who are sent greater than the one who sent them. Since you know these things, you will be happy if you do them.
—John 13:14-17

Unfortunately, the idea that something is "not my job" has permeated every area of life. The server at the restaurant doesn't bring the water because that's the hostess's job. The person on the street corner doesn't pick up the trash and put it in the bin because that's the street cleaner's job. The little things we could do, and most of the time could do pretty easily, end up not being done because we've got the not-my-job disease.

Today, remind yourself that you are always invited to do the job, whatever it is, as soon as you see the need or have the opportunity. You can wash the feet of others just as easily as you can be served by them.

Your job is always changing and your work for the Lord is always ongoing. If you think it's somebody else's job, give that another thought today and lead on!

IN THE FLOW

Lord, thank you for reminding me that I have the job to be aware of others and their needs and that I can pick up the baton and move forward to get things done no matter how big or small the job may be. Amen.

TIME TO SHINE YOUR ARMOR

Put on God's armor so that you can make a stand against
the tricks of the devil. . . . Therefore pick up the full armor
of God so that you can stand your ground on the evil day
and after you have done everything possible to still stand.
—Ephesians 6:11-13

Have you tried on your armor lately? Does it still fit? Getting a
little rusty? These days you may have to suit up more than you
once did because the world is just a bit this side of chaotic and
crazy and the devil is dancing everywhere you turn.

Some of us wear our armor like we would a tuxedo or a ball
gown, because we pull it out for special occasions and moments
when we're more sure it will be called for. Others of us give it
a passing nod as we pick out our morning jeans and tee-shirts.
After all, we're just staying home today and can't really get into
any trouble.

The truth is that you need your armor all the time, every
day. It's your best defense against the moments when someone
suddenly challenges your thinking, questions your faith, or makes
you feel uncertain about why you believe the way you do. It's
your protection against self-doubt or mild depression that can
hit you unexpectedly. It's God's gift to you and it really looks
great on you. Pull it out today and shine it up a bit. You may be
surprised at just how comfortable it feels.

IN THE FLOW

Lord, I haven't been aware of putting on my armor much lately,
but I realize you gave it to me to help me get through each day. Walk
with me today no matter where I go. Amen.

WHAT'S STOPPING YOU?

*I assure you that if you have faith the size of a mustard seed,
you could say to this mountain, "Go from here to there,"
and it will go. There will be nothing that you can't do.*
—Matthew 17:20

What keeps us from going after the bigger seeds of faith? Why
don't we go for apple-seed faith or all the way to watermelon-
seed faith? What if we really planted our faith, grounding it in
Christ in such a way that nothing could shake us? Maybe then we
could grow it into something sizable enough to make the earth
move or to influence the direction of a stream.

Jesus could raise people from the dead, stop the winds and
waves, and heal the blind. He told his disciples that with the help
of the Holy Spirit, they could do greater things than even he had
done. Either we're not tapping into the most powerful Source in
the universe or we're walking around with tiny little bits of faith.

If you examine your own faith, perhaps you can identify
the things that stop you from wanting more of it. You may be
concerned that if you had those powers, God would expect you
to use them. You may also be slightly challenged by the idea that
your faith should serve not only you, but others. Let's learn to
practice mustard-seed faith and see what grows from it.

IN THE FLOW

*Lord, you know how much I rely on you and on the faith you've
given me. Grant me more faith and a heart that is open to taking it
in and sharing it with others. Amen.*

HANG IN, HANG ON, DON'T HANG UP!

*Offer prayers and petitions in the Spirit all the time. Stay
alert by hanging in there and praying for all believers.*
—Ephesians 6:18

Make a list of the things you do "all the time." Perhaps you'll list
things like sleep, eat, love your spouse and kids, clean the house,
walk the dog, and pay your bills. How many of us would actually
list "prayer" as a thing we do all the time?

Sure, we pray fairly regularly, perhaps in the morning to
start the day, at mealtime, and then again before bed. We have
times of prayer and God loves to hear from us at those times.
The writer of Ephesians, though, is asking us to consider praying
constantly.

Clearly our minds need to function in other ways throughout
the day, so we can't literally spend every moment in prayer,
but can create windows in the day when we invite the Lord's
Spirit into whatever we're doing. We ask him to be our quiet
companion, protecting us through the day, challenging us to
listen more closely for his voice. Perhaps we could surrender
our lives and our thoughts in such a way that we would indeed
be praying without ceasing, hanging in there for the sake of
ourselves or someone else.

IN THE FLOW

*Lord, I guess I am a rather stop-and-go prayer person. I stop to
pray quickly and then go on, forgetting to wait to hear your voice,
forgetting to let the Spirit intervene on my behalf. Help me be more
constant in prayer today. Amen.*

MAKE UP YOUR MIND ALREADY!

Elijah approached all the people and said, "How long will you hobble back and forth between two opinions? If the LORD is God, follow God. If Baal is God, follow Baal." The people gave no answer.
—1 Kings 18:21

You may not have a split personality, but it can be pretty perplexing to be uncertain about something that really affects your life. You can waffle back and forth to such a degree that days go by, months even, and still you're on the fence, not moving forward, not going back, simply stuck in the middle somewhere.

Before we marvel at the Israelites' indecision, though, we might want to face the question squarely for ourselves. After all, how often do we get sidetracked by the current versions of Baal that exist in our world? How often do we procrastinate about whether we'll get more involved with the world or whether we'll follow the path God intends?

As you make choices today, remember that time slips on and some of your choices won't have the opportunity to present themselves to you again. You must act and take a stand to embrace your Savior in all that you do.

IN THE FLOW

Lord, time really does get away from me and sometimes, I'm sure, I make a mess of things when I don't handle them with your help. Let me always choose you as the most important decision I make on any given day. Amen.

STRETCHY, FLEXIBLE, OPEN HEARTS!

We are partners with Christ, but only if we hold on to
the confidence we had in the beginning until the end.
When it says, Today, if you hear his voice, don't have
stubborn hearts as they did in the rebellion.

—Hebrews 3:14-15

You probably don't think of yourself as stubborn. Oh, you may
have a few quirks about how things are done or you may have
some definite opinions about issues that are neither black nor
white, but still, you're not stubborn.

Martin Luther admitted to his own stubbornness and
said stubbornness should have been his middle name. We can
probably relate because we too are pretty inflexible about certain
things in our lives. We believe we've already cornered the market
and that there's no other valid opinion beyond the one we hold.
In fact, we can usually find a good Scripture to support our point
and make it seem like a divine revelation.

Even if we could find another Scripture to support the exact
opposite view, we would be too stubborn to admit it's there. So,
the reminder to us here is to listen today for the authentic voice
of our Savior, and be open to wherever he would lead us. We
have to stretch our minds and hearts to meet him even halfway.

IN THE FLOW

Father, help me understand when I'm holding on to something
that is not your truth. Help me live with an open and loving heart.
Amen.

HANG ON TO THE GOOD

Rejoice always. Pray continually. Give thanks in every situation because this is God's will for you in Christ Jesus. Don't suppress the Spirit. Don't brush off Spirit-inspired messages, but examine everything carefully and hang on to what is good.
—1 Thessalonians 5:16-21

Do you ever feel less than thankful for a situation you find yourself in? Maybe your son just quit college without giving you a reason why, or you lost your job without any notice or severance. Maybe you just got diagnosed with a serious illness, or you've been told you won't be able to have a baby. Some situations don't immediately bring feelings of gratitude.

When everything feels topsy-turvy and you wonder what you're going to do next, the answer is simple. You're going to run to your Father in heaven and explain everything you know about the issue you face. Then you're going to thank him. You're going to thank him for helping work out a solution that's perfect for you. You're going to also thank him for his Spirit that he gives you so generously to help you in any situation.

Hang in there with God. He won't let you down and he'll make sure you have what you need. Be thankful you have him to face whatever happens to you today.

IN THE FLOW

Lord, thank you for being there with me no matter what happens today. I put all my worries, all my joys, all my heart and life into your merciful hands. Amen.

REFRESHING RAINS

*If we live by the Spirit, let's follow the Spirit. Let's not become
arrogant, make each other angry, or be jealous of each other.*
—Galatians 5:25-26

As we follow the Spirit, breathe in the Spirit and are filled by the
Spirit, we are more prepared to embrace the gifts of the Spirit.
Arrogance, anger, and jealousy have a chance to be replaced with
more godly virtues, such as patience, kindness, goodness, and
self-control.

If you want to follow the Spirit more closely today, invite
him in to your daily routine, asking him to bless your home, your
work, and your heart. Listen for his urging when he suggests that
it's time to pray or time to relax. Thank him for giving you the
incredible peace and comfort and sense of connection you feel
with God's Word and with your faith.

You're bathed in the Spirit as surely as if you were swimming
in a small pond or floating in a great ocean. You're awash with
his presence and grace and made whole again. You simply have to
create the opportunity for him to come into your awareness.

Today, relax with the Spirit of God and receive the gifts of
faithfulness and love, joy and peace. Be his voice, his arms, his
opportunity to speak with someone who may yet long for his
embrace.

IN THE FLOW

*Lord, I invite your Holy Spirit into my life, my heart, my work, and
all that I am and all that I do today in Jesus' name. Amen.*

June 26

The Right Utensils

Doesn't the potter have the power over the clay
to make one pot for special purposes and another
for garbage from the same lump of clay?
—Romans 9:21

Sometimes we may wonder why God has us working in a certain job or living in a certain town. We feel more like a fish out of water than like a clay pot set in the window for a special reason. We may begin to question our Creator about his plans, even suggesting he may have made a mistake giving us the task at hand. In our worst state, we might even suggest he didn't do a very good job making us. After all, we're not as smart as some, not as attractive as others. We're not as skilled as our neighbor or as strong as we might be.

The truth is God designed you and he believes you're some of his best handiwork. He sees you as good and knows what you can do. You have a purpose and he's excited to see you thrive as you do his work. It's a new day and rather than wonder or question why you were created, give God thanks and praise for making you exactly as you are, and ask him to guide you into doing all that you can to fulfill your purpose.

In the Flow

Lord, I know I don't always understand what you want from me,
but I'm grateful to be here. Help me give you the best of me every
place I happen to be today. Amen.

YOU ARE GOD'S ACCOMPLISHMENT!

Instead, we are God's accomplishment, created in Christ Jesus to do good things. God planned for these good things to be the way that we live our lives.
—Ephesians 2:10

It always feels good to get something accomplished, to feel like you did something worthwhile and well. That's what God must have experienced when he made you. God gave you a very particular set of skills so that you would be well equipped to accomplish the tasks he put before you. He allows you to work in the same manner a consultant does in the sense that you can work the plan in a variety of ways and he'll be pleased with it as long as you get the intended result. In fact, the more creative you are with how you get to the goal, the more enjoyable it can be. The key is simple. You have to keep God informed of your steps.

As long as you go back to God with your game plan and give him a chance to make suggestions and bless it, things will go well, but we often walk off and start doing things without God's blessing.

Today you have another opportunity to go back to God and ask him to guide you, offer insights, and bless your work. If you do, then together you'll be able to enjoy some major accomplishments.

IN THE FLOW

Lord, I know I often make plans and forget to invite you into them. Please see what I'm doing today and help me carry out the mission we have together. Amen.

CALMING THE STORMY SEAS

When evening came, Jesus' disciples went down to the lake.
They got into a boat and were crossing the lake to Capernaum.
. . . The water was getting rough because a strong wind was
blowing. When the wind had driven them out for about
three or four miles, they saw Jesus walking on the water.
He was approaching the boat and they were afraid.
—John 6:16-19

Sometimes we ride along on calm seas. Life seems to be going smoothly, nothing feels like it's in crisis and we're headed in the right direction. Then suddenly, a storm comes up and black clouds hang over our heads. We do our best to manage the waves of fear and frustration that wash over us. Those times bring us to our knees, causing us to ask Jesus to draw closer.

The disciples were bouncing in the waves a few miles from shore, anxious because Jesus had not yet joined them and a storm was brewing. Knowing their anxiety would be high, Jesus took the shortest route to aid them. He walked on the water and reminded them to not be afraid. They were awed by the experience, but what's more, once they acknowledged it and prepared to bring their Lord on board with them, they discovered another amazing thing. They were safely back at the shore.

Whatever is causing you to feel the rising tide today, stay calm. Know that your Lord is even now drawing closer to you. It is his will to always keep you safe from the storms.

IN THE FLOW

Lord, thank you for helping me remain calm, no matter what is
going on around me. Amen.

GIVING YOUR WHOLE HEART

He replied, "You must love the Lord your God with all your
heart, with all your being, *and with all your mind. This is
the first and greatest commandment. And the second is like
it:* You must love your neighbor as you love yourself."
—Matthew 22:37-39

Do you ever notice how many things you do with kind of a half-
hearted approach? You go to a job that pays you well enough to
keep going, but not enough to make you stop wishing you could
come up with another plan. You go to Bible study on Tuesdays,
but most of the time you feel only partially present because life
issues are in the forefront of your mind.

Jesus told us that God wants the whole of us, the whole
heart and mind of us. He wants our whole being to love him.
That means we have to wake in the morning with him as our
first thought, our first love. It means we come to him before
we let anything get out of hand. We surrender our days, our
relationships, our children, and our jobs to him. We give him
thanks and praise for all we have.

Overflowing with that kind of love, we're ready to give
more. We can embrace our neighbors and friends, our co-
workers and even acquaintances with a love that comes from the
heart, from the depth of our being.

IN THE FLOW

*Lord, I come to you today with my whole heart, surrendering all
that I am, all that I can be, and all that I dream about, knowing
I'm safe in your love. Amen.*

June 30

Finding Your Bliss

I'm not saying this because I need anything, for I have learned how to be content in any circumstance. I know the experience of being in need and of having more than enough; I have learned the secret to being content in any and every circumstance.
—Philippians 4:11-12

Most of us go in and out of that feeling. We have good days and great days, bad days and horrible days, and we grow slightly cynical, assuming that it's just the way life is, that there really isn't much we can do about it. Well, the truth is we can't really do a lot about the external world, or sometimes even the events that take place in our own households, but we can do something about our internal worlds. We can come to the well, come to the Source of living water and be refreshed at any time. We can be content to bask in his presence if we just take the time to stop and let his peace wash over us.

It's a good day to find your bliss. Cut away from the busyness of life, step aside from your cares and concerns and do just one thing. Set your mind and your heart on heavenly things. Go to the One who bids you to thirst no more, but to receive the peace that only he can bring. He gives you his peace to help you manage the things of the world. All you have to do then is receive it.

In the Flow

Lord, I come to you today, ready to receive your gift of peace, ready to be content in you. Amen.

July

The fruit of the Spirit is love, joy,

peace, patience, kindness, goodness,

faithfulness, gentleness, and self-control.

Galatians 5:22-23

HARVESTING THE GOOD STUFF

But the fruit of the Spirit is love, joy, peace, patience,
kindness, goodness, faithfulness, gentleness, and self-
control. There is no law against things like this.
—Galatians 5:22-23

Imagine a fruit of the Spirit market, much like a farmer's market, where you could go amid the throngs of people and find a rich assortment of love in one booth, a soothing waterfall of peace and patience in another, and some tender sprouts of goodness and kindness just ready to blossom. You're invited into this kind of market every day and the fees are very reasonable. In fact, when you choose the Savior of the world to be your very own, he gives you this bounty as part of the deal.

Oh, you may find yourself shying away from some of the vendors. You may not want to have total self-control, for instance, having to be totally responsible for all your actions, because then it would be hard to pull out those old excuses that have carried you for so long. The truth is you no longer need the old excuses. You've already been excused from all the things that held you back and didn't allow you to bloom. Your life is meant to be fruitful. It's time to reap the harvest!

God saved all the good stuff just for you. Enjoy!

IN THE FLOW

Lord, thank you for your incredible gifts to me. Help me receive
them and utilize them for the good of others today. Amen.

HERE COMES THE SUN!

Stay awake, stand firm in your faith, be brave, be strong. Everything should be done in love.
—1 Corinthians 16:13-14

Some mornings it's a struggle to wake up. The alarm blasts out its signals and you keep hitting snooze. God respects your sleep time, your much needed rest at night, but he always has his trumpets nearby, ready to sound out his presence, because he wants you to wake up to him.

Most of the time, you can hear his voice faintly in the background as you go through the day. You can hear him, but you're still kind of sleepy as you do your best to please your boss at work or struggle to get things done on your to-do list. You wander around dimly aware of his presence and his willingness to help you get through the things that bring your faith to a standstill. He knows you have a lot to deal with and that's one reason he wants you to wake up. If you just knew you could reach out to him at any given moment of the day, you wouldn't have to be in such turmoil. You wouldn't have to feel so all alone.

This is the day the Lord has made and he wants you to wake up your sleepy head, wash your face, and open your eyes to all that he has for you. Here comes the sun, so be brave and strong and see God's glory.

IN THE FLOW

Lord, thank you for waking me up today and offering to walk with me and help me in all that I do. My strength is in you. Amen.

THE 5000-PIECE PUZZLE OF YOU!

*God has made everything fitting in its time, but has also
placed eternity in their hearts, without enabling them to
discover what God has done from beginning to end.*
—Ecclesiastes 3:11

If you've ever put together a large jigsaw puzzle, you know that
it can be pretty time consuming. There are many pieces that look
the same, so you have to keep searching for the one right piece
that will make everything come together. You can try several
times before you make that happen.

Your life story is something like that. God designed you,
gave you all the pieces you need to make a beautiful picture of
yourself. You started out with great enthusiasm. You knew you'd
go to college, get married, and have a family. At least, that's what
you thought when you started putting the pieces together.

In the meantime, life happened. Some of your pieces never
did fit well and some are still in the box waiting for you to figure
out where they go. You may feel like you will never get the pieces
finished and accomplish your goals. The truth is that every piece
you discover moves you closer to that achievement.

So today, remember that you have more pieces to find, more
to try, and that with each one, God is creating his masterpiece
through you. He already knows how beautiful you are!

IN THE FLOW

*Lord, help me discover more of what you want for my life. I know
with your help and your love, I can put it all together. Amen.*

Free, With Purchase!

No one should look out for their own advantage,
but they should look out for each other.
—1 Corinthians 10:24

Some of us celebrate today as Independence Day, the day
when individual freedom became a household idea. But your
independence day started a long time before that one. You
became free the day Jesus chose to be your Savior. You became
free with a purchase. He purchased you!

Now that you're free, then, what do you do with your
freedom? You have the freedom to choose to make life whatever
you want to make it. You can use your gift of being free to create
more ways to get ahead of the other guy or you can create the
chance to walk alongside the other guy. That's a choice of the
freedom you have been given. You can do for yourself alone, or
you can do for others.

Today, consider your choices in light of God's love for you.
Will you run so fast to get ahead that you leave others in the
dust, or will you invite others to walk with you? How will you
foster independence today?

In the Flow

*Lord, it's not always easy to remember that I'm not here alone in
this game of life trying to make the most of it for myself. Help me do
the things that will benefit others as well. Thank you for setting me
free. Amen.*

Struggles of the Heart

Little children, let's not love with words or speech but with action and truth. This is how we will know that we belong to the truth and reassure our hearts in God's presence. Even if our hearts condemn us, God is greater than our hearts and knows all things.
—1 John 3:18-20

Your heart is a critic. It reminds you when you miss an opportunity, when you don't do well, or when you fall flat on your face. It's relentless! It may even keep you from trying to do good. It can make you believe that your contribution is meaningless and that no one really needs the things you do.

God is greater than your heart's critic. He sees the effort you make over and over again and he is thrilled with you. He knows you and he loves you and today he wants you to trust that your purpose is great in his eyes.

This is your day to do one small thing with great love, and when you do your heart will soar. God designed you for good and he loves to see your heart take wing. Do something that will make him proud today!

In the Flow

Lord, I don't always feel like I'm making much of a contribution to the world or even to the people around me. Help me stop judging myself so much and keep believing that the little things I do mean a lot to you. Amen.

WATERS OF JOY

The earth will surely be filled with the knowledge
of the LORD, just as the water covers the sea.
—Isaiah 11:9

Although Isaiah wanted us to realize that God did not hide himself and that he made it easy for us to access him, easy to find him, we might still miss the boat. We could find ourselves marooned on dry land, waiting for the day when he'll rescue us from ourselves, waiting for the living waters.

It may be of interest to also note that potable water, fresh water that we can drink, only covers about 2.75 percent of the earth. That means we can be aware of the water, but we may not yet be able to drink it, to refresh and renew ourselves through it. Jesus is the fresh water. He is the living water that will allow you to never thirst again, to never be dry-docked. He is your fountain of life and will keep you covered in joy.

Today, as you consider the waterways that are near you, imagine the great oceans filled with the knowledge of the Lord, and remind yourself once again how much joy you receive from the fresh water that comes to you every day, through the gift of your faith in Christ.

IN THE FLOW

Lord, I thank you for filling me with fresh water to replenish my spirit and help me through this day. Thank you for your grace and mercy. Amen.

MAKING A FOOL OF YOURSELF!

So be careful to live your life wisely, not foolishly.
—Ephesians 5:15

Someone once said that wise people learn more from the fools in this world than fools learn from those who are wise. So what about you? If this is a two-sided coin, which way do you want the coin to fall? You can choose. You can be wise or foolish on your own.

Your goals and dreams are yours. Some would call them foolish and remind you that you need to take a wiser course of action. Others would call you wise for believing and trusting the God of your heart even when things look improbable, or even impossible.

Jonathan Swift, that fabulous author of *Gulliver's Travels*, said this: "A person should never be ashamed to own being wrong, for it simply means you are wiser today than you were yesterday." If you need more wisdom today, then start your day with the Source of all knowledge, the one who knows you perfectly.

Embarrassing moments happen to everyone. You can survive a red face and a moment of discomfort, but you'll discover the best wisdom comes when you seek God's Word and his guidance.

IN THE FLOW

Lord, I am a little crazy sometimes and I'm so glad you hold me up and keep me strong. Help me desire more of your wisdom in every choice I make. Amen.

I'M SORRY, I'M SORRY, I'M SORRY!

He doesn't deal with us according to our sin or repay us according to our wrongdoing, because as high as heaven is above the earth, that's how large God's faithful love is for those who honor him. As far as east is from west—that's how far God has removed our sin from us.
—Psalm 103:10-12

Forgiveness is not an easy thing, and perhaps one of the hardest struggles has to do with forgiving ourselves, especially when we've done something that is a total departure from who we really are or who we want to be. We can't forgive ourselves so we imagine that God can't forgive us either.

The truth is this. God sent his Son for you on purpose. He sent his Son so that he could take all your foolishness, all your crazy decisions, and all the things that you struggle with to the cross. He nailed them right there and that's where they are. You don't have to keep going back and getting out the hammer to take the nail out and then post it up there again. You're forgiven! God accepted your apology the day you accepted his Son.

IN THE FLOW

Lord, I do have a problem forgiving myself for things I can't even believe I did now that I'm past them. I'm glad you see all of me and forgive all of me, because I couldn't carry the burden of these foolish choices without you. Thanks for wiping the slate clean again. Amen.

Shaking Off the Dust

*Like a parent feels compassion for their children—that's how
the LORD feels compassion for those who honor him. Because
God knows how we're made, God remembers we're just dust.*
—Psalm 103:13-14

No doubt, we all appreciate the idea that God is compassionate
about his children. He watches over each of us with great
interest and concern for our well-being. Like a good parent, he
sometimes lets us go out on our own. He sees every step we take,
lifts us up again when we fall, and brushes off the dust when we
stumble.

In the same way, he wants us to see each other with merciful
eyes. He did not put us here to judge another person's way of
life or someone else's looks. He did not ask us to determine right
and wrong except for the choices we make for ourselves. No,
what he wants is for us to go out into our neighborhoods or sit
down to the dinner table with our families and remember one
thing: we're all dust. We're a creation of God's hands and we live
because of his great love for us.

When we see each other through compassionate hearts, we
see the whole person, the whole possibility, the reason God is her
or his Father as well as ours. Let your compassionate heart enrich
the lives of everyone around you now.

In the Flow

Lord, help me have a kind heart toward all your children. Amen.

Those Lessons From Kindergarten

All the believers were united and shared everything.
They would sell pieces of property and possessions and
distribute the proceeds to everyone who needed them.
—Acts 2:44-45

Remember when you were learning about sharing and getting along with others? Your teacher made a point of telling you to share your toys, to be nice to the person next to you, and to help someone whenever you could.

The classroom has gotten bigger, but the lessons are still the same. Share with others, be kind, and help when you can. It's pretty simple, and yet the grown-up version of us doesn't always aspire to do those things.

Take a look at any area of your life today where you're still withholding, still stocking all the toys you can even if you never play with them. Also, you may discover that you've been really adept at sharing and that kindness is so natural to you that you could still make the sandbox set proud.

You may find that you crave the simple acts of kindness and love that you once knew more than you ever realized. You may want those days to come back again.

Guess what? Those days have never gone away. Share your heart today.

In the Flow

Lord, thank you for all that you've done to give me simple joys and
pleasures. Open my mind and heart to new ways to share with
others. Amen.

Spiritual Muscle Fatigue

*Dear friend, I'm praying that all is well with you and that you
enjoy good health in the same way that you prosper spiritually.*
—3 John 2

How are your spiritual muscles today? Are they fatigued by all
the working out you've been doing the past few days or are they
somewhat limp from a lack of use, somewhat less developed than
they might be?

Your health is good when it is good emotionally and
spiritually as well as physically. You can run five miles every
morning and eat a lot of whole grains and raw vegetables and still
feel somewhat fatigued, somewhat disconnected to your heart.
If that's the case, take a look at the last time you ran the race for
the prize that never perishes, fought the good fight for all that
pleases your Creator, and managed to exercise your privilege to
worship any way that you choose.

Add to that the spiritual food that comes from the fruit of
the Spirit and the living waters of Jesus. Nourish yourself with
kindness, goodness, and self-control and see if your muscles
don't feel stronger, your smile brighter and your day happier.

Tap into God's training program and really develop your
spiritual muscles. They will sustain you and keep you strong all
the days of your life.

In the Flow

*Lord, I know I don't exercise nearly as much as I should either
physically or spiritually. Help me strengthen myself in you. Amen.*

A Black-Tie Event

*God . . . has clothed me with clothes of victory, wrapped
me in a robe of righteousness like a bridegroom in a
priestly crown, and like a bride adorned in jewelry.*
—Isaiah 61:10

When was the last time you went to something that required a
great suit, a tux, or a long gown? It may have been your child's
wedding or your last cruise when you sat at the captain's table.

Now you may be wearing blue jeans and a tee-shirt or maybe
even a bathrobe, but you're wrapped in God's clothes of victory.
You're adorned with love and you sparkle in a way that you
never did before. In fact, you look a bit like royalty! He'll give
you jewels like you've never seen, and by the time he's done,
you'll feel like a bride on her wedding day, or a groom peacefully
waiting at the altar.

Since this is a black-tie event, there will be grand music in
the hall and photographers with their flashbulbs bursting. The
best caterers will have created exquisite tables and the King
himself will be there to greet you. Yes, it is a day of incredible
celebration.

The good news is you can begin the celebration right now,
because you've already been clothed in his righteousness. Just say
"yes" to his invitation.

In the Flow

*Lord, thank you for treating me in such a grand way and giving
me a chance to come to your party. Help me live so I reflect the best
of who I am in you. Amen.*

FREE AT LAST!

He rescued us from the control of darkness and
transferred us into the kingdom of the Son he loves. He
set us free through the Son and forgave our sins.
—Colossians 1:13-14

Slavery in any form brings a desire to be free. Whether we acknowledge it or not, many of us are slaves to something . . . perhaps a relationship, a job, an addiction to food or drugs, or even a desire to accomplish important things. We set those things up as either the obstacles to get through or the objects of our affection, and sometimes they become our addictions in a way that keeps us continually tied to them. We yearn to be free!

It's important to know the difference between what you control and what controls you. Perhaps one way to recognize this difference is to hold it up to the light. Hold the thing that keeps you captive up to the light and see if it strengthens you to navigate the darkness. See if it frees you from all that works to pull you down.

Whatever keeps you enslaved, in big ways or small ways, steals your freedom. Today, pray to be free in the way that only the Son can provide. It's your day to feel the light of his love on your life.

IN THE FLOW

Lord, I thank you for the freedom to worship you, to love you, and to let go of those things that no longer serve you or me. Help me live free and safe today. Amen.

BELIEVING IS SEEING

*By faith Enoch was taken up so that he didn't see death,
and he wasn't found because God took him up. He was
given approval for having pleased God before he was taken
up. It's impossible to please God without faith because the
one who draws near to God must believe that he exists
and that he rewards people who try to find him.*

—Hebrews 11:5-6

Many of us approach God with a kind of "seeing is believing"
mentality whereas God has more of a "believing is seeing"
mentality. The more you believe, the more you'll see. The more
you see, the more God draws near to you and is able to approve
your plans and dreams.

How can you practice believing? God must know that
you believe in him, have complete faith in him, and are totally
connected to him regardless of what you see or don't see. God
must be a witness to your faith. When he is, then he can reward
you and approve your future plans and dreams. To help you
practice believing, try this simple exercise and repeat it until you
have truly taken it in as your own idea.

Say to yourself, "Lord, I totally believe in you and in your
love for me. I believe that you are ready to approve my hopes
and dreams. Thank you for loving me so much. Amen."

IN THE FLOW

*Lord, I'm faithful most of the time, but I admit I don't always have
the assurance I wish I had. I know that sometimes I want you to
give me signs of your presence so I know I'm right. Lord, just help me
believe more fully in you today. Amen.*

July 15

You're a Shining Star!

Do everything without grumbling and arguing so that you may
be blameless and pure, innocent children of God surrounded by
people who are crooked and corrupt. Among these people you shine
like stars in the world because you hold on to the word of life.
—Philippians 2:14-16

If you stay still for just a moment and lean in, you might be able
to hear it. Can you hear the applause, the ones surrounding you
cheering you on because they are so excited you've gotten this
far? You've managed against all odds to stay the course in a world
where the grumblers and mumblers are abundant; you stand out.
You're like a shining star in the middle of a big dark sky.

Sure, you may wonder whether it's all worth it, or whether
you want to keep trying. There are days when you could just
hide your light under a bushel, but you allow his word to be an
actual lamp to your feet, a light to your eyes, and a halo over
your head and you keep going.

Oh, there it is again—more cheering, more angels
surrounding you, rejoicing with you over the good you've
accomplished and the things you've done. People may tease you
a bit about your innocent ways, but more than that, they may
wish they could be more like you. Yes, they can all see what a
difference it makes. Bravo for you!

In the Flow

Lord, you keep me steadily on the path of your love, helping me stand
even when everything around me feels shaky. You're my rock. Thank
you. Amen.

FOLLOW THE LEADER

Therefore, if there is any encouragement in Christ, any comfort in love, any sharing in the Spirit, any sympathy, complete my joy by thinking the same way, having the same love, being united, and agreeing with each other.
—Philippians 2:12

Did you ever play a game called "Follow the Leader"? You wanted to do everything to be just like the leader.

You're not a kid anymore, but you're still invited into the game. You can play the game best when Jesus is your leader and you strive to follow him in all that you do.

When you find someone suffering from any form of sorrow, you can bring encouragement in a way that no one else can. When you see someone who doesn't have a smile, who is depressed by the shadows of life, you can offer your smile, your positive spirit, and your gift of joy, because you offer it to them just like Jesus would.

Whatever you do today, be a faithful follower and a wonderful friend. Be more like Jesus!

IN THE FLOW

Lord, help me follow in your footsteps and offer the mercy and grace and peace of heart and mind that only you offer to people just like me. Amen.

WHEN YOUR WORLD FALLS APART

God is our refuge and strength, a help always
near in times of great trouble.
That's why we won't be afraid when the world falls apart, when the
mountains crumble into the center of the sea, when its waters roar
and rage, when the mountains shake because of its surging waves.
—Psalm 46:1-3

In recent years, our planet has been experiencing a lot of tumultuous episodes that cause it to quake, shake, and break in various places and yet, we know that God is still in control.

The same thing is true when our personal world begins to fall apart. We realize that things are not going as smoothly at the job as they once did or that our spouse isn't really talking to us in the same way.

Unfortunately, those rumbles of change often blast into full-blown whirlwinds, engaging us in ways we never dreamed possible. Remember God is always right there at your side, helping to calm the storms and smooth the waves. If you're going through big changes, know he has you wrapped in his embrace and he won't let anything happen to you. He has a plan and he has your back. He knows how to make the world turn right side up again.

IN THE FLOW

Lord, it's not always easy for me to recognize your presence in the
midst of my storms. I guess I focus more on the storms than I do on
you. Please help me trust that you're part of all that happens to me
today. Amen.

FRIENDS TO THE END

*This is God, our God, forever and always! He is the
one who will lead us even to the very end.*
—Psalm 48:14

Did you ever do a "pinky swear" with a friend? You know, the
moment when you both made a commitment to be friends
forever. A pinky-swear moment is very serious because those
who make that vow expect to honor it their whole lives.
Unfortunately, things change and people grow apart. It happens
and we all accept it as part of life.

Aren't you glad, though, that God doesn't get another job
and move out of the country or make new friends and forget about
you? He's with you all the way to the end. He's always your friend.

Dr. David Livingstone, the Scottish pioneer and missionary
to Africa, said, "Would you like me to tell you what supported me
. . . among a people whose language I could not understand, and
whose attitude to me was always uncertain and often hostile? It was
this, 'Lo, I am with you always, even unto the end of the world.'
On these words I staked everything, and they never failed."

No matter where you are today, or what kinds of obstacles
you face, remember that God is always with you. He never leaves
your side. He sees you, loves you, and is working with you for
your good in every situation. Pinky swear!

IN THE FLOW

*Lord, thank you for being with me today. Remind me that there is
nothing that can happen to me that we won't face together. Thanks
for your faithfulness to me. Amen.*

WHAT PART OF *NO* DON'T YOU UNDERSTAND?

Let your yes *mean yes, and your* no *mean no.*
—Matthew 5:37

Most of us are ambivalent. We often say *yes* when we mean *no* or perhaps *maybe* and we sometimes say *no* before we understand what we mean by that as well. We struggle then with letting our *yes* mean yes and our *no* mean no. One writer said, "Yes and No are the two most important words that you will ever say. These are the two words that determine your destiny in life."

Wow! That puts the full responsibility back on your shoulders, doesn't it? You've probably straddled the fence now and then, hoping that waiting long enough would present yet another option, but eventually the problem came back again. You had to make a choice.

Owning our choices is the rub, then. It's the place where salt sometimes enters the wound, the place where we wonder at our wisdom or our stupidity to have gotten into the circumstance we're in. We can wonder all we want, but the truth is, we chose it.

Consider your choices today. It's time for you to believe in your own ability to choose, to know when your *yes* means yes, and your *no* means no. Hold steady to the God of your heart in the process. He already said *yes* to you!

IN THE FLOW

Lord, thank you for holding on to me when I make choices. Help me see the wisdom of my thinking so that I can really mean it when I declare yes or no in any situation. Amen.

IT'S OKAY TO BE HAPPY

*So I commend enjoyment because there's nothing better for
people to do under the sun but to eat, drink, and be glad.
This is what will accompany them in their hard work,
during the lifetime that God gives under the sun.*

—Ecclesiastes 8:15

Sometimes as believers, we miss the fact that God really wants us
to be happy. He provided everything we need to live here on this
planet and he provided our talents and our livelihood and our
friendships. We really do have it all. So why aren't we happy?

Perhaps the best way to really be happy is to know who we
are in Christ. When we understand all that he has done for us
and live our lives as fully aware of his presence as possible, then
nothing can really undermine us. Nothing can really steal our
happiness away. We are content no matter what the situation
might be, and when we're content, we can smile at life and be
happy.

It's a new day and no matter what your happiness quotient
looked like yesterday, try to adjust your perspective to being a
truly happy child of God no matter where you go or what is on
your plate. If you have something to do, something to love, and
something to hope for, you're on the way to true happiness.

IN THE FLOW

*Lord, I am happy that you are in my life, in fact, that you are the
reason I can be content at any time. I'm smiling today, and it's all
because of you. Amen.*

Who Are Your Enemies?

Instead, love your enemies, do good, and lend expecting
nothing in return. If you do, you will have a great reward.
You will be acting the way children of the Most High
act, for he is kind to ungrateful and wicked people.
—Luke 6:35

Luke was trying to convince us here that we need to be willing to take care of other human beings, simply because that's what they are, human beings! We don't have to agree with them and we don't have to become best friends, but we do have to care. We have to recognize that God also cares about the people we put in our enemy camp.

Enemies may exist inside you too. Perhaps you are too critical of your body, or too critical of your failures, so that you're your own worst enemy. Perhaps you are still trying to figure out forgiveness, never mind love.

"Love your enemies" is the guideline. You may find yourself giving time and attention to people you don't especially like, or you may find yourself stopping your inner critic in mid-thought and working instead toward acceptance and even love.

In the Flow

Lord, help me identify my enemies so that I can discover ways to serve them and love them. Help me look at those that exist within my own heart too. Amen.

HUMILITY AND ARROGANCE

Are any of you wise and understanding? Show that your actions are good with a humble lifestyle that comes from wisdom.

—James 3:13

Humility and Arrogance
Did not see eye to eye—
One was full of self-importance,
The other full of humble pie.
They chanced upon a mirror
Hanging halfway down the hall
And stopped for just a moment
To check their countenance and all.
Arrogance was rather pleased
At the reflection he took in,
But Humility saw only Christ
Who had paid for all his sin.

—Karen Moore

Augustine of Hippo remarked, "Unless humility precede, accompany, and follow up all the good we accomplish, unless we keep our eyes fixed on it, pride will snatch everything right out of our hands."

Today, if you will be proud, be proud of who you are in Christ and all that he can do through you.

IN THE FLOW

Lord, remind me that all I have came from you. For that I offer you my life, any good I might do, and my humble heart. Amen.

THE BIGGEST BLESSING

*The LORD bless you and keep you. The LORD make his
face shine on you and be gracious to you. The LORD
lift up his face to you and grant you peace.*
—Numbers 6:24-26

Isn't it awesome to think that the Creator of the entire universe
keeps you in his heart in such a way that he can shine a light in
your direction and bless you abundantly any time at all? You may
receive his gracious light and peace whenever he looks your way.

Imagine now the light of the Son, shining on you, lifting
you up, giving you a peace that passes all understanding. Imagine
receiving the blessing right now, today. Once you have received
it, take it into your heart and hold it just for a few moments. Let
it radiate through your body and mind. Let God's grace lead you
forward.

We're so accustomed to the rat race, so plugged into the
busyness of life, that we seldom really give ourselves the chance
to stop, listen, and invite the King of the Universe to join us,
to smile upon us, to help lighten the load we carry all the time.
It's a good day to be refreshed, reenergized by his glorious
countenance, and then step into the day with great faith and joy.

May the good Lord bless you in a big way, every day and
always.

IN THE FLOW

*Lord, thank you for the gifts that come with your gracious blessing.
Thank you for seeing me right where I stand. Help me walk more
closely with you today. Amen.*

BUSY AS A BEE

As a result of all this, my loved brothers and sisters,
you must stand firm, unshakable, excelling in the
work of the Lord as always, because you know that your
labor isn't going to be for nothing in the Lord.
—1 Corinthians 15:58

Did you ever watch honeybees as they buzz from flower to flower, focused on drinking their fill of glorious nectar, designed to help them produce sweet, succulent, golden rich honey? Interestingly, a single bee only creates about one twelfth of a teaspoon of honey in its lifetime. The bee is very purposeful, though, and never stops trying to get the job done.

How we approach our work, our attitude toward what we do, makes a huge difference in what we're able to accomplish. More than that, it makes a huge difference in how we perceive the importance of our role to get the job done.

Whether you're a street cleaner or a school teacher, your work makes a difference. There's a team out there that totally depends on the work you do. When you adopt an attitude of joy about your work, you make the angels smile because you show without a doubt that you are doing your work for the Lord. Hope you're busy as a bee today.

IN THE FLOW

Lord, I am happy to do the work I do, knowing that it pleases you
and that you bless the work of my hands with your grace and mercy.
Amen.

SEEK FIRST TO UNDERSTAND

Fools find no pleasure in understanding,
but only in expressing their opinion.
—Proverbs 18:2

Some people never tire of sharing their opinion on the topic of the day, whether anyone asked them for it or not.

Wisdom doesn't care so much about opinions. Wisdom always seeks first to understand. Understanding something is a layered process. You can understand the first layer, but once you've peeled it off, somewhat like an onion skin, and gone to the next layer, you may have to start again to grasp the deeper concept. God designed us to strive to understand each one another. He wanted us to dig in and work for a clearer meaning to things.

Intellect may help, but intelligence doesn't necessarily bring true understanding to the table. We must seek understanding like thirsty explorers, hoping to come upon nuggets of truth that we simply couldn't see before even if they were right in front of us.

For a person of faith, understanding is a treasure to be sought after, precious in all that it brings. Today, keep your heart and mind in Christ Jesus that you may have greater understanding and be blessed with peace and joy.

IN THE FLOW

Lord, I do seek to understand more of you today and to be more closely attuned to others as I go about my work. I ask you to help me offer an attitude of understanding more than an ungrounded opinion. Amen.

AWASH WITH THE SPIRIT

*Jesus answered, "I assure you, unless someone is born of water and
the Spirit, it's not possible to enter God's kingdom. Whatever is born
of the flesh is flesh, and whatever is born of the Spirit is spirit."*
—John 3:5-6

It is summertime, and for a lot of people that means paying extra
attention to watering the lawn and working to keep the garden
nourished and growing. Some days, when the sun beats down in
an unforgiving way, you may find yourself wilting, and then you
appreciate more fully the gift of water. Nothing quite hits the
spot as well as a cold, frosty glass of iced tea or cool lemonade on
a summer's day.

Imagine how parched and dry your life would be without the
refreshing Spirit of the Living God. Imagine getting through the
dry spells that happen and not having a resource, a place to go to
find shade and peace. Jesus told Nicodemus that a human being
needed to be washed in the Spirit in order to come into the
kingdom of heaven. The body on its own remains thirsty until it
is given the living water of God's grace and love.

As you water your garden, or sit on the deck with a thirst-
quenching beverage, remind yourself about the gift God has
given through his nourishing and refreshing water for your spirit.
His love renews you every day and keeps you growing in the
garden of his kingdom.

IN THE FLOW

*Lord, I am grateful for your refreshing Spirit and the way it touches
the dry parts of my life, renewing my soul and reminding me that
I never have to be thirsty again. Help me live in a way today that
reflects your great love and mercy. Amen.*

It's Okay to Talk to Yourself

The LORD is merciful and righteous; our God is
compassionate. The LORD protects simple folk; he saves me
whenever I am brought down. I tell myself, You can be at
peace again because the LORD has been good to you.
—Psalm 116:5-7

In this psalm, we're reminded to talk to ourselves in the midst of our trials, to tell ourselves that all is well because we can trust that God will be good to us. We can trust that because he is merciful and compassionate. He sees who we are and he knows we need him to be part of everything we do.

Most of us engage in negative self-talk more than anything else. We don't like our hair, our hips, and our limited skills. We imagine that everyone else is smarter, prettier, wealthier, and anything else we might not be at the time. We simply have an endless stream of chatter that will keep us bogged down.

Today, go along with the psalmist. When things start to drag on you and bring you down, stop the worries and the pessimism. Stop the doubts and the what-ifs and the attitude that only results in more chaos. Instead, tell yourself that all is well because God is good and he has always taken care of you. He always has and he always will. Tell yourself the good news!

In the Flow

Lord, thank you for always being there for me even when I forget to
acknowledge you. Forgive me when I say those negative things that
separate me from you and my faith. Bring me closer to you today.
Amen.

You're a Piece of Cake!

We know that God works all things together for good for the ones who love God, for those who are called according to his purpose. We know this because God knew them in advance, and he decided in advance that they would be conformed to the image of his Son.

—Romans 8:28-29

Before you had a resume or a bio that could impress anybody, you were known. God knew all about you in advance. He designed the very purpose for which you were born.

We might think of your relationship with God like a recipe. You know that you'd love to make a homemade chocolate cake. You can see an image of the cake in your mind and taste it from past experience. God didn't picture you as a chocolate cake, but, in the same way, he knew there was a very special recipe that would make you the beautiful person you are.

He then prepared all the ingredients. He gave you just the right DNA and just the right family to nurture you for his purposes.

You may not yet be all that he designed you to be, but he knows you have everything it takes to get there. He knows that you were made for an important reason. He knows because he knew you way before you were born. He thinks you're beautiful!

In the Flow

Lord, I'm not always sure if I have everything it takes to do what you want me to do, but I'm willing to try. I ask that you would reshape me in any way you need to so that I can fulfill my reason for being in this world. Amen.

July 29

Quiet, Please, Exam in Progress!

Examine yourselves to see if you are in the faith. Test yourselves.
Don't you understand that Jesus Christ is in you?
—2 Corinthians 13:5

If Jesus Christ is inside of you, he is there to help you develop your faith. He wants you to know the Father more fully. He wants you to get to know him too. The idea here is that you may need to test yourself now and then, making sure you're on the path and that your faith is growing. How might you do that today?

One writer said, "God does not require you to follow His leadings on blind trust. Behold the evidence of an invisible intelligence pervading everything, even your own mind and body."

In other words, God hasn't made it difficult for you to determine he is there. He is in everything, the evidence of his presence is in all things, even your body. If that's the case, the test is for you to observe, to feel, and to invite a greater awareness of him into your life. The test of your faith is about desiring even more of what God has to offer you on one hand, and then on the other hand working in a way that gives him back all that you came here to do. Your faith is in God, not in your work, not in your possibilities, and not in yourself—just in him.

In the Flow

Lord, thank you for being the force that sticks with me even when I forget to listen or act. Help me be faithful in everything I do. Amen.

LET GOD BE THE JUDGE

So every single one of you who judge others is without any
excuse. You condemn yourself when you judge another person
because the one who is judging is doing the same things.
—Romans 2:1

It would be great to imagine that you're not a person who judges others. It would be great, but the chances are slim because as soon as you decide to be generous and forgiving toward one group of people that you might have once been biased against, another opportunity shows up and you find yourself judging another group.

Hundreds of illustrations could come up for how quickly we assess situations and put our judgment stamp upon them, never knowing for sure if we're right, and worse yet, not really caring.

It's safe to say that culturally, we're finding our moral fiber eroding from the place we once wanted it to be. Judging others, though, is still not our job. God didn't ask us to judge any more than he asked us to determine someone else's salvation, because those are things that belong strictly to him. Our job is all about love. Let's step out in love and help each other today.

IN THE FLOW

Lord, I know that it is easy to see someone else and believe that I can
see what is wrong in their life. I also know that most of the time I'd
be wrong about the assessment I made. Help me learn to reach out
with an attitude of love wherever you lead me today. Amen.

Now, Isn't That Tempting?

So those who think they are standing need to watch out or else they may fall. No temptation has seized you that isn't common for people. But God is faithful. He won't allow you to be tempted beyond your abilities. Instead, with the temptation, God will also supply a way out so that you will be able to endure it.
—1 Corinthians 10:12-13

It would be great to believe that we're too smart to get caught up in the things that tempt ordinary people. After all, we're believers and so we know we will make better choices.

Big temptations can strike us when we least expect them. It may come in the form of not being fully transparent with the IRS at tax time, or withholding affection from your spouse so that you can manipulate a situation to get the outcome you want. It's a form of temptation because it's contrary to what helps to create a loving relationship.

We receive help for the dilemma of temptation through our faith. Thomas à Kempis said, "Little by little, with patience and fortitude, and with the help of God, you will sooner overcome temptations than with your own strength and persistence."

You're not alone today as you face the temptations that may spiral around you. Call on the God of your heart to help you any time you feel tempted.

In the Flow

Lord, I don't even know sometimes that I'm vulnerable to temptation and then suddenly it rears its ugly head. Help me stay faithful and true to you and to myself in you. Amen.

August

May the God and Father of our Lord
Jesus Christ be blessed! On account of his
vast mercy, he has given us new birth.

1 Peter 1:3

ENERGY BOOST

But those who hope in the LORD will renew their strength;
they will fly up on wings like eagles; they will run and
not be tired; they will walk and not be weary.
—Isaiah 40:31

Been dragging your heels a bit lately? Wondering where you'll get the moxie to keep doing the things you do when nothing seems to be going in your direction?

It's time to spread your wings! It's time to get out there and put your hope in the Lord. Oh sure, that sounds like what you do all the time, but is it? How often do you really come to him in prayer and surrender your daily walk, surrender your own ego, and look to him to renew your strength?

You may hope in the Lord in small ways or hope timidly. You can take a tiny cup to the ocean and hope God would allow you to fill it up. You can, but why would you? Instead, go to the One who made the ocean and ask to be filled from head to toe, ask for buckets unending of his strength. You're sure to find your wings. It's your day for a great energy boost.

IN THE FLOW

Lord, thank you for renewing my hope. Help me rise again in joy knowing that you are working all things out for my good. Thank you, Lord, for loving me so much. Amen.

SIMPLY NO COMPARISON

*Each person should test their own work and be happy with
doing a good job and not compare themselves with others.*
—Galatians 6:4

From your first day at school, you were compared with others.
You may have heard your teacher remarking about how well
some other kid could draw, or you may have heard your parents
compare you to your siblings. You discovered there were kids
who were more praised than you were because they could read
or they could play the piano. You learned you might not be good
enough for the world, and you were only six years old.

You moved on to high school and college, doing your best
to be yourself. You looked at others and envied the ones with
the brains or the charm or the beauty and wished you could be
more like them. You went on to work and discovered that the
comparisons hadn't stopped. The person who had the job before
you was beloved. You looked for a life partner, only to find out
that people were chosen for a lot of superficial reasons.

Where does it stop? When does it happen that you can be
totally happy being yourself, being uniquely the person God
wanted you to be? The answer is right now! Right now, you
can stop all the stories in your head about what else you should,
could, or would be, and simply be a person where there is no
comparison, because you are fabulous just as you are!

IN THE FLOW

*Lord, thank you for making me unique. Help me have confidence
in all that I am and try to not compare myself to others. Thanks for
loving me so much. Amen.*

Something More Than Romeo

But God shows his love for us, because while we
were still sinners Christ died for us.
—Romans 5:8

When those star-crossed lovers, Romeo and Juliet, decided
they couldn't live without each other, it was a story of intrigue,
deception, and romance. Shakespeare brought us full circle with
a love story unlike any other.

The fact is that you also have a true love, someone who
loved you so much he was willing to die for you. He didn't see
all your flaws, he didn't see the craziness that you inherited from
your family, he simply saw you, beautiful you. He looked at all
you are and all you would become and said, "I love you so much,
I'm willing to die for you." Whew! That's pretty big love.

God loves you, then, because he has chosen to do so. What
a wonderful thought to carry around with you today. What a
glorious idea that you could not and did not have to play a part
and attract him like a Romeo or a Juliet, but simply had to be
exactly as you are, and he chose to love you. Walk in his love
today.

In the Flow

Lord, I don't always recognize what it means to have your gracious
love, but I am so thankful that you know me and love me just as I
am. Amen.

THOSE LITTLE WHITE LIES

"LORD, deliver me from lying lips and a dishonest
tongue!" What more will be given to you, what more
will be done to you, you dishonest tongue?
—Psalm 120:2-3

Some of us have mastered the art of word games. We know what someone wants to hear and we say the right thing. We smile when we might feel like frowning and we say yes when we wish we would say no.

We may not think about the many ways we lie to ourselves as being dishonest, but what else can we call it? If we really want to be delivered from lying lips, it's not just about the lies we might tell to or about someone else, it's about those little white lies we so often tell ourselves.

That ancient philosopher Demosthenes put it this way: "Nothing is so easy as to deceive oneself; for what we wish, we readily believe." Ask God to lead the way, to direct your thoughts so that you discover the kind of truth you really want to live, the kind that allows you to be authentically and fully yourself. The truth is, you're God's ambassador and he wants the best possible you to represent him in the world.

IN THE FLOW

Lord, thank you for forgiving me those little lies I make even
unconsciously. Help me be very aware of the choices I make when I
talk to myself or speak with others. Amen.

August 5

The Big Seven

*Then Peter said to Jesus, "Lord, how many times should I
forgive my brother or sister who sins against me? Should I
forgive as many as seven times?" Jesus said, "Not just seven
times, but rather as many as seventy-seven times."*
—Matthew 18:21-22

Maybe it will work if we forgive someone seventy-seven times, or
seventy times seven times, or a million times. The point is that we
need to forgive each other. If someone offends you repeatedly,
doesn't it seem reasonable that you could actually stop forgiving
them?

It does, until you consider what God does. What if God had
a quota of how many times he would forgive you for something
you had done or for all the things you do? What if God cut you
off and left you with no avenue for forgiveness even for one day?

Consider this. Forgiveness doesn't change the past, but it
can surely change the future. If you can think of one person
who has offended you seven times, you can choose to keep
counting the errors, you can sever the relationship, or you can
choose to forgive seven more times, and seven more times after
that. Forgiveness allows a relationship to keep going toward the
future. Nothing else can do that so well. Open your heart to
greater joy and love and forgiveness today.

In the Flow

*Lord, help me be able to forgive those who offend me. Remind me
to let go of old stories and move on. Walk with me today, Lord, and
forgive me all that I do to offend you. Amen.*

TEACHING PEOPLE HOW TO TREAT YOU

Treat people in the same way that you want them to treat you.
—Luke 6:31

You can find a lot of self-help books designed to build relationships, to resolve conflict, and to give you insights and strategies about dealing with difficult people. These books are popular because we all struggle with the way someone else treats us. We are baffled when we give them our best and show them concern and love and they still find ways to offend and annoy us. We wonder at their audacity to treat us unfairly.

Jesus tried to help us with this understanding when he reminded us that a good step is to consider what we want back in a relationship and then to give that to someone else. Think about the way we want to be treated, and be a great example of what we hope for in return. It sounds simple enough in theory, and yet in practice we often fall short.

If you want friends, be a friend. If you want kindness from others, be kind. If you want love, be loving. It's a good day to let others see you for who you really are, so they can love you with joy because they really know you well.

IN THE FLOW

Lord, help me be myself and share who I am with others in ways that please you and allow others to treat me as I also treat them. Bless this day. Amen.

GETTING A GOOD PORTION

Give, and it will be given to you. A good portion—packed down, firmly shaken, and overflowing—will fall into your lap.
—Luke 6:38

Wouldn't you love a windfall? Maybe a sweet surprise, or some unexpected funds, or some good news from someone you love. If you hope for those things and anticipate them, you actually have a part in causing them to come to fruition. Your part is to ease up on others, stop making judgments about what they should be or what they aren't, and start forgiving.

It would be interesting to keep a running tally of the ways we think about others during the day. Would we be able to balance the score at all with how much we were willing to forgive others or how much we were willing to give to those in need? Would we find that our generosity would surprise even us?

When you tip the scales in the direction of doing good, in the arena of giving whatever you can of your time and money and resources, then there's a promise attached. You'll cause something wonderful to happen. You'll find a windfall suddenly appearing in your lap. God will reward you for your kindness and your generosity. He'll see to it that you receive according to the level at which you give.

IN THE FLOW

Lord, thank you for giving me the things I have. Thanks for the multitude of blessings you so often send my way. Amen.

OPENING THE EYES OF YOUR HEART

*I pray that the God of our Lord Jesus Christ, the Father of
glory, will give you a spirit of wisdom and revelation that
makes God known to you. I pray that the eyes of your heart will
have enough light to see what is the hope of God's call, what is
the richness of God's glorious inheritance among believers.*
—Ephesians 1:17-18

The light comes flooding in. As the room gets brighter, you
can see everything that it contains. You can see the beautiful
tapestries, the delicate floral prints, the incredible furnishings. It's
an amazing sight and you're part of it. It's beyond any richness
you ever imagined.

This little imaginary journey has just been presented to you
by the God of all glory, the one who has an amazing inheritance
to bestow upon his children. Your eyes have been opened and
the light has dawned.

As a believer, you know that God's storehouses are full. His
faithfulness is steadfast and his ability to lavish his love on you
is without comparison. All that he needs is for you to desire to
know more of the hope to which he calls you.

As you go about your business today, pray with a focused
kind of intention that the eyes of your heart will be open to all
that God has for you. Smile at his generous spirit and his pleasure
in giving you all good things.

IN THE FLOW

*Lord, thank you for all that you give me. Help me stay mindful of
what I have in you forever and always. I am awed by you. Amen.*

Put Your Heart Into It!

Whatever you do, do it from the heart for the Lord and not for people. You know that you will receive an inheritance as a reward.
—Colossians 3:23-24

Few of us have glamorous jobs or the kind of lives that will end up on virtual reality TV shows. We seldom have more money than we know what to do with and we're not so destitute that we have to stand on street corners doing a song and dance with our hat in our hands.

As believers, though, we might conclude that wherever we are today, we're in exactly the right place. We're in the place God called us to be in for right now. We're his field soldiers, his eyes and ears. More than any of that, though, we're his heart.

Billy Graham once said that "you might be the only Bible some people ever read." What that means, perhaps, is that when someone spends time riding in your car, or calls you with a concern, in need of your friendship and patience, or your skills at any level, they need to see God's heart reflected in you.

Whatever work you have to do today, lift your arms in praise to God and declare that anything you do, you do for him. Your work will seem lighter, and your heart will feel brighter. May you work with all your heart today.

In the Flow

Lord, I thank you for the work I get to do each day according to your plan, your design, and your grace. Help me do what pleases you today. Amen.

How Can I Serve You?

*You were called to freedom, brothers and sisters; only
don't let this freedom be an opportunity to indulge your
selfish impulses, but serve each other through love.*
—Galatians 5:13

When we walk into a restaurant, we expect the waiters to be
enthusiastic about our arrival, pleased to take our order, happy to
get us anything we ask for, and thrilled to get our tip at the end
of the meal, and then send us on our way smiling.

What if we took it upon ourselves to spend our days
treating each other in a similar fashion? We would be creating an
opportunity for doors to open through this encounter. We would
do this because we are free to offer others a hand as we choose.
And we can't help getting something back from our kind deeds
because we'll have a genuine sense of satisfaction that we might
have made a difference.

Imagine today that you can brighten someone's day just
because you showed up. That's your calling. That's the reason
you've been gifted with all you are and all you have. That's how
you give back to God a small piece of all he has given you. It's
your day to cheer up a few more people. Enjoy it!

In the Flow

*Lord, thank you for giving me an attitude of graciousness and a
spirit of love. Help me serve others as you would have me do. Amen.*

LIFE IS NOT ALWAYS A PICNIC

*Go to the ant, you lazy person; observe its ways and grow
wise. The ant has no commander, officer, or ruler. Even
so, it gets its food in summer; gathers its provisions at
harvest. How long, lazy person, will you lie down?*
—Proverbs 6:6-9

When we observe the ants as the writer of Proverbs has done, we
witness the work ethic to which they subscribe. Ants work for
a living and though they go round and round, they don't wait
to be told what to do. They know that if they don't work, they
don't have food, and so they keep working, from sun up to sun
down. They keep going even though the only boss they have to
please is themselves. They work to live and live to work.

Most of us work hard. We do our best to keep up with all
that is required of us. So what can we learn then from the ants?

We can learn not to rest on our laurels. We can learn to
prioritize our work, to do the right work, and then to reap the
rewards when the harvest comes. Life isn't always going to be a
picnic, it won't always be easy to gather what we need into our
nests for the winter. We need to prepare and to be ready.

IN THE FLOW

*Lord, you know the work that I do and you know what else you want
to see me do. Keep me in a place where I am ready and willing to
serve you at any moment. Amen.*

IT'S BLACK AND WHITE

*Anyone who tries to keep all of the Law but fails at
one point is guilty of failing to keep all of it.*
—James 2:10

There are few things in this world that truly are black or white.
According to James, the fact that breaking the law makes a
person guilty of the whole law is one of those things. We might
be able to say we kept the nine Commandments, but the one we
missed out on keeping actually throws us back into the pot of
breaking the whole law.

If you've ever tried to keep one of the Commandments for
even a day, you can quickly see how easily they are broken and
how difficult it really is to achieve salvation through them. The
Ten Commandments then are the perfect guides to why we need
Jesus. With him, we are rescued from the dilemma. With him, we
are saved from the law because there is a new law in our hearts
that he alone can put there. We are saved, pure and simple . . .
black and white.

Today, give Jesus your heart and your mind and your soul
and thank him for helping you work out your salvation through
his rescue efforts on your behalf.

IN THE FLOW

*Lord, help me remember that I can't survive in this world or the
next without you. You're my only redeemer and friend. I praise you
and thank you. Amen.*

RED, WHITE, AND BLUE!

*Come now, and let's settle this, says the LORD. Though
your sins are like scarlet, they will be white as snow. If
they are red as crimson, they will become like wool.*
—Isaiah 1:18

God has provided the way for you to come back to him. He's
taken your sins and changed them from a raging red to a
beautiful white. It's settled and nothing can change it.

Perhaps nothing can change it but you. Martin Luther said
this: "Either sin is with you, lying on your shoulders, or it is lying
on Christ, the Lamb of God. Now if it is lying on your back, you
are lost; but if it is resting on Christ, you are free, and you will be
saved. Now choose what you want."

You have a lot of choices to make every day of your life. You
can choose to go on alone, walk as far as you can and carry the
burden of sin. You can choose to carry it all the way to your final
resting place. You can. But, why would you? Jesus has already
taken the sins that are as scarlet and made them white as snow.
He has already given you a blue chip, a passport to heaven. You
simply have to choose him and let him know you want to be on
his train.

IN THE FLOW

*Lord, I thank you for taking all my sins on your shoulders. I thank
you for keeping me in your fold, allowing me to be a sheep in your
pasture. Amen.*

The Source of All Power

By now I could have used my power to strike you and your people with a deadly disease so that you would have disappeared from the earth. But I've left you standing for this reason: in order to show you my power and in order to make my name known in the whole world.

—Exodus 9:15-16

Niagara Falls is powerful. It generates enough electricity to light up a good share of the North American continent.

Gravity and electromagnetism are also powerful forces. They not only keep you safely walking around on the ground, but they keep the earth in its orbit around the sun. The forces of nature keep everything balanced. They are powerful things.

Love is powerful. It draws you into its grasp, like a moth to a flame, or metal to a magnet, and you can feel powerless to resist it. Love is the medicine that heals wounds and broken hearts, the tonic that makes everything in life feel better. Love is a powerful thing.

Many things are powerful, from the physical things that God created to make the planet work well, to the simple things that you can generate, like love and compassion. Many things are powerful, but there is only ONE source of real power. God is all there is when it comes to power. He rules. Aren't you glad to be one of his children?

In the Flow

Lord, there are so many things that make me feel powerless. Yet, you love me, simple as I am, and give me the power to be your child. Thank you for loving me so much. Amen.

August 15

Life on the High Seas

Some of the redeemed had gone out on the ocean in ships,
making their living on the high seas. They saw what the
LORD had made; they saw his wondrous works in the depths
of the sea. God spoke and stirred up a storm that brought the
waves up high. . . . None of their skill was of any help.
So they cried out to the LORD in their distress. . . . God
quieted the storm to a whisper; the sea's waves were hushed.
So they rejoiced because the waves had calmed down; then
God led them to the harbor they were hoping for.
—Psalm 107:23-30

Your life may not feel like it's sailing along very well, or it may
feel like you've been cruising quite a while with nothing but
smooth waters. The seas of life are churning all the time, though,
and you never know when another storm may come up on the
horizon. You have an anchor, a steady Captain at the helm of
your lifeboat who knows exactly what to do to get you to a
better place.

You call on the Lord and ask him to quiet the storms. You
call on his name until you can breathe in the salty air and feel his
presence. You give up the situation and let your heart and mind
melt into oneness with the Creator.

This is your day to call on his name. This is your day to
understand fully that all is well in the Lord.

In the Flow

Lord, help me remember that you are always with me and that you
won't allow me to be shipwrecked without warning. Wash over me
with your peace that passes all understanding. Thank you, Lord.
Amen.

No Competition

*But the one who is greatest among you will be your
servant. All who lift themselves up will be brought low.
But all who make themselves low will be lifted up.*
—Matthew 23:11-12

Jesus' disciples wrestled with the idea that their master was
going to one day be the chief, the head honcho, the big man on
campus, and so they wondered where that would leave them.
Where would they be sitting when their master came into his
own? After all, they had worked hard for him, so clearly they
were meant to sit on either side of him.

We all know people like this. They expect to be called to the
First Class section and it doesn't matter if they earned a special
place, they simply feel it belongs to them. In fact, they are pretty
sure that others don't deserve to squeeze in ahead of them.

Ah, but the tables keep turning and God has other plans.
He doesn't really care about who thinks they are worthy of
the best seats in the house, he only cares about what motivates
their hearts. He cares about how much they love and provide to
others. Jesus entered Jerusalem on a donkey and went out on a
cross. He is number one! Where we are in the line doesn't matter
at all. It's being in the line that matters. Give God thanks and
praise that you get to be in line with him.

In the Flow

*Lord, it is fine with me to simply show up in line with you. I am
grateful that you have chosen me to be one of your followers. Amen.*

August 17

Remembering Easter

*May the God and Father of our Lord Jesus Christ be
blessed! On account of his vast mercy, he has given us
new birth. You have been born anew into a living hope
through the resurrection of Jesus Christ from the dead.*
—1 Peter 1:3

Today is not a holiday. It's not close to anything for which you're
getting ready to decorate the house or send out greeting cards.
It's just a good day that the Lord has made. It's a day that he
alone designed and planned with you in mind. It's a good day to
remember what he has done for you.

You wake up a little differently from some other people. As
a believer, you wake up to a living hope every morning. You're
reborn each and every day to new possibility, new options, new
opportunities that only come about because of your relationship
with Jesus Christ.

In the words of Cyril of Alexandria, "The Only Begotten
Word of God has saved us by putting on our likeness. Suffering
in the flesh, and rising from the dead, he revealed our nature as
greater than death or corruption. What he achieved was beyond
the ability of our condition."

It's a new day to praise and thank the Lord.

In the Flow

*Lord, you are the only One who claims us, who loves us even as we
are. I thank you for loving me so very much. I praise you for all
you've done in my life. Amen.*

SHAME GAME

Then they both saw clearly and knew that they were naked. So they sewed fig leaves together and made garments for themselves.
—Genesis 3:7

Ever since Adam and Eve, we have found ourselves standing naked before God. We have no ability to hide anything from him, but we still try. We still sew our own version of fig leaves together so that we're not quite as embarrassed to walk close to him.

In our humanness, we convince ourselves that there are little things we can do, and no one will ever find out. We think we can get away with things and we take this attitude all the way up to heaven's door. We look God right in the face and hope that we got away with the things that bring us shame.

Well, hold on to your fig leaves, because no matter how hard you try to cover things up, God already knows everything you've done, thought, or said, and he has one thing to say to you. "Come over here, talk to me, ask my forgiveness." When you do that, he can then wrap his arms around you and say, "I love you so much and I am glad that you told me of your troubles. You don't have to try to hide anything from me."

IN THE FLOW

Lord, I am awed by your willingness to forgive me every time I have to add a new fig leaf, every time I want to hide what I've done. I'm grateful to you for loving me so much. Help me keep trying to please you. Amen.

TWO EARS, ONE MOUTH!

Wise are those who restrain their talking; people with
understanding are coolheaded. Fools who keep quiet are
deemed wise; those who shut their lips are smart.
—Proverbs 17:27-28

Someone once said that "wisdom is knowing when to speak your mind and when to mind your speech." You may have been around people who share their thoughts about your personal story, mostly without invitation, in a way that's aimed like an arrow right at your chest. They may not have thought for thirty seconds about what they are saying, but they can make you feel that what they're saying is important. Perhaps you've done it yourself, reacting emotionally to someone before actually seeking to understand them. It's a common denominator for most of us. We forget that we have two ears for a reason, so that we can listen twice as much as we speak.

As a believer, it's great to pray for more wisdom, to ask God to guide not only your life direction, but your thoughts and your speech. Ask his help before you give someone else feedback or advice. Listen more than you talk. The best wisdom sometimes comes in the form of silence. It allows the situation to speak for itself. Be wise in all that you do today.

IN THE FLOW

Lord, it isn't always easy for me to step back and be quiet when I am
so used to jumping right in with an opinion. Help me stop, pray,
and seek your guidance before I ever make an attempt to guide
someone else. Help me be wise. Amen.

BRING ME ANOTHER ADVIL!

Everyone's head throbs, and everyone's heart fails. From head to toe, none are well—only bruises, cuts, and raw wounds, not treated, not bandaged, not soothed with oil.
—Isaiah 1:5-6

Did you ever notice how many commercials for pain relievers follow the nightly news or the TV shows about crimes? We're addicted to news and we bring it in on our TVs and our computers and in our newspapers. We bring in the world's difficulties and struggles, couple them with our personal stories, and before we know it, all we can do is take another Advil.

It's not just getting another headache that's the problem, though. It's getting so fearful that we grow weaker and uncertain about what God is doing and how he'll help us manage all the grief we see everywhere.

Rest assured, God is in control of all the troubled waters that exist in the world today. Only he knows the remedy that will bring peace again. Our job is to cling to him like never before, even if it means shutting off the TV now and then so that we can recover. Let the Word of God bring you peace today.

IN THE FLOW

Lord, I can hardly take in all the sad news that exists around the world. I pray for all the people who suffer unfairly and without cause at the hands of those who are evil. I pray too for love to fill me so I can be a light when I'm needed. Amen.

Hey, It Wasn't My Fault!

The man said, "The woman you gave me, she gave
me some fruit from the tree, and I ate."
—Genesis 3:12

If there's one thing few of us are good at, it's taking the blame. We just hate having to own our screw-ups. We're likely to do the same thing Adam did: try to point the finger at someone else. In his case, there was only one other human being. "The woman you gave me" did it. In some measure he might have even been blaming God because God had given him the woman.

We might like to think we'd be bigger than that, that we wouldn't blame someone else and that we certainly wouldn't blame God, but we probably wouldn't be telling the truth.

Fixing the blame is never going to fix the problem. Facing the problem, owning the experience, allowing it to educate and prosper your spirit, is the best way to keep moving forward.

God has already made provision for our mistakes. He just wants us to learn from them and be willing to admit when we make them. Celebrate his gift of forgiveness today.

In the Flow

Lord, I am certainly aware of my own mistakes and am so grateful that you forgive me when I do things that are just plain wrong. Help me take responsibility for my actions, and when I fail bring me back again with your forgiveness. Amen.

FROM DRIFTING TO UPLIFTING

*But you need to remain well established and rooted in faith and not
shift away from the hope given in the good news that you heard.*
—Colossians 1:23

Our ancestors came to the United States to start life over again,
to put down new roots, enjoy religious freedom, and carry on
with the hope of all that new possibility brings. They established
the root system that still nourishes us today.

If you look at your root system, the one that helps keep
your faith growing and keeps you blossoming in the Lord, how
effective is it? Does it run deep and hold you when the tempests
of life come in and keep you from drifting away?

If you are rooted in faith, you're protected by the
Vinedresser, nourished and sustained and able to stay strong in
the best and worst of times. If you're tempted to go on alone,
uproot yourself for a time and drift along, remember that you
may well be bounced along on some craggy banks, some stony
places where the peaceful rivers can't flow. As soon as you realize
that you are no longer rooted to the source of life, turn again to
him, for only he can keep you growing healthy and strong. He is
your hope for all eternity.

IN THE FLOW

*Lord, forgive me when I step out there on my own, thinking I know
best, that I can take care of myself. Thank you for always keeping me
rooted in faith, connected to your Divine vine. Amen.*

A Little Weak in the Knees

He said to me, "My grace is enough for you, because
power is made perfect in weakness."
—2 Corinthians 12:9

God is always willing to act on your behalf. The problem is that when you're in your own strength, you sometimes forget who is actually providing the ability and the possibility of the things you're doing. You might even imagine that you are doing it yourself. It is only when you're in pain or when you're feeling weaker that you turn to God for help, that you ask him to create a way for you to move forward.

It's no wonder then that he reminds you that he can bring more power to your situation when you're weak. In other words, when you take yourself off the throne, off the center, and realize that you aren't doing anything alone, then God can act on your behalf. He has the freedom to uplift you and strengthen you.

As one writer said, "Make every effort to let God be great and to ensure that all your good intentions and endeavors are directed to him in all that you do and in all that you refrain from doing." Keep God in the loop of all that you do today and he will strengthen you step by step.

In the Flow

Lord, I pray that you will uphold me today, strengthen and renew
me, and help me be mindful of you in all that I do. Help me see you
more clearly with every step I take today. Amen.

WHEN YOU DON'T KNOW HOW TO PRAY

*We don't know what we should pray, but the Spirit
itself pleads our case with unexpressed groans.*
—Romans 8:26

Our instincts are heightened, our thoughts are somewhat vaguely tuned in to someone we love or something that we just can't put our fingers on, and yet we have a feeling we should stop everything and pray. But for what, or for whom?

When the Holy Spirit nudges you to pray with some insistence, it's good to listen. You may come to the Lord with a vague awareness that you were meant to pray only to discover that you still don't know exactly what brought you to your knees. All you know now is that you haven't hit on whatever it was and so you wait, hoping it will come to you.

The good news is that your obedience is all that was needed. The Spirit has directed it so that your heart and God's will are aligned. You have served as a prayer warrior for someone out in the world.

John Calvin wrote, "God tolerates even our stammering, and pardons our ignorance whenever something inadvertently escapes us." We are blessed with a freedom to address our God at any time. We can put all things in front of him because he cares so much about us. Prayer is one of your best habits.

IN THE FLOW

Lord, I thank you for hearing me and accepting my most humble prayers. Thanks for all your blessings to me. Amen.

August 25

With Every Reason to Hope

We even take pride in our problems, because we know that trouble produces endurance, endurance produces character, and character produces hope. This hope doesn't put us to shame, because the love of God has been poured out in our hearts through the Holy Spirit, who has been given to us.
—Romans 5:3-5

When you try to imagine the Holy Spirit, what comes to mind? Do you think of him as a friend, a teacher, a confessor, or a ghost? The person of the Holy Spirit actually comes to you in many ways. He's there with his arms around you when you suffer over losses, or grieve over someone who is precious to you. He is your divine Guide, the one who works to help you stay connected to the God of your heart in all the right ways.

Troubles will come to us, but we have the gift of the Holy Spirit to help us endure them. We know that we're not alone when we face trials that seem too big for us or too uncomfortable to handle.

We are conquerors through the work of the Spirit of the living God. He sees all that we face today and he steps right up beside us and says, "Let's go . . . there's not anything we can't take on together." Walk in the Spirit today.

In the Flow

Lord, thank you for sending the Holy Spirit to guide me and comfort me. Thank you for making a way for me to get through my problems with your help. I praise you in Jesus' name. Amen.

YOU'RE PART OF A TEAM!

Each one had a role given to them by the Lord: I planted,
Apollos watered, but God made it grow. Because of this, neither
the one who plants nor the one who waters is anything, but
the only one who is anything is God who makes it grow.
—1 Corinthians 3:5-7

Most of us like the idea of finding something meaningful to
do that provides a way to give back to our families or to the
community for the greater good. We hope to leave a legacy of
sorts by doing at least one thing that we realize wouldn't have
happened if we weren't in the picture.

God wants that for us too. He gave us an assignment and he
looks forward to us getting it done. We have a job to do because
we're part of his team. What we have to keep in mind, though, is
that we're able to play just one position on the team.

It's not always easy to recognize what your part might be
in the process, but you can be sure it's important. Without
you, someone isn't going to get properly nourished, carefully
prepared, ready to grow into a deeper faith. It's a big job, but
God knows you can do it.

IN THE FLOW

Lord, help me do my job for you today with great joy and
thanksgiving. Thank you for letting me be part of your incredible
team! Amen.

AUGUST 27

BEING CONTENT

*Do not desire your neighbor's house. Do not desire and try
to take your neighbor's wife, male or female servant, ox,
donkey, or anything else that belongs to your neighbor.*
—Exodus 20:17

Let's get things straight. The people in big houses, medium-sized
house, tiny houses with tin roofs, are not any better or any worse
off than you are, unless they don't have Jesus. Everything anyone
else has is nothing in comparison to what you have in him. You
have every reason to feel like royalty and to make your home a
palace, because you're a king's kid.

When you're content with what you have, you're not going
to be wishing for what someone else has. Paul said that he had
learned to be content in every situation because he knew what
it was like to have a lot, and he knew what it was like to have
a little. You know too. Benjamin Franklin commented that
"contentment makes poor men rich; discontentment makes rich
men poor."

We're rich in the things that really matter. We're wealthier
than anything when it comes to what we inherit from our
Heavenly Father. We have every reason to stop wishing we were
someplace else, and start loving that God has put us right where
we need to be. We have every reason to be content.

IN THE FLOW

*Lord, thank you for putting me right where I am. Help me not envy
those people or those things that are so fleeting, but be content with
all that you give me right here and now. Amen.*

Because of the Cross

But as for me, God forbid that I should boast about anything except for the cross of our Lord Jesus Christ. The world has been crucified to me through him, and I have been crucified to the world.
—Galatians 6:14

Thomas à Kempis suggested that you "carry the cross patiently, and with perfect submission, and in the end it will carry you." We can wear a cross around our necks, admire a cross in a beautiful cathedral, imagine the three crosses on the hills of Golgotha, but none of those images will serve to substitute for what our hearts must understand about the cross of Christ.

Submitting to the cross means you're unique. You're known by the God of the universe and by Jesus. You're in the world, but not of the world, able to bring something to it that couldn't have ever happened without the events on Calvary.

M. Lloyd-Jones wrote, "The preaching of the cross of Christ was the very center and heart of the message of the apostles, and there is nothing I know of that is more important than that."

The Good Friday message that leads to Easter is made new every time you remember what God has done to bring you back to himself. You inspired him to give his only Son so that you might live in relationship to him. Today and every day, live your life as a person who is highly aware of being redeemed.

In the Flow

Lord God, I thank you for loving me more than I can even comprehend. I thank you for redeeming my soul. Amen.

Finding the Oasis

Just like a deer that craves streams of water,
my whole being craves you, God.
My whole being thirsts for God, for the living God.
When will I come and see God's face?
—Psalm 42:1-2

You've probably gone through some dry spells, those times when you weren't feeling especially connected to God. You didn't realize just how dry you could get until one day, you started feeling a little choked, like your throat was full of sand and your heart had lost its flexibility. You began to seek water. You began to recognize your thirst was overpowering and you needed to take care of it.

You wandered around, taking a little sip from the pool at Sunday morning worship, but heading right back to the sand dunes as soon as you left. You left still thirsty, still wanting more. David felt like that too. He told the Lord in no uncertain terms how much he thirsted for the connection they shared.

How are you doing today? Are you dry again? The Source of Living Water is ready to nourish and refresh you any time you ask. The Oasis is near. You simply have to open your eyes to see it and to drink from it.

In the Flow

Lord, thank you for letting me drink from your precious springs of
living water. Thank you for filling me with all I need to get through
a new day. Amen.

WHAT'S STEALING YOUR HEART?

Stop collecting treasures for your own benefit on earth. . . .
Instead, collect treasures for yourselves in heaven, where moth
and rust don't eat them and where thieves don't break in and
steal them. Where your treasure is, there your heart will be also.
—Matthew 6:19-21

It's good to have treasures. Yours have probably changed over
the years. You've gone from treasuring your baseball cards or
your ballet shoes to treasuring the little things that make your
house a home. God delights in giving you the things that make
you feel joy in living.

The only issue comes in when the treasures start to consume
your time and energy so much that they steal your heart away
from God. When you live to add to your collection of beautiful
things, instead of living to do the work God brought you here to
do, you might find yourself treading on dangerous ground.

A. W. Tozer said, "The man who has God for his treasure
has all things in one."

It's okay to love your things. It's better yet to love your
Creator, who gave you all that you have and who has even
greater treasures in store for you in heaven. Help him to stock
those shelves every day you live.

IN THE FLOW

Lord, thank you for giving me such an abundant life. Thanks for
all you do to help me grow in awareness of the treasures that I truly
have in you. Amen.

THE PSALM OF TRUST

*The LORD is my shepherd. / I lack nothing. / He lets me
rest in grassy meadows; / he leads me to restful waters.*
—Psalm 23:1-2

If you consider the very first thought of the psalmist, that the
Lord is his shepherd, you might feel yourself sighing just a bit,
relieved from the pressures of life, ready to lie down in the grass
and rest. A shepherd's whole purpose is to be there for the sheep.
Imagine your shepherd watching over you at this very moment.

Now couple that thought with this one, "I lack nothing."
Say it out loud. I lack nothing. Give God a happy shout and
thank him that you indeed lack nothing. He has provided
everything for you to rest right where you are.

As he leads you to rest by the peaceful waters, your life is
refreshed, your heart is renewed, and your spirit is revived. You
follow him wherever he goes because you trust him implicitly.
You know that there is nowhere that he would go that would get
you into trouble, you simply have to follow his voice.

Can you hear him as he calls you to come away today? Come
away, my child, and breathe in the fresh air, rest by the cooling
waters. That's what the psalmist wants you to know today: the
Lord is your shepherd and he will lead you for his name's sake
for the rest of your life. Be refreshed in him!

IN THE FLOW

*Lord, there is nothing better than knowing you're with me. I know
that I can't get too far away, because you'll come after me and
bring me safely home. Thanks for loving me so much. Amen.*

September

Be glad in the Lord always! Again I

say, be glad! Let your gentleness show

in your treatment of all people.

Philippians 4:4-5

WHO CAN YOU TRUST THESE DAYS?

*It's far better to take refuge in the LORD than to
trust any human. It's far better to take refuge in
the LORD than to trust any human leader.*
—Psalm 118:8-9

According to the psalmist, it's best for us to not put too much
trust in anybody other than the Lord, even if that person is in
leadership. That being said, how do we know when we can trust
someone else? Jesus Christ is the same yesterday, today, and
forever, but that's not true of us. We change. We change all the
time, and sometimes that means we're trustworthy and other
times it means we're not so sure where we're going, so we may
not be worth following.

The social network called Twitter invites users to "follow"
each other. You can keep up with someone else's ideas or a
group's activities or an author's work. You can follow whoever
you want, but can you trust them?

God is trustworthy and faithful all the time. He is consistent
in his ways and offers grace, salvation, and blessings for all
time. He will not go back on his word. Even if you don't quite
understand his direction, you can lean on him and believe he
wants what is best for you.

Today, put all your trust in the Lord and he will guide you to
those people on earth that you can deem to be trustworthy.

IN THE FLOW

*Lord, please help me be careful about the people I trust. I know that
I'm not always the best judge of other people's agendas or motives.
Help me trust you in all I do! Amen.*

YOU'RE SO BRAVE!

*But we aren't the sort of people who timidly draw back
and end up being destroyed. We're the sort of people who
have faith so that our whole beings are preserved.*
—Hebrews 10:39

Faith gets the credit for doing a lot of things. It gets you through the weird things, the tough times, the craziness that life can bring. It gives you reasons to keep hoping for the good things and challenges you when you're somewhat dismayed. It's your friend, your confidante, your strength partner. Faith is the living, breathing essence of what makes you a believer. It's your lifeline!

It's not always easy to put faith ahead of fear, but it's possible. God has given you a way to get past those things that strike fear into your heart. The closer you get to him, the more he can do. The greater your weakness, the more he sends in the cavalry, marshalling the troops to give you whatever you need to keep going. When fear tempts you to run, run toward the One who has the ability to help you get through any obstacle, who loves you just as you are and works to put all things together for your good.

God thinks you're brave. He sees you coming from miles away, knowing exactly what you need, and he runs toward you with lightning speed. That's what his love does. Nothing can be greater than that!

IN THE FLOW

*Lord, thank you for taking care of me when I'm fearful. I come
to you and lean in so I can hear your voice strengthening me and
helping me bravely go forward. Amen.*

September 3

You Plus God Is a Majority

Your way of life should be free from the love of money,
and you should be content with what you have. After all,
he has said, I will never leave you or abandon you. *This*
is why we can confidently say, The Lord is my helper,
and I won't be afraid. What can people do to me?
—Hebrews 13:5-6

Do you ever stop to think about what it really means when God says, "I will never leave you or abandon you"? There's nothing equivocal about that statement. It's a promise you can count on.

We can read the promise God gives us and still not hang on to it when we hit the rough seas. When the water is coming into our little boat and we're bailing as fast as we can, we only imagine that we'll drown. We don't look for the life preserver God put in the boat before we got in.

Whether we're drowning in debt or drowning in sorrow or grief or addiction or loneliness, we're not alone. Our first step is to believe that God is there with us, to trust that he is so strong nothing can happen to us as we hang on to him.

Embrace the promise of God. Let him know how glad you are that he has climbed aboard with you on this amazing trip you're taking through life. Let him know that you believe that there is nothing that can't be handled as long as the two of you face it together. Take him at his word and stand on his promise.

In the Flow

Lord, thank you for being there even when I forget. Thank you for loving me so much that you would never leave me in the midst of any trouble I might face. Be with me today. Amen.

In the Heat of

I know that good doesn't live in me—that is,
to do good is inside of me, but I can't do it. 1
I want to do, but I do the evil that I don't
the very thing that I don't want to do, then I'm not the one doing
it anymore. Instead, it is sin that lives in me that is doing it.
—Romans 7:18-20

You may not think of it this way, but you're in a constant struggle, a tug of war between the you that wants to do things that will please God enormously and the you that will disappoint God. You want to do the right thing, and God knows you try. He's pulling for you and trying to help any way he can.

Fortunately for you, he already helped in the best possible way. He freed you from having to do everything absolutely right because he accepted his Son's sacrifice on your behalf. He knows you can't come to salvation all on your own.

Decisions don't come easily, though. Choices are constantly coming up, and the battle rages between keeping you on the path or pulling you off.

C. S. Lewis said, "Good and evil both increase at compound interest. That is why the little decisions you and I make every day are of such infinite importance." Be aware today of all the choices you make, seek God's help, and offer your options to him. He'll help you move forward with wisdom to achieve his purposes.

In the Flow

Lord, be with me in the choices and decisions I make today. Help me move ahead only when I hear your affirmation for what I choose. Amen.

ᴏME TO THE PARTY!

There are different spiritual gifts but the same Spirit;
and there are different ministries and the same Lord;
and there are different activities but the same God who
produces all of them in everyone. A demonstration of the
Spirit is given to each person for the common good.
—1 Corinthians 12:4-7

When God invited you to his party, he already had in mind just
what you could bring. He knew what you'd be good at and what
talents you could share with others. He knew your personality
style and who else would be there who might need time just
with you. He gave you everything you need to enjoy yourself
immensely.

Your gifts and talents are fabulous, but if you stay in your
house and never come out, very few people will ever get to
appreciate them. You can be wonderful in isolation, but you were
made for community. You're a piece of somebody else's puzzle.
Somebody else holds a piece of your puzzle. It works that way
because we're meant to be interconnected, sharing what we have
and what God has blessed us with for the good of us all.

Every day we're invited to share our talents and offer seeds
of wisdom so that God's love will flourish everywhere. Keep
blossoming.

In the Flow

Lord, thank you for your standing invitation to come and share the
many gifts you've given me. Help me bless others as you have blessed
me. Amen.

LAYING A STRONG FOUNDATION

By wisdom a house is built; by understanding it is established. By
knowledge rooms are filled with all precious and pleasant wealth.
—Proverbs 24:3-4

When we build something, anything, we need to position it
on a strong foundation. Certainly a house needs to be built on
land that will support it. A marriage needs to be built on ideals
and dreams and realities that will give the couple all they need
to grow and strengthen each other. A business can't be built
without a good business plan.

We're always building a new house in one sense because the
body we live in houses who we are and provides the support we
need to live and grow and change. We definitely need wisdom
as we create blueprints for the life we hope God will honor and
bless. Our greatest assets, then, our building blocks, must start
with Jesus, the cornerstone of all that really matters.

As we branch out from there, steadying ourselves through
prayer, digging into the Word for a stronger foundation, we're
filled with wisdom and knowledge. The more we reach out to
God to receive his direction, the more he can clear the way for us
and help us develop into the beings he meant for us to become.

Only Christ can offer a foundation that is true. Build with
wisdom on the rock that can support you forever.

IN THE FLOW

Lord, thank you for guiding me and helping me grow in knowledge
in the work I do. Help me then apply wise choices for the good of
others. Amen.

NAME DROPPERS

A good name is better than fine oil, and the
day of death better than the birthday.
—Ecclesiastes 7:1

Some people just love to establish their own importance by
dropping the names of celebrities or people of influence. They
love knowing the head chef at a great restaurant or the mayor
of their city. It reflects well on them to have connections with
people in high places. What about you?

You certainly know some people in high places. There can't
be a higher name throughout heaven and earth than the name of
Jesus Christ. He doesn't mind if you become a name dropper on
his behalf.

As you reflect on the beauty and the value that comes from
the name of Jesus, consider your own name. How might you
build it in a way that it brings joy to others and is received as
honey and sweetness? The day you were born brought a moment
of celebration in the heavens and the day you return will bring
even greater joy for the journey you have been on.

Consider your name today and what it means to those
around you. Think even more about what it means to you and
to your family and friends. Your name is an honorable one and it
deserves to be respected and protected.

IN THE FLOW

Lord, thank you for giving me a name that brings honor to me and
to my family. Remind me that it is a gift worthy of respect and
protection. Bless my family name today and always. Amen.

FIGURING OUT THE GOOD GUYS

*A good tree can't produce bad fruit. And a rotten
tree can't produce good fruit. Every tree that doesn't
produce good fruit is chopped down and thrown into the
fire. Therefore, you will know them by their fruit.*
—Matthew 7:18-20

It's not always easy to figure out the good guys from the bad
guys. They can dress pretty much the same. They can show up
on the church board or the corporate executive roster. They can
appear to be giving and charitable and kind. The important thing
to discover is whether they bear good fruit. You have to find out
just what the results are of the things they do.

We've let the idea of good and evil become washed out
in our culture. We live in a virtual reality most of the time,
never really focusing on the real truth as God might have us
understand it. Discernment then is kind of scary. It asks us to pay
attention. It reminds us that we can best understand others by
looking at what they plant and what they harvest.

Good judgment comes from good motivation. When we
are motivated by God's Spirit, seeking to know more of him and
how he would have us see the various aspects of life, we can be
sure that we'll recognize the good guys from the bad guys. Seek
the kind of wisdom that helps you recognize the real fruit that
someone produces. It's okay to go ahead and shake the tree.

IN THE FLOW

*Lord, thank you for helping me see people as you reveal them to me.
I know I don't always get it right, but I pray that you will help me
focus on the things that reveal the truth in any situation. Amen.*

September 9

Setting Your Heart on Him

I have fought the good fight, finished the race, and kept the faith. At last the champion's wreath that is awarded for righteousness is waiting for me. The Lord, who is the righteous judge, is going to give it to me on that day. He's giving it not only to me but also to all those who have set their heart on waiting for his appearance.
—2 Timothy 4:7-8

You wished for a pony when you were a kid. You hoped it would happen any day, and even though you knew it was going to be hard to have a pony in the middle of a city, you still hoped. Your mother told you that it might be best to not "set your heart" on that hope. Over time, you learned that you had to adjust the things you set your heart on and give them more of a reality base.

The good news for all of us is that we can set our hearts on God. We can totally believe that he is coming again and that when he does, we'll be awarded the champion's wreath for all we've done here. So how do we make sure we are "fighting the good fight"?

We turn faith into actions. We don't want to just run the race mindlessly, or run for the goal of the prize we want, but we want to run it well with the kind of integrity that will please God.

Go and serve the Lord!

In the Flow

Lord, you have blessed me abundantly. Please forgive me when I lose sight of my direction and when I don't serve you well. Bless each step I take today. Amen.

GAINING A NEW PERSPECTIVE

*Aren't five sparrows sold for two small coins? Yet not one of them
is overlooked by God. Even the hairs on your head are all counted.
Don't be afraid. You are worth more than many sparrows.*
—Luke 12:6-7

The good news for you is that God is in the details. He knows
your thoughts, your heart, your hopes, and even the number of
hairs on your head. That must mean he's very close to you all
the time, since that number most likely changes every few hours.
God is near you all the time for only one reason.

He chose you. He values you. He knows that with his help
you can do amazing things for his kingdom. He bought you for
a great deal more than two small coins. He knows what you're
worth.

If all that is true, you need to be in the details too. You need
to stay closely connected to your Creator so that you know at any
moment what he wants you to do in any situation. Does he want
you to lend a hand to a stranger or give a talk to your friends at
church? Does he want you to give to a specific charity or pray
more? You can only know those things when you're willing to
look at the little, even mundane things to see what they might
mean or how you might use them for God's glory.

Remember how much value God puts on the life of each
person you meet. Walk right beside him today.

IN THE FLOW

*Lord, you take care of me so well that I sometimes don't realize how
often you've been there in the smallest detail of my life. I praise and
thank you for being there every time I need you. Amen.*

THE WORLD IS SCARY!

*I've commanded you to be brave and strong, haven't
I? Don't be alarmed or terrified, because the LORD
your God is with you wherever you go.*
—Joshua 1:9

Few of us can come to this day, September 11, and not think of
the tragedy of the falling World Trade Center Towers in New
York. That horrible experience has changed life for so many of us
ever since.

Because of that day, we're more suspicious of others than
we've ever been before. Because of that day, we've lost a sense of
security that we once thought was ours.

Perhaps as we remember the sadness of all that we lost that
day, we might also look toward what we carry with us now. Now,
more than ever, we see that our lives, our homes, our work, and
everything about us rests in one place—the hand of God.

Only God can calm our fears and remind us that he is with
us wherever we go. When terrible things happen, we cannot
control the event. All we can control is our response to it and
then do what we can to have an effect on the outcome.

As we face this day, let us go forward with courage, knowing
that our souls belong to him and that he is with us everywhere
we go.

IN THE FLOW

*Lord, please watch over your children on the earth today and keep
them safe from those who would harm them, free to live and breathe
and have their being in you. Amen.*

RUNNING TO WIN

*Don't you know that all the runners in the stadium run,
but only one gets the prize? So run to win. Everyone who
competes practices self-discipline in everything. The runners
do this to get a crown of leaves that shrivel up and die,
but we do it to receive a crown that never dies. So now
this is how I run—not without a clear goal in sight.*
—1 Corinthians 9:24-26

We live in a competitive world. We play a board game and our
opponents do all they can to beat us. We work in an office and
we do all we can to get ahead of the person in the cubicle next
to ours. We sometimes even try to out-give each other so that
we can claim to be the most charitable or the most Christian. We
run to win!

But if we have the right goal in sight, we aren't in the race
to get the prize that needs to be dusted, or the one that will be
spent in just a few days. We're seeking greater treasures, greater
rewards. We want to run the race with the kind of integrity that
makes God proud of us.

We want the prize that only he can offer . . . a place with him
in the kingdom of heaven. We're all out to win that one, and the
only competitor in the race is the one you see in the mirror every
morning. Run to win according to God's will and purpose for
you.

IN THE FLOW

*Lord, I want to give you my best self. I want to please you today in
all that I do. Please bless my efforts and help me be a contender for
the prize only you offer. Amen.*

BUZZ! THANK YOU FOR PLAYING!

*I fight like a boxer in the ring, not like someone who is
shadowboxing. Rather I'm landing punches on my own
body and subduing it like a slave. I do this to be sure that I
myself won't be disqualified after preaching to others.*
—1 Corinthians 9:26-27

Whether you think of it this way or not, every day you step into
the ring. You take on the opponents who are out there ready to
punch you, take you out, discourage you, and keep you down. It
takes a lot of accurate movement of your feet and a few indirect
hits to keep standing. As you prepare to get into the match, you
have to have a lot of self-discipline. That's where the work really
is. That's where you have to learn to stand.

It's up to us to be disciplined in our daily routines enough
that when something blindsides us or knocks us for a loop, we
can stand back up again and keep going. One way we protect
ourselves is by putting on the full armor of God. We get that
armor by staying entrenched with our Creator, stuck to the Word
like it's our last avenue of defense, holding on to it for dear life.

God is with you as you enter the arena, even more as you
step into the ring. He will guide your steps, give you strength,
and keep you standing according to his grace and mercy. Give
him thanks and praise.

IN THE FLOW

*Lord, thanks for being with me in the daily battles, the moments
when I'm not always prepared for what comes next. Help me stay
close by your side today. Amen.*

TEMPORARY BLINDNESS

*The god of this age has blinded the minds of those who
don't have faith so they couldn't see the light of the gospel
that reveals Christ's glory. Christ is the image of God.*

—2 Corinthians 4:4

Remember the story of the three blind men and the elephant.
Each man touched a part of the elephant and thought he could
see just what it was. One was sure the sturdy side was a wall and
one thought the trunk was a snake. It was clear to each of them
that he knew exactly what the elephant might be like though all
of them were blind.

Sometimes, we're not even aware of our own blindness. We
imagine that what we think and what we know is so black and
white that we're seeing things clearly. We imagine our own truth
and we believe it. God is not working with us to create our own
truth, though. He wants us to know his truth.

If the god of this age has blinded our minds, we have to
work even harder to be diligent in our approach to faith. We
have to get close to the Word so that we are able to define each
situation we encounter in the right way. We want to be able to
see with the eyes of faith.

Our job is to put our trust in the One who wants us to see
him clearly. Let's walk closer to him today.

IN THE FLOW

*Lord, I know I don't always see you and understand what you want,
partly because I'm so sure I already have it figured out. Help me see
you and look for you with open eyes. Amen.*

Talk About a Positive Attitude!

*Teach the wise, and they will become wiser; inform the
righteous, and their learning will increase. The beginning
of wisdom is the fear of the LORD; the knowledge of the holy
one is understanding. Through me your days will be many;
years will be added to your life. If you are wise, it is to your
benefit; if you are cynical, you will bear it all alone.*
—Proverbs 9:9-12

We've long equated wisdom with age, meaning that we assume
that the older we grow, the more we've learned, and that we put
our learning to good use. That would be an ideal assumption,
but not necessarily a true one. Some of us are wise at any age;
some of us not so much.

Your teachers didn't go away when you left high school or
college. In fact, some of your best teachers may have had nothing
to do with your formal training at all. Some of your best teachers
came in the form of big, ugly mistakes. Falling down doesn't feel
good unless you pick yourself up again and learn what tripped
you up so you don't do it again.

The good news is we eventually become wiser. The wiser
we are the more we have the opportunity to create an abundant
life. Whether God adds more years to your life or more life to
your years, you win either way. Ask God to give you the proper
attitude adjustment today.

In the Flow

*Lord, you have given me so much to appreciate about my life. When
I get a bit down or cynical, help me rise up again and seek your
face. Amen.*

The Spring of Life Even in the Fall

Within you is the spring of life. In your light, we see light.
Extend your faithful love to those who know you; extend
your righteousness to those whose heart is right.
—Psalm 36:9-10

Perhaps the leaves are turning where you live. Perhaps you're preparing for the winter now, gathering your warmer clothes, maybe canning some fruits and vegetables or raking the yard. The fall is a great time of year when the sunlight seems to reflect differently off the hillsides as we move forward. Yet, even as we approach the dimness of winter, comes the spring of life, the light of the world.

Since God doesn't change with the seasons, since he doesn't get weary at night or tired in the middle of the day, we can look to him as our wellspring. We can find his love bubbling up around us when we least expect it, shedding light on a bit of darkness that took us by surprise. He extends his faithful love to us season after season, sunrise to sunset, day after day.

All we have to do is set our hearts on the right path. He'll help us in our efforts to walk the right way, to come into his light, as long as we seek his truth, as long as we yearn to know more of him.

God is the spring of life, the one who daily leads you toward the light of his love.

In the Flow

Lord, thank you for shining a light in my direction and helping me see more clearly the things that are really important. Amen.

A GRACIOUS SUFFICIENCY

*A person's steps are made secure by the LORD when they delight
in his way. Though they trip up, they won't be thrown down,
because the LORD holds their hand. I was young and now I'm
old, but I have never seen the righteous left all alone, have
never seen their children begging for bread. They are always
gracious and generous. Their children are a blessing.*
—Psalm 37:23-26

Life can feel like you're walking a tightrope sometimes. You're
not sure if there's a net below you to catch you if you fall, and all
you can do is put one foot in front of the other. Every now and
then your balance gets a little shaky and you wonder if you're
going to be able to keep going, if you can make it to the place
just up ahead.

If you turn the tightrope into a trust walk, it makes the
whole thing easier. If you move with the confidence of one who
is holding the hand of God, the steps suddenly become more
certain no matter how far off the ground you might be.

Whether your feet are on solid ground or you're on a bit of a
tightrope today, remember that you do not walk alone. You have
the support through grace of the One who designed you to do
good works. Just take it one step at a time!

IN THE FLOW

*Lord, thank you for guarding my steps and holding me steady on
the course. I lean on you today, trusting you to be my strength and
support. Amen.*

SHARING YOUR JESUS

Therefore, everyone who acknowledges me before people,
I also will acknowledge before my Father who is in
heaven. But everyone who denies me before people, I
also will deny before my Father who is in heaven.
—Matthew 10:32-33

Probably most of us are comfortable sharing our faith in those settings where such discussions are natural and easy. We can talk about Jesus freely at church or at our weekly Bible study, but what about those unexpected places? What about talking about Jesus with your new friend over coffee at Starbucks or with your old friend at the football stadium?

It's hard in the same way that getting up in front of a crowd of people and making a speech is hard. It's hard because we're suddenly feeling almost naked as we reveal something about ourselves that those people might not have known about us before. We are suddenly vulnerable to their ridicule or to their assertion that religion is a private matter.

The truth for us is that God wants us to talk about him. He wants us to share the incredible gift we have in him, our future in heaven, our present opportunity for forgiveness, our sense of well-being because we have a great relationship with him.

It's okay to talk about the love of your life. You have an open invitation to do so.

IN THE FLOW

Lord, you are the love of my life and I am awed by all that you do
for me. Help me be willing to share what I know about you any time
a good opportunity comes my way. Amen.

GIVING FROM THE HEART

I don't want you to feel like you are being forced to give anything.
What I mean is this: the one who sows a small number of seeds
will also reap a small crop, and the one who sows a generous
amount of seeds will also reap a generous crop. Everyone
should give whatever they have decided in their heart.
—2 Corinthians 9:5-7

Giving isn't just about how many dollars you put into the collection plate on Sunday morning, or how much of your paycheck goes to United Way each month. It's about you. It's about you having the opportunity to give to those things and those people that you choose.

Sometimes we see someone on the street in need and we pass them by, not because we don't want to help, but because we don't know where it ends. We have our own bills to pay and our own families to take care of. How can we figure out what it means for us to give to others in a way that comes from the heart?

Giving from the heart means you feel joy and even a sense of privilege for being able to give. You can give your money, you can give your time, your talent, or your kindness, and whatever it is you give, your heart feels better. You give the best you have to offer and you hardly think twice about it.

When you give, you share your heart. The more you share, the bigger the return. It's that simple.

IN THE FLOW

Lord, you have given so generously to me that I am overwhelmed by
your grace and goodness. Help me be a generous giver in return to
the people you put in my path. Amen.

HEROES—RELUCTANT AND OTHERWISE

Offer yourself as a role model of good actions. Show integrity,
seriousness, and a sound message that is above criticism
when you teach, so that any opponent will be ashamed
because they won't find anything bad to say about us.

—Titus 2:7-8

You may not think of yourself as a superhero. In fact, when
it comes to rescuing others you may be more of a reluctant
bystander. The truth is that you're in the spotlight sometimes
whether you want to be or not. You are someone else's only
example of what it means to be a believer. You're the one they
are trying to emulate.

If others are trying to follow your example, then you have to
work doubly hard to follow the example of Christ. You have to
watch him closely, listen to his voice, and follow him everywhere.

If a good example is the best sermon, you might want to be
aware of where you are when you flash your cape and enter the
room ready to save the lost and the broken-hearted. God knows
why he sent you into the midst of the people you work with or
the people you bowl with on Sunday nights.

You're God's example, his hero to the people he wants to
bring into the kingdom. He chose you to get the job done and
all you have to do is be a good example of his love.

IN THE FLOW

Lord, thank you for being my role model, for giving me the divine
examples that keep me safe in God's hands. Help me be a better
example of your love to those around me. Amen.

AND GOD SAW THAT IT WAS GOOD!

Let's not get tired of doing good, because in time we'll
have a harvest if we don't give up. So then, let's work
for the good of all whenever we have an opportunity,
and especially for those in the household of faith.
—Galatians 6:9-10

When God was busy creating the world we know, he looked
at each step he took and was pleased. He thought it was good.
He looked forward to what the world would be like given the
amount of goodness he put into it. Because all goodness can only
be measured against his standards, we sometimes weary of doing
good. We sometimes wonder if the good we do matters at all, or
if it even makes a difference.

God sees your work and your good intent. He sees your
heart and what motivates you to do good things, and it pleases
him. Meister Eckhart said, "Do what good you can, and do it
solely for God's glory, as free from it yourself as though you did
not exist. Ask nothing whatever in return. Done in this way, your
works are spiritual and godly."

The world needs more good. We're somewhat off kilter,
out of balance, and hungry for the things that bring truth and
meaning to life. We need to see goodness as the beautiful thing it
was meant to be. We need to do all the good we can for as many
people as possible.

IN THE FLOW

Lord, thank you for giving me opportunities to do good. Help me be
more generous every day with all the gifts you've given me. Amen.

THE STRENGTH OF GENTLENESS

Be glad in the Lord always! Again I say, be glad! Let your
gentleness show in your treatment of all people. The Lord is near.
—Philippians 4:4-5

Most of us really appreciate being around people who exude
kindness and gentleness. We may wonder what it is they have
that gives them the strength to be like that. We may marvel that
they are so consistent in their mannerisms, so quietly confident in
who they are. They treat everyone they meet as though they were
lifelong friends. They're strong, and we admire them.

Those who are confident in who they are, who lead with
integrity and fight the good fight, have no need to come out in
a raging fury. They know that more can be accomplished for the
good of all others by a gentle spirit. As it says in Proverbs 15, "A
sensitive answer turns back wrath, but an offensive word stirs up
anger."

May gentleness stir in your heart today, coming to your aid
when someone is unkind, standing up for you when someone
bruises your spirit, and guiding you when you can't quite find
your way. May the gentleness of Jesus permeate your soul and
fix itself on those who come into your midst. As you show them
your gentle spirit, God will show them his.

Do all the good that you can do today, coupled with a spirit
of gentleness and love.

IN THE FLOW

Lord, you so often deal gently with me. Help me keep my head
around others today, giving them a gentle touch of love according to
your will and purpose. Amen.

Blowing Out the Winds of Anger

Be angry without sinning. *Don't let the sun set on your*
anger. Don't provide an opportunity for the devil.
—Ephesians 4:26-27

Anger loves to tell its story. In fact, it will tell the story to
everyone and anyone who will listen. It feeds on itself. It gets
hotter with every retelling, smoldering in its righteous gravy,
certain of its veracity. Before you know it, you'll be overcome by
its masterful skill at taking you in. You may not even remember
what brought anger to the table, but you let the fire burn every
time you open anger's door.

Sure, you have a right to be angry sometimes. You have
every reason to be offended when someone does something
deliberately against you. You have reason to be livid at betrayal
in any of its ugliness, but your rights only last for one day. At
sunset, you need to hand any of those toasty embers over to
God. Let him figure out the best plan for bringing out some
sense of justice.

Be angry if you must, but at the end of the day, let it go
and give it to God. Share your heart and your emotions about
the things that make you angry the same way you do about the
things that make you happy. God cares what is happening to you
all the time. Don't give Satan even five minutes of your life.

In the Flow

Lord, I don't always get my angry feelings under control. Sometimes
I nurse them, pamper them, and hope to make my case stronger.
Help me let go of anger any time it is near. Amen.

WHAT DOES YOUR HEART SAY?

*God doesn't look at things like humans do. Humans see only
what is visible to the eyes, but the LORD sees into the heart.*
—1 Samuel 16:7

What if we only saw each other as human beings doing our best
to make our way in the world? What if we truly saw each other
from the perspective of our heart's view? If we did that, we'd be a
lot closer to following the example of Jesus. We'd be more open
to meeting people where they are in their walk of faith or their
search for meaning. We could let go of doubt and misguided
judgments. We could stop searching for hidden motivations.
We could simply let people breathe and live and be all they were
meant to be. We could give them what we want for ourselves.
We'd be on the cusp of understanding what real love is all about.

Do an experiment today. Make it your intention to look past
the way someone is dressed, or the way someone pronounces or
mispronounces their words. Look beyond the fact that someone
isn't necessarily attractive in your usual terms, and look inside
. . . yourself. Look within yourself and see what your heart knows
that you have yet to discover. At the end of the day, think about
the people you met and pray for them. Ask God to open your
heart even more for the day after this one. Look to the eyes of
your heart and see if you can make a difference.

IN THE FLOW

*Lord, thank you for not seeing us the way we often see one another.
Remind me that I need to do more looking with my heart when it
comes to being a better friend and a better servant. Amen.*

THE SPITTING IMAGE OF YOUR FATHER

Then God said, "Let us make humanity in our image to resemble us so that they may take charge of the fish of the sea, the birds of the sky, the livestock, all the earth, and all the crawling things on earth." God created humanity in God's own image, in the divine image God created them, male and female God created them.
—Genesis 1:26-27

Sometimes we puzzle about what God looks like. If we were able to take the supernatural form that he holds and put it into an earthly vessel, we'd be surprised to discover that he looks a lot like us. As it says in Genesis, God created humanity in the divine image. We're the spitting image of our Father.

If you think about it, there are a lot of things that cause you to be "like" your family. Beyond your DNA are things like social skills, talents, and cultural mannerisms you've learned from living in your family. You may use a lot of the same phrases, or you may nod your head in a similar way when you're thinking about things. Being the image of your family is about a lot more than simply the shape of your nose.

So what about you reflects the image of your heavenly Father? What would make people say that you were a lot like him? As you look at who you are right now and what you want others to see, imagine God looking at you, straight at you, and remarking at how well you've grown, how much you look like the rest of the family. You are sure to make him proud.

IN THE FLOW

Lord, I hope I look a lot like you. I hope I reflect you to others in the things I say and do. I want to be your child in every way. Amen.

FLIM-FLAM FAITH

Be careful that you don't practice your religion in front
of people to draw their attention. If you do, you will
have no reward from your Father who is in heaven.
—Matthew 6:1

You know about the flim-flam man? He's the one who shows
up like the Music Man shouting and gathering crowds, defining
trouble with a capital T. He addresses an audience simply to take
hold of their thinking and to get them to dig down deeper into
their pockets. He's not just defining trouble, he is trouble.

Some apostles of faith today can be like that. There are some
who attract huge crowds, pandering with their message, creating
opportunity for dramatic events and getting people to give more
of their hard-earned pensions. They're the flim-flam masters of
faith. They may have started out with an honest hope of spreading
the gospel, but they ended up only spreading their own fame.

God doesn't want a show. He doesn't want more drama.
He's got enough of that to contend with in the world. What he
wants is you with a sincere and devout heart, coming to him in
prayer with thanksgiving. He wants your love and your integrity,
and if you witness for him, he wants you to do it from the
abundance of faith that flows through your veins. He wants your
actions to be motivated at all times with love.

IN THE FLOW

Lord, I've never been particularly showy about my faith, but I'm
a little turned off by those people who are. Help me be me about
expressing my faith honestly in front of you and other people. Amen.

September 27

Waking the Dawn . . . With Praise!

Wake up, my glory! Wake up, harp and lyre! I will wake the dawn itself! I will give thanks to you, my Lord, among all the peoples; I will make music to you among the nations because your faithful love is as high as heaven; your faithfulness reaches the clouds. Exalt yourself, God, higher than heaven!
—Psalm 57:8-11

Some places just overwhelm you with the Creator God. If you sit on the deck of a ship and observe the vastness of the ocean, or view the Grand Canyon or any of the other remarkable sites created by God's hand, you feel awed. Praise comes quickly to your lips and spills out over the landscape, echoing in words and phrases you didn't even know were inside you. That's you . . . waking up. That's you, recognizing God in a way that you are barely aware of at other times.

Sit back a moment and close your eyes. Anticipate the morning sunrise, the first hint of light that begins to touch the sky, offering a warm pink glow to the clouds, slowly giving rise to the horizon in a way that catches your breath. Imagine then that some music comes wafting through the air and you're humming the song without knowing the words. All you can do is sigh, giving God thanks for what you behold, praising him with every fiber of your being.

You are awake now. Go and share your heart for God with everyone you meet.

In the Flow

Lord, thank you for waking me up today. Thank you for the magnificent and breath-taking world you have created. Bless everyone I meet today in your name. Amen.

JUMPING INTO THE WAVES

The LORD your redeemer, the holy one of Israel, proclaims: I am the LORD your God who teaches you for your own good, who leads you in the way you should go. If you would pay attention to my commands, your well-being would be like a river, and your righteousness like the waves of the sea.
—Isaiah 48:17-18

Imagine standing on the banks of one of the world's largest rivers, the Amazon or the Nile, or perhaps the Mississippi or the Po. You see it coursing its way, over the rocks, reflecting the landscape, ever moving and strong. Imagine your well-being floating along on that river and taking you places you never thought you would go. For once, you're free of all cares and anxieties.

God has only your good in mind. He leads you and directs your path as surely as the mighty rivers find their way to the sea. He's your fountain of everlasting truth and joy.

It's a wonder with all that help and support that we fill our little boats up with one fear, one loss, one rejection, and a bit of chaos—and we keep on until the boat is practically overflowing with the weight of our concerns. We do that even though we know we don't have to.

Today, let your troubles float away with the current and rest in his tender care. He's with you now and forever.

IN THE FLOW

Lord, help me really jump into the waves and go with the flow today, knowing that you are there directing my course, keeping me safe. Thank you for watching over me. Amen.

September 29

Life in the Spirit, the Spirit in Life

But you aren't self-centered. Instead you are in the Spirit, if in fact God's Spirit lives in you. If anyone doesn't have the Spirit of Christ, they don't belong to him. If Christ is in you, the Spirit is your life because of God's righteousness, but the body is dead because of sin.
—Romans 8:9-10

If you're off center, that's a good thing. In your life with Christ, you aren't intended to be in the center, he is! He is your engine, your power, the thruster that gets you into the day. He's your, pardon the expression, Holy Smoke!

When you're in the Spirit, you're on fire for God. You may remember that holy fire from when you were first baptized in the Spirit. It was almost overwhelming to have that sense that you were somehow connected to the Creator of the universe. It was more joy than you knew what to do with and made you want to tell everybody about your faith. You may have even been somewhat obnoxious about it.

That fire may have cooled some by now, maturing with you into more of a peaceful flame, an eternal flame that will never be extinguished. It's good to get to where you are now, not only off center, but pleased to be so. Your life is given over to the Spirit, and you couldn't be happier. Now, doesn't that just make every new day more exciting?

In the Flow

Lord, I remember when we first met and how in love I was. It was a great feeling, but the relationship we share now feels even better, steady and more whole. Thanks for giving me the Spirit. Amen.

LET ME GIVE YOU A HAND

*Christ is just like the human body—a body is a unit
and has many parts; and all the parts of the body
are one body, even though there are many.*
—1 Corinthians 12:12

When we think of ourselves as the body of Christ, we need to
remember that all the churches who worship Jesus everywhere
in the world are part of that body. We're all part of the same
Lord and, therefore, we're still each other's hands and feet. What
affects one of us, really affects all of us.

It's the ripple effect. What happens to one member of the
body has a consequence for the rest of the body. We have a love
of creating labels in our culture, and we have traditions based in
theology for the many churches that make up the body of Christ.
One of them may be a "hand" and one may be a "leg," but each
one represents the same God, the author of each of us.

Today, let's celebrate the fact that God has such a diverse
body, linked together by the blood of Christ. Let's thank him
for one another and the work that each church does to make
the world a better place. Wherever you live, wherever you work,
wherever you worship, you are an important member of the body
of Christ and we need you to do the wonderful things you do to
make us one. Celebrate God's love for his church today.

IN THE FLOW

*Lord, thank you for creating your church here on earth and for all
the people who belong to you. Help us be good hands and good feet
and good hearts for you and help us serve each other well. Amen.*

October

I have great joy and encouragement

because of your love, since the hearts of

God's people are refreshed by your actions.

Philemon 7

THE CHAMELEON IN YOU!

*I act weak to the weak, so I can recruit the weak. I
have become all things to all people, so I could save some
by all possible means. All the things I do are for the
sake of the gospel, so I can be a partner with it.*

—1 Corinthians 9:22-23

You're pretty adaptable! You change your stripes when you need
to. You're comfortable in most settings, whether they're formal
or easy-going. You can hike a little, dance a little, and cheer on
your favorite baseball team. You've got a little chameleon in you.
It's a good thing!

In this letter to the Corinthians, Paul says that is what he
tries to do too. He tries to adapt to the situation in the hope
that he'll be able to serve or lead, as the need may be, the people
who are around him. Jesus was a great example of that for us as
well. He met people right where they were and, without judging,
shared his heart and his spirit. He gave them what they needed,
even if sometimes they weren't really sure what that was.

You have what it takes to become what you need to so that
you can relate in very positive and uplifting ways to the people
around you. You may not know what they need. They may not
know what they need, but God does. Today be ready to change
your direction, your thoughts, and your heart at a moment's
notice for the good of someone you meet.

IN THE FLOW

*Lord, you always are there to meet us where we are. You are all
things to all people. Help me be more of what you would have me be
in any situation I face today. Amen.*

October 2

We're All in the Same Boat

When Jesus got into a boat, his disciples followed him. A huge storm arose on the lake so that waves were sloshing over the boat. But Jesus was asleep. They came and woke him, saying, "Lord, rescue us! We're going to drown!" He said to them, "Why are you afraid, you people of weak faith?" Then he got up and gave orders to the winds and the lake, and there was a great calm. The people were amazed and said, "What kind of person is this? Even the winds and the lake obey him!"
—Matthew 8:23-27

If you've ever been in a frightening storm, gone to a shelter during a hurricane, or had to find a safe place during a tornado, you can probably identify with the disciples as they rolled around on the waves waiting to capsize. Here they are with Jesus, watching the storms all around them, getting scared out of their minds, and they find Jesus asleep.

He had a faith that was bigger than the boat they were in. He had faith that nothing would happen to him because he was on a mission. He rested in knowing his relationship with the Father.

We're always in a rocking boat when we don't give up our fear and get more closely connected with God. Let's plan today to rest in God's hands no matter what the day brings.

In the Flow

Lord, you are my rock, my strength, and the One in whom I put all my faith. Help me rest in you today, trusting you for every aspect of my life. Amen.

WHAT'S IN THE SMALL PRINT?

Whoever believes and is baptized will be saved, but whoever doesn't believe will be condemned. These signs will be associated with those who believe: they will throw out demons in my name. They will speak in new languages. They will pick up snakes with their hands. If they drink anything poisonous, it will not hurt them. They will place their hands on the sick, and they will get well.
—Mark 16:16-18

When you signed up to be on God's team, to follow Jesus and put your life in his hands, you might not have noticed the small print. You might not have realized that believing and being baptized came with some perks. Just take another look.

Are there still people who believe in demons? Aren't most of those descriptions from the Bible personality disorders? What about speaking in new languages?

What are these signs of belief really about? They're about you! They're about you realizing that because of God, because of your belief in Jesus, there is nothing that God can't do through you. You are a vessel for his Spirit, and in that Spirit you can do all things through Christ. You can do good things like heal the sick and encourage the weak. You can do amazing things that you never dreamed were possible. With God all things are possible. His possibility is made even stronger because you believe.

IN THE FLOW

Lord, help me believe so much that I can do anything that you would have me do. Help me have no fear because I believe in all that only you can accomplish through me. Amen.

October 4

What Time Is It for You?

There's a season for everything and a time for every matter under the heavens: a time for giving birth and a time for dying, a time for planting and a time for uprooting what was planted, a time for killing and a time for healing, a time for tearing down and a time for building up.
—Ecclesiastes 3:1-3

Time always wins. Every decade we live influences the way we think about time. When we're young, it seems like forever before we're old enough to have the independence we crave and go on and do the things we dream about. As we move up the scale, time just simply gets shorter until it finally seems to evaporate.

What time is it for you? Is it time to get past a fear that has held you back for years? Is it time for you to get off the sofa and meet the new neighbors down the street or time to remind your spouse how grateful you are to have such a loving relationship? Is it time to renew your connection to God?

We might think that we can keep putting things off until tomorrow, keep waiting for what might be a better time, but the truth is "there is no time like the present," and in fact, there is no time BUT the present. It's a new day, a new time, a new opportunity for you to make the most of it. You're already on borrowed time!

In the Flow

Lord, I know I take time for granted. I don't use it wisely and I let it melt away. Then, I find myself rushing everywhere to get things done. Help me invest my time wisely. Amen.

FAMILY MATTERS

He replied, "Who is my mother? Who are my brothers?"
Looking around at those seated around him in a circle, he
said, "Look, here are my mother and my brothers. Whoever
does God's will is my brother, sister, and mother."
—Mark 3:33-35

Blood relatives are the ones we refer to as family. Those are
the people we spend most of our time with, the ones we walk
with and talk with each day. Our siblings, our parents, and our
children are defined as family.

What is Jesus saying in this Scripture, then? Is he adopting
the whole world as being part of his family? Well, yes, he is, as
long as those people are mindful of doing God's will. So family
isn't so much about DNA as it is about our actions of faith, our
efforts to align with the will of God.

As members of his family, we're always in a better place when
we treat God like a Father, a confidante, and a friend. When
we come before him and put our hopes at his feet, we place
ourselves within his will. As a special member of his family, see
what you can do today to align your heart with his.

IN THE FLOW

Lord, thank you for accepting me into your family and help me be
mindful of you in everything I do today. I lay down my life's work
in front of you to establish a path in accordance with your will.
Amen.

October 6

Rooted in Faith

But now he has reconciled you by his physical body through death, to present you before God as a people who are holy, faultless, and without blame. But you need to remain well established and rooted in faith and not shift away from the hope given in the good news that you heard.
—Colossians 1:22-23

Are you aware of the way the Aspens in Colorado are all rooted to each other underground? They are literally all connected, holding on to one another and helping one another to sustain life because of their incredible root system.

What difference might there be if human beings were as rooted to one another as the Aspens? What if we were then that deeply rooted to our faith in God?

Some roots run so deep you can hardly dig them out with heavy-duty machinery. Some pull out without any effort at all. It can be a matter of not being rooted in the right kind of soil. If you're rooted in the soil of faith, held in place by the community you experience with other believers, then it will be much more difficult for the Adversary to pull you away. God will hold on to you all your life because of his great love.

It's your day today to get back to your roots and let the Gardener take care of you.

In the Flow

Lord, thank you for everything you do to nurture my faith, to protect me, and to keep me rooted in your love. Help me keep growing in you. Amen.

GOT PLANS? TAKE 'EM UP A NOTCH!

My plans aren't your plans, nor are your ways my ways, says the
LORD. Just as the heavens are higher than the earth, so are my
ways higher than your ways, and my plans than your plans.
—Isaiah 55:8-9

Making plans can seem like a simple enough act. You create
your to-do list and make a vow to yourself to check off at least
three things on it before the day is done. You get to number
one, smooth sailing, looking like you'll be in port in just a few
moments, when suddenly the winds of change start blowing and
before you know it, you're totally off course.

Of course, it's good to make plans. It's just better to realize
that your plans and God's plans may not come together. He is,
after all, the Creator. He creates change as he sees it so that you
accomplish what he has in mind. He may not cross off the things
he wanted you to accomplish in a day because he carries a life
planner and checks your progress with that. You're here on a
mission and he wants to be sure you get things done.

As you look at your plans today, consider taking them up
a notch. Start by planning time to spend with your Creator,
getting his blessing for the things you'll accomplish today, things
that you and he can do together.

IN THE FLOW

Lord, thank you for having big plans for my life. Help me stay
connected to you in a way that keeps the path clear for me to achieve
the goals you have set for me. Amen.

GOBBLING UP THE WORD

*Just as the rain and the snow come down from the sky and
don't return there without watering the earth, making
it conceive and yield plants and providing seed to the
sower and food to the eater, so is my word that comes
from my mouth; it does not return to me empty.*
—Isaiah 55:10-11

Splash! Another cascade of raindrops is moving down the
window. As you look past it out into the backyard, you can see
the grass soaking in its goodness. The birds are shaking the rain
off their wings, getting some nourishing sips as they go, and the
flowers are closed up a bit, letting the water wash over them,
preparing to open up and be even more radiant when the sun
comes back again.

You may feel too busy some days to go and renew your Spirit
with Bible reading. If you do, think of what you're missing in the
same way you would miss having dinner or drinking a glass of
water when you're thirsty. God knows you're always thirsting for
him in one way or another, and so he has provided a way to be
close to him. Like the birds and the flowers dancing amidst the
raindrops, growing and flying and trusting their Creator, you are
the object of his love. Go ahead, take in the refreshment he offers
right now. It'll do you good!

IN THE FLOW

*Lord, thank you for giving me your Word to help renew my trust, my
faith, and my sense of all that is possible with you. I praise you and
thank you for showering me with continual blessings. Amen.*

FASHIONABLE FAITH

Since we belong to the day, let's stay sober, wearing
faithfulness and love as a piece of armor that protects
our body and the hope of salvation as a helmet.

—1 Thessalonians 5:8

If you're wondering just what to wear today, this Scripture offers
you some guidance. Sometimes when we approach our clothes
closet, we're already certain we won't find a thing that will really
appeal to us. Everything seems so "yesterday" and so used. Sure,
some of those clothes are old comfortable friends and it's always
good to see them, but what to wear today still doesn't seem to
jump out at you.

It may not come with shiny beads or added colorful
swatches, but one suggestion is to wear some faithfulness. In fact,
wear faithfulness like it's a full body suit, a bit of stretchy armor.
Armor is a protector, something that will come to your defense
if you need help, and faithfulness acts the same way. It's such a
great body suit!

Faithfulness fastens itself to you and changes your approach
to the day. It opens doors, raises hopes, and shelters spirits. It
protects you and does its job even more fully when you couple it
with love. You may not be on the next magazine cover of *Vogue*
or the society page, but your outfit will be stunning. It will stun
those who belong to the darkness. It will stun those you need to
keep at a safe distance. It's a great thing to wear!

IN THE FLOW

Lord, thanks for dressing me in the things that really matter. Thanks
for your constant love and faithfulness to me. Amen.

YOU GET BY WITH A LITTLE HELP FROM YOUR FRIENDS

*So continue encouraging each other and building
each other up, just like you are doing already.*
—1 Thessalonians 5:11

Look at the headlines of the daily paper in the morning and you
may feel the weight of the world on your shoulders. Everywhere
you look there is one disaster after another. You read about
tornados raging through small towns and leaving a path of
desolation, teenagers going on a killing spree just for fun, or
homeless people needing shelter in zero-degree weather. The list
goes on and the heartbreak is endless.

So what is your job? You can't save the world. God already
made provisions for that. What you can do, though, is offer help
in the form of encouraging words or volunteering some time.
You can make a difference right where you live, right where you
are.

Be an angel to someone today and offer him or her an
encouraging word or a cheerful smile. Offer a little light that
only you know how to give.

IN THE FLOW

*Lord, the world seems so heavy, so dark sometimes that it's hard
to take in the pain reflected in every news broadcast and daily
headline. There's too much CNN and not enough TLC. Help me
remember to offer whatever encouragement I can in the things I do
today. Amen.*

THAT LITTLE HOUSE ON THE PRAIRIE

Aim to live quietly, mind your own business, and
earn your own living, just as I told you.
—1 Thessalonians 4:11

Do you ever dream of having a little house in the mountains, or perhaps near a beach town, somewhere where you can escape all the chaos of the world and just live in peace? You have probably already discovered that the best remedy for that feeling is to create sacred spaces in your own home, a simple spot where you can slip away and be with God, meditate, read, and just feel his peace and comfort.

If you aim to live quietly, mind your own business, and earn your own living, you're on the right track. Believers have to stay informed, but they don't have to get entrenched in the troubles of the world. They do have to pray every chance they get for those in need, help where they can, and be responsible hands and feet and hugs of Jesus, though.

But today, you might consider just stepping aside for a few moments, running away to your quiet spot and simply taking in the peace that only God can give you. Create your own little house on the prairie even if it's in your living room.

IN THE FLOW

Lord, thank you for reminding me to keep things simple. I get overwhelmed with the doing and the trying and the giving that takes up so much of my time. Help me stop and just spend time with you today. Amen.

BEFORE TIME BEGAN

Their faith and this knowledge are based on the hope of eternal life that God, who doesn't lie, promised before time began.
—Titus 1:2

God made a plan with love and he did it before Genesis, before he even started speaking all things into existence. Wow! He has always known us and with that knowledge created a promise that he keeps forever . . . that he'll bring us back to himself one day and give us the hope of eternal life.

Now that we know where we're going, what difference does that make in our day today? What can we do today that we'll be pleased to share with him when we get to see him face to face? We're not always conscious of our choices in light of that moment when we're talking with our Creator, but sometimes it's good to look at things from that perspective.

After all, we're finite and we're pretty good at squandering time. We know we don't have forever and yet we don't always make our moments count. This is the day the Lord has made and we are glad. Let's walk with him and work with him and grow in him today so that we have more faith and more knowledge and more hope than we have had in years. It's your day to shine!

IN THE FLOW

Lord, thank you for this new day and thanks for making plans to bring me hope and faith and the way back to you someday. Help me make today count so that I'll be glad to share my stories of today when we're standing face to face. Amen.

ALL WASHED UP!

But "when God our savior's kindness and love appeared, he saved us because of his mercy, not because of righteous things we had done. He did it through the washing of new birth and the renewing by the Holy Spirit, which God poured out upon us generously through Jesus Christ our savior."

—Titus 3:4-6

We have unique phrases in English that can carry almost opposite meanings, so we always have to be aware of the context of them. "All washed up" is one of those phrases. Often when we say it, we know it's not a very good time in some person's life.

Then there's the way our moms used it when they asked, "Are you all washed up for dinner?" Of course, that meant go wash your hands and get ready for the main meal of the day. It was time to get washed up.

When God looked at us with his saving grace and loving kindness, he saw that we were definitely all washed up. We were shipwrecked. Out of his goodness, he renewed our hearts by washing us up in the Holy Spirit and giving us a chance to be born anew. Now we're "all washed up" in his Spirit. Now we're new again in him.

Today, as you step into the shower to get ready for the day, send some love up to God and thank him for making you whole and clean again. Thank him that you are now "all washed up."

IN THE FLOW

Lord, I know I'd be hard-pressed to clean off some of the dirt and grime I've managed to collect in my life. Thanks for washing me in your love and in your Spirit. Amen.

October 14

Getting a Good Look at the Spirits

Dear friends, don't believe every spirit. Test the spirits to see if they are from God because many false prophets have gone into the world. This is how you know if a spirit comes from God: every spirit that confesses that Jesus Christ has come as a human is from God, and every spirit that doesn't confess Jesus is not from God.
—1 John 4:1-3

We can be lulled into thinking that demons are imaginary beings from a Harry Potter movie, or simply the uneducated response to those who didn't really recognize the various types of personality disorders back in biblical days. In fact, it seems that demons were everywhere in Bible stories and Jesus was always having to deal with them directly.

You may not wrestle with demons on a regular basis, but you might meet a false prophet now and then, or you may be duped into believing someone who has a good story, even if they can't in any way confess Christ as their Lord and Savior. You might do that because most of us try to stay open to other philosophies and ideologies. Openness is a good thing, because God designed all that is, but the fact remains that we could be misled, blinded, if we don't keep our eyes and hearts on the work of Christ. Test the spirit of someone before you agree to follow them.

In the Flow

Lord, I must admit that sometimes I don't recognize false teaching for what it is. I see other voices as simply trying to offer a point of view. Protect me during those times and help me understand when a false teacher is near me. Amen.

WHAT DO YOU DO FOR GOD'S PEOPLE?

I pray that your partnership in the faith might become effective
by an understanding of all that is good among us in Christ. I
have great joy and encouragement because of your love, since
the hearts of God's people are refreshed by your actions.
—Philemon 6-7

Take a few moments and think about the people who make a
difference in your life. They may be family members who have
helped you through hard times, celebrated with you through
great times, or simply lent you a hand when you had a big
household project to do. You may think of your church family
and the people you see Sunday after Sunday whom you don't
know well, but you've come to count on seeing because you all
belong there. Who else? Maybe you think of a good friend who
has been with you through thick and thin.

These are the people who have given meaning to your life,
contributing to you in ways that enrich your days and give you
reasons to be happy. These are the people you may well thank
God for because of their love and their faithfulness.

In the same way, we can lead others to Christ any time we
open our hearts in a way that allows a person to get close enough
to us to see God's light within us. The more they see of his light,
the more they want to know. Shine your light today for all of
God's people.

IN THE FLOW

Lord, thank you for loving me so much and for reminding me to see
every person I meet as one of your children. Help me open my heart
in such a way that others see you. Amen.

A WORTHY HOUSE

*When you go into a house, say, "Peace!" If the house
is worthy, give it your blessing of peace. But if the
house isn't worthy, take back your blessing.*
—Matthew 10:12-13

What is a worthy house? Is it one that is kept neat and tidy,
where everyone speaks kindly to everyone else? Is it one where
the woman does all the cooking and the cleaning and the man
does all the yard work and washes the car? Are they deemed
worthy if they read the Bible or if they read Shakespeare?

What about your house? Is it worthy? Chances are it is and
that any visitors to your door would be more than happy to offer
a blessing on your house, asking God for his favor, and informing
others that you have a house that embraces visitors.

Perhaps what we seek then is to be at peace with God. When
we are, the feeling of joy and acceptance and love permeates the
house and so when others come into our homes, they feel it too.
We have created a home worthy of blessing because Christ is the
true center of all we do.

IN THE FLOW

*Lord, most of the time I am at peace in my heart and I do my best to
share that sense of joy and gentleness that comes from you. Help me
create a home that is worthy of your peace. Amen.*

HOW CAN WE UNDERSTAND THE SPIRIT OF GOD?

But this is precisely what is written: God has prepared things for those who love him that no eye has seen, or ear has heard, or that haven't crossed the mind of any human being. *God has revealed these things to us through the Spirit. The Spirit searches everything, including the depths of God. Who knows a person's depths except their own spirit that lives in them? In the same way, no one has known the depths of God except God's Spirit.*
—1 Corinthians 2:9-11

Fortunately, God is well aware that some of us really love the hunt. We love the idea of getting out there, looking for clues, figuring out bits and pieces that others might not get, and then coming up with the solution. We love that so much that God didn't give us that option when it comes to finding out all about him. He gives enough clues to keep us curious, but he saves the best till last. He knows how to intrigue us and keep the mystery going.

Our job then is to keep searching, keep learning, keep desiring to know more of God and to become more of what he designed us to become. God knows we are not really capable of being fully in his presence while we are in our human form. That is why someday, he will bring us to himself in a place he has already prepared for that purpose and we will see each other clearly. May he keep us ever in his grasp until then.

IN THE FLOW

Lord, help me always seek to know more of you so that I can become more of what you dreamed me to be. Amen.

I CAN'T BELIEVE YOU SAID THAT!

*Jesus called the crowd near and said to them, "Listen
and understand. It's not what goes into the mouth that
contaminates a person in God's sight. It's what comes
out of the mouth that contaminates the person."*
—Matthew 15:10-11

Did you ever hear someone say something that just caught you totally off guard, made you stop everything and wonder that such a thing came out of her or his mouth? We've probably all done it, said things we regret, maybe even wondering why.

It's interesting how careful we are about some things. We wash our hands before we eat dinner. We wash off the vegetables before we cook them after we bring them home from the store. We look at the expiration dates on the stuff in our refrigerators, not wanting to put anything in our mouths that might be contaminated. Then what gives? Why aren't we just as concerned about what comes out of our mouths? Why don't we scrutinize the things we say that could hurt others and even change their lives forever?

Whether we witness for God directly or our behavior witnesses for God indirectly, we are responsible for the things we say and do. Let us always be aware of what comes out of our mouths that will not benefit others.

IN THE FLOW

Lord, I'm as guilty as the next person about not always being fully aware of what I say that may be hurtful or unkind. Help me be a witness for you in all the best ways. Amen.

YOUR HEART AND MIND

*More than anything you guard, protect
your mind, for life flows from it.*
—Proverbs 4:23

God created you with a great sensitivity to life. You have empathy
for those who struggle and you offer encouragement to those in
need of hope. You have a good heart.

It's not always easy to protect your heart and mind, though.
You can be drawn off in a variety of directions with every news
report, every job loss, every relationship that goes down the
tubes. It's not easy to protect yourself, so people who seek after
God have to stick close to him.

When you have a heart for God and for humankind, you
seek to make a difference in the lives of those around you. You
seek to become more than you were before, and you even seek to
embrace the concept of holiness.

You are his work of art and you are even more, a work of
his heart. As you embrace the day, ask God to walk with you
and watch over you. Ask him to protect your heart from the
cacophony of worldly news and views. Ask him to show you
where you can open your heart more fully to receive more of
what he has for you. Share your heart with God and those you
meet today.

IN THE FLOW

*Lord, thank you for helping me become more of what you created
me to be. Help me be willing to share my heart and share your love.
Amen.*

October 20

How Many Terabytes Is That?

This is the disciple who testifies concerning these things
and who wrote them down. We know that his testimony
is true. Jesus did many other things as well.
If all of them were recorded, I imagine the world itself wouldn't
have enough room for the scrolls that would be written.
—John 21:24-25

Imagine trying to record all that Jesus did and then running it on a computer program. Let's say you could give him a trillion bytes of space. Would that be enough? Would you have enough space left to record the story that is going on even today?

As believers we're still giving testimony to the things we've seen and done because of the life and death and resurrection of Jesus. We're still standing in his light and sharing his heart with others. We do this by living the best life we can and working to be a good sermon. We're walking stories of what faith is all about.

Are you aware of moments when you shared your faith lately? Sometimes you are when you share with someone who still struggles to believe and you can tell you've opened the door a little, giving them more to think about and causing them to want to hear more. Those are fabulous moments and make your heart rejoice.

If you're doing your part, someone is reading your faith story with every encounter they have with you. Make it a good one.

In the Flow

Lord, I know I don't always think about how well I'm telling your
story. Help me be aware of all the ways I can help someone else see
your light. Amen.

BREAD AND WATER, PLEASE!

*"The bread of God is the one who comes down from heaven and gives
life to the world." They said, "Sir, give us this bread all the time!"
Jesus replied, "I am the bread of life. Whoever comes to me will
never go hungry, and whoever believes in me will never be thirsty.
But I told you that you have seen me and still don't believe."*
—John 6:33-36

Nothing teases the senses and invites you to the table quite as
quickly as the smell of freshly baked bread. Whether laden with
herbs or just hot enough to melt the butter so it slides down
your fingers, it's a joyful experience. It's hard to know if Jesus
was thinking of these kinds of things when he compared himself
to bread, offering himself as the bread of heaven, but perhaps so.
What else could be so welcoming and so necessary to sustaining
life as the miraculous bread that only he can provide?

Imagine for a moment what it would mean to never thirst or
to never be hungry again. Imagine what it means even for a few
hours. Today, every time you drink a glass of water, give some
praise to Jesus. Every time you lift a fork to your mouth, or make
a sandwich, send him some love. He is all you need. He is all that
will sustain your life. Thank him for all that he has provided for
you right now.

IN THE FLOW

*Lord, I am so thankful that you are the bread of life, the
nourishment that feeds my spirit and keeps my soul safe and strong
in every way. Amen.*

WHO'S SHAKING THE FAMILY TREE NOW?

Look at how good and pleasing it is when
families live together as one!
—Psalm 133:1

Families are incredible microcosms of culture. Each one represents an aspect of the greater cultures found throughout the world. The dynamics are similar, but not the same. There's everything . . . the good, the bad, and the ugly.

Someone is always shaking things up in most families. It might not be the nuclear family; it may be more of the extended family; but that sense of real peace and harmony only lasts for moments at a time, if indeed it is attained at all.

It's certain that there will be times when someone in your family will make you feel on edge, will hurt your feelings, or will make you angry. But those are just times that you learn to love through, to live through, and to remind yourselves that nothing is more important than knowing you have each other. Put a little extra love and harmony into your family life today.

IN THE FLOW

Lord, thank you for giving me such a wonderful family. When we don't get along, help us come back to you and to one another so that we can find peace again. Amen.

To Know God Is to Love God

Dear friends, let's love each other, because love is from God, and everyone who loves is born from God and knows God. The person who doesn't love does not know God, because God is love.
—1 John 4:7-8

Remember a song written by Phil Spector called "To Know Him Is to Love Him?" It's actually a great song to sing to God. Whenever you feel his presence and sense his smile on your life, it makes everything worthwhile. It's your turn to smile back because nothing is better than that.

Once you finish singing your heart out to God, then take the next step. Start seeing the people that you love already as people you could also sing that song to. After you've sung to all the people you know well, then look at people you work with who also need more love and change up the song for them.

Then, take a giant leap and see if you can sing the song to your enemies. That's right. See if you can put in the name of someone you don't especially feel fond of, but someone that Jesus died for just the same as he did you.

God wants you to love others. He wants you to love your families and your friends and those you don't even know yet. He wants you to love everyone he loves. He has a very big Christmas card list. See if you can love others with his heart today.

In the Flow

Lord, thank you for loving me. Give me the insight, the desire, and the ability to love others the way you love me. Amen.

October 24

Put Down That Heavy Load!

*Come to me, all you who are struggling hard and carrying
heavy loads, and I will give you rest. Put on my yoke, and learn
from me. I'm gentle and humble. And you will find rest for
yourselves. My yoke is easy to bear, and my burden is light.*
—Matthew 11:28-30

It's a new day and you're waking up as though you never went
to sleep. Your thoughts instantly fly to the things you're trying
to tough out, the challenges that never seem to end. You wonder
where God is and why all this business hasn't gone away by
now. You finally get out of bed, strap the weight of worry and
frustration on your back, load your arms with grief and anger,
and set out to see if there's a smile to be found anywhere.
Everything is a mess.

A yoke is a device that puts two oxen or other animals
together so that they can use their weight to pull heavy loads.
They have to work in tandem because if one of them gets into a
different rhythm from the other, they may tip over the cart they
are pulling.

In this case, what Jesus needs is for you to come close to
him, lean into him, hook up with him in such a way that he can
help you carry the load. In fact, he will gently and humbly walk
beside you the whole way and take on the bulk of the burden if
you let him. It's time to lighten up!

In the Flow

*Lord, I know I need your help. I'm not always good at leaving my
messes in your hands, but I want you to be near me today to guide me
and help me carry the weight of everything in front of me. Amen.*

THE REAL JUSTICE SYSTEM

Let the sea and everything in it roar; the world and all its inhabitants too. Let all the rivers clap their hands; let the mountains rejoice out loud altogether before the LORD because he is coming to establish justice on the earth! He will establish justice in the world rightly; he will establish justice among all people fairly.
—Psalm 98:7-9

If you had a sibling while you were growing up, you probably recall more than one occasion when you didn't think things were done fairly. Of course, now you've grown up and you know that those slights, those seemingly unfair and unjust issues, are nothing compared to the amount of injustice suffered worldwide. Our ability to hurt each other, hurt animals and children, and hurt the planet goes beyond imagination. A sense of justice rarely occupies our minds because we can't see it being delivered in any arena of life.

But hold on! There's a new day coming! Justice will prevail, and when it does . . . look out! Get out the brass bands and the bass drums because there's going to be a noise going up to the heavens like no one has heard before. The whole of creation will join in on the song, shouting and shifting, raising waves of triumphant joy, moving and shaking loose every sad story, every hard tale because the victory has come. The King of Justice has entered the courts and a new day dawns.

IN THE FLOW

Lord, things are so out of balance that I don't often know just how to think about them. I pray for the right things to happen and I pray for your justice to win out over all that brings such misery to others. Amen.

UNEXPECTED COMPANY

Happy are those whom he finds alert, even if he comes at midnight or just before dawn. But know this, if the homeowner had known what time the thief was coming, he wouldn't have allowed his home to be broken into. You also must be ready, because the Human One is coming at a time when you don't expect him.
—Luke 12:38-40

Are you the kind of person whose house is always spotless, always in great shape no matter what? If so, you probably don't mind the occasional visit by someone you weren't expecting, someone who just dropped by without calling first.

This Scripture is a little daunting because it's suggesting to us that it might be a good idea to get our house in order and keep it that way. After all, we never know when company is coming, and in this case, it could be the King of the Universe.

Are you ready then? Any time now the One who created you is coming back and he wants you to be ready for him. He wants you to have your affairs in order in a way that shows him how happy you are to see him. He'll be expecting you to anticipate his arrival and to be ready on a moment's notice to offer a warm embrace.

Might be a good day to take a little inventory of just how ready you are for his visit.

IN THE FLOW

Lord, I have to admit that some days, I'm sure I'm ready for you to come and visit and other days, I'm hoping you delay a little. Help me be ready and waiting with open arms for your return. Amen.

You're in Good Hands

I also observed under the sun that the race doesn't always go to the swift, nor the battle to the mighty, nor food to the wise, nor wealth to the intelligent, nor favor to the knowledgeable, because accidents can happen to anyone. People most definitely don't know when their time will come. Like fish tragically caught in a net or like birds trapped in a snare, so are human beings caught in a time of tragedy that suddenly falls to them.
—Ecclesiastes 9:11-12

Most of us carry some kind of catastrophe insurance. We don't expect to be caught in a hurricane or we don't anticipate that our house will be struck by lightning and burn to the ground, but in some measure we try to be prepared.

One insurance carrier has a slogan that assures customers that signing up with them means the customer will be "in good hands." If you think about it, your slogan could well be "you're in good hands" with Jesus. When you signed up with him, you signed up for a lifelong partner in disaster insurance. He will take every claim and begin to work with you immediately. He'll assess the situation, size up the difficulty, and then have you nail the problems to a tree, because he has already worked out the victory.

Accidents happen. They can happen to you and devastate you. Or, you can put yourself in good hands. You won't be trapped like a bird in a snare. Instead, you'll have wings to fly and rise above anything this world brings your way.

In the Flow

Lord, thank you for holding me up, sustaining me, and protecting me. Thank you for giving me the opportunity to place my life in good hands . . . your hands. Amen.

YOU ARE LOOKIN' GOOD TODAY!

So then, from this point on we won't recognize people by human standards. Even though we used to know Christ by human standards, that isn't how we know him now. So then, if anyone is in Christ, that person is part of the new creation. The old things have gone away, and look, new things have arrived!
—2 Corinthians 5:16-17

Have you ever run into an old friend and been awed at how much they had changed since the last time you saw them? Maybe they had lost a lot of weight or they had blossomed into a confident, strong person. Maybe they now carried the weight of the world on their shoulders when they used to be light and carefree. Whatever it was, it was amazing to you to see them in this new way.

That's how God sees you. You are in a new light because you're standing in the light of his Son. The reflection is awesome and God sees you as a whole new being and he loves you. You're one of his favorites.

Who is the new you? It's the perfect you, the one aligned as a child of God. It's the you who strives to do the right thing, to trust when the odds are against you and to believe when most would fall away. It's the new you who knows you have one eternal flame that burns brightly enough to guide you through the day and give you peace. It's a brand new day and you are lookin' good!

IN THE FLOW

Lord, thank you for walking with me into this new day. Thank you for making me new again in you. Help me reflect you as beautifully as I can. Amen.

"IT'S FOR YOUR OWN GOOD!"

*Now in light of all that, Israel, what does the LORD your
God ask of you? Only this: to revere the LORD your God by
walking in all his ways, by loving him, by serving the LORD
your God with all your heart and being, and by keeping
the LORD's commandments and his regulations that I'm
commanding you right now. It's for your own good!*
—Deuteronomy 10:12-13

Have you ever been aghast by the things that were done "for
your own good"? For one thing, they never felt good. When
your mother said it, you knew before anything happened that
you were not likely to appreciate the fact that you had to learn to
like spinach or you had to skip the party everyone else could go
to because, well . . . you know.

How is it different with God? How is it different when he
wants you to do things that are for your own good? For one
thing, the request is coming from your Father, not just someone
who hopes you won't embarrass them, but someone who actually
knows the absolute best ways for things to be done. He's got
the caring and love of your mother, but ten times over. His only
agenda is you, and everything is designed for your good.

Love him, rejoice in him, serve him . . . and you'll know his
infinite goodness!

IN THE FLOW

*Lord, thank you for loving me beyond my understanding and for
working things out for me in ways that I'll probably never even
know simply because you wanted me to know your goodness. Amen.*

October 30

Haven't We Met Before?

As water reflects the face, so the heart reflects one person to another.
—Proverbs 27:19

Do you ever spot someone you think you know and then realize you don't? They remind you of someone, but you can't quite place them. You wonder what it is about them that is so familiar.

Perhaps what you're seeing has more to do with the spirit than the body. Perhaps what you're seeing is something holy . . . a reflection of their Father and yours. If so, it stands to reason that they would seem familiar, because they reflect the heart of the one you love as well.

Today, when you catch a glimpse of yourself as you pass by a big plate-glass window, or perhaps see your face in the waters of the fountain on the square, imagine seeing Christ's face alongside yours, even coming through yours. Imagine his kind smile, his generous spirit, and his sparkling eyes and reflect on the joy you share in knowing that you are in him and he is in you.

You're not only his face and his reflection, but you're his hands and feet, and his eyes and ears. You are a reminder of his love and his heart, and that makes you important to him today. It makes you essential to those around you.

Offer his smile to everyone you meet today.

In the Flow

Lord, you are so kind to me. You bring such joy to my heart. Thank you for loving me and living within me. Help me be a better reflection of you. Amen.

WHAT HAVE YOU DONE FOR ME LATELY?

"When did we see you sick or in prison and visit you?"
Then the king will reply to them, "I assure you that when
you have done it for one of the least of these brothers
and sisters of mine, you have done it for me."
—Matthew 25:39-40

Some days we are overwhelmed with life and we can barely take care of ourselves. Giving to others doesn't come up on our radar. We don't put ourselves out of the way. If we're lucky, though, God will put someone in our path who is in greater need than we are. He will help us to see that we still have something to give and that we're still in his care and keeping as well. That one person will remind us that we may not be able to take on a whole load of people, but we can take on at least the one who is in need.

Mother Teresa said, "If you can't feed a hundred people, then feed just one." Feeding one person may simply mean offering a kind word or a smile. It may mean helping them get a seat on a crowded bus. It can mean many things, but each time you respond, each time you say yes to helping another person, you say yes to God. He sees what you do and rewards you for it.

It's a great day to do something good. What will you do?

IN THE FLOW

Lord, you have blessed me and I am grateful. Help me bless others in any way that I can today. Amen.

November

Comfort the discouraged. Help the weak. Be patient with everyone.

1 Thessalonians 5:14

INVISIBLE MEANS OF SUPPORT

If you love me, you will keep my commandments. I will ask the Father, and he will send another Companion, who will be with you forever. This Companion is the Spirit of Truth, whom the world can't receive because it neither sees him nor recognizes him. You know him, because he lives with you and will be with you.
—John 14:15-17

In an effort to look reality squarely in the face, we sometimes overlook another reality, the very supernatural reality that is part of being a believer. God is spirit, and as well as operating with us physically as we wander about in our temporal bodies, he also works on our spirits. We work on our spirits too, praying to be faithful, hoping to be more like the One who created us.

It's natural for God to talk with us about recognizing his Spirit that he placed within us. He knows we are finite. He knows we are human. The only real hope we have, then, is that the incredible human spirit he gave us will mix and mingle with the Holy Spirit he also gave us. He knew we couldn't get through life without an invisible means of support. He sent a Companion, the Spirit of Truth, to live with us on a full-time basis.

A companion, any companion, is someone that you love to pal around with. You may not think of the Spirit of Truth as that kind of companion, but as you reflect on that today, get a little closer to him and thank him for all he does to help you navigate your walk here on earth.

IN THE FLOW

Lord, I am amazed that you would give such a glorious part of yourself to me, to live with me and teach me and comfort me. I love you and I thank you for your beautiful Spirit. Amen.

THE CHILD WITHIN YOU

People were bringing children to Jesus so that he would bless them. But the disciples scolded them. When Jesus saw this, he grew angry and said to them, "Allow the children to come to me. Don't forbid them, because God's kingdom belongs to people like these children."
—Mark 10:13-14

You probably know people who are seriously adult. They carry their "grown-up-ness" around like it's a badge of honor. They've got weighty matters on their minds all the time and they've somehow forgotten to smile, to ease up on themselves and others, and simply to play.

When was the last time you gave yourself a play date? When was the last time you let the kid in you have fun and laugh for almost no reason, or hope in something that just seems crazy ridiculous to the adult mind? Remember the kid who hoped for a pony?

Make it a point today to look for those people who smile for no apparent reason. Discover those who befriend you in an instant because they simply trust in the good will and the good nature of others. Notice how freely they allow the love within them to flow and how quickly others respond to even their smallest gestures. It's childlike faith. The kingdom of heaven is made for people like that.

IN THE FLOW

Lord, help me reconnect with the child within me. Help me notice the little things that bring such joy to every day. I thank you for loving me so much. Amen.

Knit One, Pearl You!

You are the one who created my innermost parts; you
knit me together while I was still in my mother's womb.
I give thanks to you that I was marvelously set apart.
Your works are wonderful—I know that very well.
—Psalm 139:13-14

If you do any knitting, you're probably a pro at the different patterns that you can create with just a few simple knit and purl stitches. It's awesome to see what the variety of wools and fibers can turn into when you're done shaping and creating something beautiful that never existed before.

The good news is that everything God creates and starts to knit comes out a perfect pearl. You started out as a gem and somewhere within you, a tiny sparkling gem still exists. It was part of the knitting process when you were being imagined.

If you haven't felt like a pearl lately, it might be a good day to do a little digging and see where that nugget of joy really is. Remember that your Savior is the "Pearl of Great Price" and that he redeemed you so that you could come back to him, not just someday, but every day. He made it possible for you to seek his face every day you live.

Today, remember how valuable you are. Remember what love went into making you the perfectly beautiful person you have become. You're his pearl all the time.

In the Flow

Lord, you have done so much for me and I can hardly take it in.
Help me remember that you see me as beautiful so that I can live up
to that image as much as possible. Amen.

November 4

Simply Divine Conversation!

*When all the people saw the column of cloud standing at the
tent's entrance, they would all rise and then bow down at the
entrances to their tents. In this way the LORD used to speak
to Moses face-to-face, like two people talking to each other.*
—Exodus 33:10-11

These days it's pretty easy to connect with the people you love. If
you're near, you stop by. If you aren't, you get on the phone or you
pull up Skype and in a matter of moments you can be talking face
to face. When we're talking to God, we might have a feeling that
our prayers are more like getting on the phone. We may not always
hear what God is saying from the other end, mostly because if
there's a bad connection, it's probably our system that is causing it.

We might wonder what it takes to have direct
communication with God. We might ask ourselves why we're
always in the fog. The truth is that even though it will be exciting
when we're able to see each other clearly, we aren't at a loss, we
aren't left without a way to be closely connected. We can always
hear God if we're willing to listen for his tender voice. He speaks
through others, he speaks through our intuitive understanding,
he reaches out any way that he can to be sure we're connected to
him and that we too are part of a divine conversation.

In the Flow

*Lord, thank you for giving me a way to talk with you and to feel
connected to you all the time. Thank you for giving me a clear
signal that you are truly there with me today. Amen.*

SHAKING YOUR PUNY FIST!

How long will you forget me, LORD? Forever? How long will you hide your face from me? How long will I be left to my own wits, agony filling my heart? Daily? How long will my enemy keep defeating me? Look at me! Answer me, LORD my God!
—Psalm 13:1-3

We've all been there! We've been praying about something, hoping with all we have, and yet we get no answers, no direction from God. Nothing is happening. God appears to have gone on vacation, at least from us, and he does not come back with anything that we can understand.

The psalmist was in that place too. Everywhere he turned, it looked like misery and defeat. He couldn't get any clear direction from God and he felt abandoned. He felt desperate. The One he was used to calling on and gaining support from just wasn't answering him.

It is easy to understand why we claim "patience" to be a virtue. We must be certain of the things we hope for, and have the faith to walk and wait, pray and cry. God sees our need and isn't being slow to answer, but is working all things together for our good.

The answers may not always be the ones we hoped for, but the One we hope in will be steadfast and true. He will be there always, even to the end of the earth.

IN THE FLOW

Lord, I have wondered sometimes why you don't seem to be there when I need you the most, and yet, in my heart, I know you are. Help me be patient and wait for the good only you can design for me. Amen.

November 6

Depressed, Stressed, and Blessed!

We are experiencing all kinds of trouble, but we aren't crushed.
We are confused, but we aren't depressed. We are harassed,
but we aren't abandoned. We are knocked down, but we
aren't knocked out. We always carry Jesus' death around in
our bodies so that Jesus' life can also be seen in our bodies.
—2 Corinthians 4:8-10

Reality TV often presents us with someone who is endeavoring to get us to vote for them so they can go on to the next level or stay in the contest a little longer. Week after week, though, someone gets voted off the show until there is just one contestant still standing, the one who wins the prize.

The truth is that God wants you to stand and win. He wants you to win the prize and trust him when the lessons come, when the heartaches happen so that you learn to rely on him for everything. The difficulty is that he can't walk the path for you, and he can't take the obstacles away. What he can do, though, is promise to be by your side every step of the way. He will guide you forward to the light of a new day.

Take him by the hand as you seek his Word and his heart to learn what you should do now. The reality of your show is that you will indeed win because he has already voted you in and made the prize available. Stand firm. Blessings will come!

In the Flow

Lord, it doesn't feel like things are ever going to change. One thing
leads to another and no matter what I do, it just doesn't get better.
I give it all to you and ask that you would watch over me and the
people I love and help us trust in you. Amen.

THE RED WAGON

My God will meet your every need out of his riches in the glory that is found in Christ Jesus. Let glory be given to God our Father forever and ever. Amen.
—Philippians 4:19-20

There's a wonderful story about a woman who was walking along the beach. She was praying to God about her earthly concerns, which mostly had to do with money and being able to take care of herself and her children. As she walked along the shore, she saw Jesus walking toward her pulling a red wagon. As she got closer, she discovered it was loaded with gold.

It was a glorious moment, but just then, a man came running across the sand and grabbed the wagon from Jesus' hand. As the woman watched the scene her heart sank. Jesus kept coming toward her and motioned for her to come closer to him.

As she got to him, she noticed that he still had his hand on the handle of a little red wagon. She was startled to see that he still had it behind him. "Lord," she said, "I just saw a man come and steal the wagon away from you. Do you have another one?"

Jesus looked at the woman and stepped aside so she could see behind him. The woman saw wagon after wagon filled with gold. Jesus took her by the hand and smiled. "There's no need for anyone to have to steal from God's treasure chest," he said, "for he has an abundance for all those who seek his help."

IN THE FLOW

Lord, thank you for sharing your abundant love and glorious treasures with me. Thank you for your Son. Amen.

More Than a Fig Tree

Jesus responded, "I assure you that if you have faith and don't doubt, you will not only do what was done to the fig tree. You will even say to this mountain, 'Be lifted up and thrown into the lake.' And it will happen. If you have faith, you will receive whatever you pray for."
—Matthew 21:21-22

When Jesus was hungry and found the fig tree without fruit, he spoke to it and caused it to wither and die. He reprimanded it for not bearing fruit as it should. It was a wonderful metaphor for what God expects of his children, but it was also a lesson for his followers. It was a lesson about faith. How do we get to the place where our ability to suspend doubt is so strong that we can speak and the things of nature will respond? For most of us, getting a mountain to rise up and throw itself into the lake, or speaking to the storm and getting it to calm down, are experiences we don't expect to ever have. We simply don't have that kind of faith.

Perhaps what we have to recognize is that we still are followers with very weak faith. We're not much further along than the disciples were when it comes to totally understanding and trusting the power of God that is unleashed in real faith.

As you venture out into a new day, examine your faith. Imagine trusting and believing so much that your faith could move mountains or even wither a fig tree.

In the Flow

Lord, I know I have weak faith. I ask you to keep working with me to help me see you in ways that strengthen and renew my faith in every area of my life. Amen.

FAITHFUL OVER A LITTLE

His master replied, "Excellent! You are a good and
faithful servant! You've been faithful over a little. I'll put
you in charge of much. Come, celebrate with me."
—Matthew 25:21

Most of us are never going to be in a position of great power or influence. We won't command armies or rule over thousands of people. We're simply going to be everyday, ordinary people who now and then do extraordinary things. The key to any of it is locked into our level of faithfulness.

You have a job to do, a mission of sorts, a definite purpose. You're continually being put into situations that bring out the best of your talents and cause you to fulfill your mission. You are always guided to the goal of getting your job done.

How much are you willing to do to answer the call you have been given? God is always faithful to you. He is always on the job and never slumbers or sleeps, never takes a day off, never unplugs the phone. He is faithful.

It stands to reason then that he wants his children to be faithful too. He wants us to be faithful in little things so he can give us the opportunity to grow in faith and take on even bigger things. Remember that God is best served by you when you desire to be more for him, when you desire to have a bigger faith. Go and serve the Lord!

IN THE FLOW

Lord, I love the way you help me to learn more of the work you want
me to do. Help me always be faithful to the tasks that you give me,
in big ways and small ways. Amen.

Might, Wisdom, and Knowledge

But God made the earth by his might; he shaped the
world by his wisdom, crafted the skies by his knowledge.
At the sound of his voice, the heavenly waters roar. He
raises the clouds from the ends of the earth. He sends the
lightning with the rain, the wind from his treasuries.
—Jeremiah 10:12-13

God shaped the world as we know it through his own inexhaustible powers of wisdom and knowledge and might. He set the clouds in the skies and spoke the rains and the mists into being. He has powers that are without peer in this universe. Yet, even so, Jesus came along many years after the prophet Jeremiah and reminded us that this God who made all things seeks a relationship with his creation, his children. It is by faith in this same God that we are told we too can come to wisdom and knowledge to do in part the things he has done.

Knowledge can be attained by much practice and study. Wisdom must partner with faithfulness in order to lead with strength and honor. Most of us strive to attain more knowledge and to lead our lives with more wisdom. Yet, one thing may still elude us. We may not discover more of what faithfulness offers.

May God grant you wisdom today as you seek to know more of him and all that he wants for your life.

In the Flow

Lord, you are the source of all wisdom and knowledge and through
your might, you created all that we see. Help me delight in your
creation and learn all that I can about you as a matter of love and
faithfulness. Amen.

GOD HAD CHOICES

*While we were still weak, at the right moment, Christ
died for ungodly people. It isn't often that someone will
die for a righteous person, though maybe someone might
dare to die for a good person. But God shows his love for us,
because while we were still sinners Christ died for us.*
—Romans 5:6-8

God had choices. He could have scratched all his plans and said
he was done with us. After all, he tried twice and the human
race still didn't seem to get it. We're still pathetic and selfish and
pretty hard to live with most of the time. Yet, even with choices,
even after the flood, God felt so bad for what he had done, and
for us, that he gave us a rainbow promise that life would go on.

Fortunately for the human race, God made a plan. He
looked at us one more time, and with more love than we could
ever possibly earn or deserve, he sent an innocent baby boy to
be our sacrifice. The Lamb of God, Jesus, would live among us,
laugh with us, cry with us, and work with us and yet know that
he would one day lay down his life so that we could live.

God didn't have to do it. He had choices. His decision was
made a long time ago and it still stands. He won't change his
mind. We're his lost sheep and he was mighty glad to send us a
Shepherd.

IN THE FLOW

*Lord, I don't know how to thank you for making it possible for me to
come back to live with you someday, but I do. Thank you for loving
me more than I can understand. Amen.*

SAVED IN HOPE

We know that the whole creation is groaning together and
suffering labor pains up until now. And it's not only the
creation. We ourselves who have the Spirit as the first crop
of the harvest also groan inside as we wait to be adopted
and for our bodies to be set free. We were saved in hope.
—Romans 8:22-24

Whether we are conscious of it or not, we all exist with hope. We
hope that the work we do will make a difference or that it will
at least be accomplished well. We hope that our children will be
strong and healthy and grow up to be kind and generous people.
We hope that we'll get to enjoy more of life as the days ahead
unfold because we've been mired in things that don't make life
easy. Whatever it is and wherever we are, we live in hope.

In Paul's letter to the Romans, though, he takes that idea
a step further. He says we were saved in hope. We were saved
in hope and we long for our spirits to be set free. We anticipate
the coming of Christ as the moment when we can be all that we
were meant to be in his eyes. We hope that we are blessed in the
harvest and picked to be with our Lord forever. We live in hope.

We are anchored in the hope of our Redeemer. Let us live
and work and play in that hope every day.

IN THE FLOW

Lord, I am so grateful for the hope I have in you. I know that if all
else fails, if I cannot accomplish all that I hope to achieve, still I am
eternally safe in your care. I have put all my hope in your hands.
Amen.

THE HEAD OF THE HOUSE

Now I want you to know that the head of every man is Christ, and the head of the woman is the man, and the head of Christ is God.
—1 Corinthians 11:3

We are familiar with the adage that the man is the head of the house, but the woman is the heart of the house. It's a lovely idea, but our culture has long since created homes where men are actually not the head of the house. The family dynamic does not favor the likelihood of that structure in many homes. Whether or not that structure exists in your home, and even if you're a single parent, look at what this passage is saying.

What God may be after here is to know that each family will come to him to be the head of the house no matter how the family unit might be constructed. Since God placed us in families so we wouldn't be lonely, he hoped the outcome would be that each person would serve him with love and other family members with joy.

You have a well-established family dynamic. Regardless of the structure, you have someone who sees you right where you are and works to create the best possible home life. You have an advocate. When you look at your home, can you recognize the head of the house?

IN THE FLOW

Lord, thank you for my family. We don't always even pay attention to matters like this one, but we need to. Help us be very clear about creating our home so that you are the head of it. Amen.

November 14

Sweating the Small Stuff

*Who among you by worrying can add a single moment to
your life? And why do you worry about clothes? Notice how
the lilies in the field grow. They don't wear themselves out with
work, and they don't spin cloth. But I say to you that even
Solomon in all of his splendor wasn't dressed like one of these.
If God dresses grass in the field so beautifully, even though
it's alive today and tomorrow it's thrown into the furnace,
won't God do much more for you, you people of weak faith?*
—Matthew 6:27-30

We're not as caught up these days in the "dressed for success"
idea, though an attitude of that sort persists in some circles. The
one we're more concerned with is the way we worry about all
the details of our lives. We worry that we aren't as well dressed
as the next person. We worry that we might not have everything
we need each day. When we can't see the result we hope for, we
begin to worry.

As you walk into a new day, take some time to pray and to
determine just how you want to handle things. Will you pick up
fear and worry, or will you handle everything with faith? It's your
life and your choice. Regardless, you don't have to worry about
whether you're dressed for the part. From God's view, you're
beautiful just as you are.

In the Flow

*Lord, help me handle my life with prayer and trust you for all the
details I'm unable to work out for myself. Forgive me when I hold on
to worry more than I hold on to my faith. Amen.*

HE WILL LIFT YOU HIGHER

*My plans aren't your plans, nor are your
ways my ways, says the LORD.
Just as the heavens are higher than the earth, so are my ways
higher than your ways, and my plans than your plans. Just as the
rain and the snow come down from the sky and don't return there
without watering the earth, making it conceive and yield plants
and providing seed to the sower and food to the eater, so is my
word that comes from my mouth; it does not return to me empty.*
—Isaiah 55:8-11

Some people are planners. They like to map out every step they'll
take on a given day. Other people are just the opposite. They run
with the wind here and there. They somehow still manage to get
along on their intended course.

The tricky part of the planning process is that God is also
planning and he's been planning your steps since the day you
took your first breath. You were designed for a certain mission,
a purpose that only you and he will actually ever know. So,
the problem with planning is that it requires more than an
action based on what you want. It requires you to listen for the
voice of the One who speaks to you often and creates the best
opportunity for his plans to come to fruition.

God knows why he made you. He planned for you to have an
abundant life, filled with joy, enriched by his guidance through the
Word. Step out in faith and leave the planning to God.

IN THE FLOW

*Lord, I always make lists of things I need to do. I hope that you help
me create those lists, but I also ask that you would help me create the
priorities. I want to work with you every day. Amen.*

November 16

Cheering You On

Let's also think about how to motivate each other to show love and to do good works. Don't stop meeting together with other believers, which some people have gotten into the habit of doing. Instead, encourage each other, especially as you see the day drawing near.
—Hebrews 10:24-25

Isn't it wonderful to have a champion? A champion is someone who cheers you on and encourages your dreams and your life direction. They see the real you and they hope and pray for you and they help you keep going. They are the wind beneath your wings as they help you reach your goal.

You have an eternal champion in Jesus Christ. He is always ready to cheer you on and to remind you of your goal. He's always interested in the things you do and in the friendships you build because he's all about relationship. After all, it's difficult to love your neighbor as yourself if you don't know your neighbor.

Whatever you do today, remember to have your radar set on high to connect in every good way with the people around you. Cheer them on and bless their work. Help them to know that what they do matters not just to them, but to you, and even more so, to God. We'll all succeed if we pull together!

In the Flow

Lord, help me recognize those moments when I can be a cheerleader for someone else. Help me plant the seeds of your love anywhere I can today. Amen.

ONGOING TRAINING

Train children in the way they should go; when they grow old, they won't depart from it.
—Proverbs 22:6

We may look at this verse as one that reminds us to discipline children so that they will grow emotionally and faithfully strong and healthy. Indeed, that is something to be taken to heart, but what else is involved with training besides discipline? What else can we give our children so that when they grow older, they will pass along the things we've taught them?

When we consider the kind of love God has for us, it's hard to imagine how we can parent in a way that reflects his desires for our good. The truth is we raise our children desiring more than anything that they grow up strong in the Lord, true to themselves, and humanitarian in their approaches to others. We want them to be kind and giving and generous to those around them.

The good news is we're all in training. We train our children and then they train others, and even as we all grow older, God continues to train each of us. We're his children always and so our training doesn't end no matter what age we might be. We're always learning more of what God wants from us and training to become the best we can be just for him.

IN THE FLOW

Lord, keep training me, because I have a lot to learn. Thank you for your patience and enduring kindness to me. I couldn't be where I am without you. Amen.

IT'S ALL GOOD!

Comfort the discouraged. Help the weak. Be patient with everyone. Make sure no one repays a wrong with a wrong, but always pursue the good for each other and everyone else.
—1 Thessalonians 5:14-15

God pursued what was good right from the beginning. He looked at each step of his creation and declared it to be good. He was pleased when he finished his work because he could truthfully say, "It's all good!"

Generally, we try to see the good in a situation. We may dismiss those parts that don't feel quite as good as the rest and simply declare that it's all okay. The truth for us, though, is that we have to actually do just what God did, we have to pursue what is good. It doesn't just come to us. In fact, we often encounter things that are somewhat muddy, things in need of an overhaul. We're given those things so we can shine a light on them and bring the good out of them.

If you haven't been called a "do-gooder" in a while, you might want to reconsider the things you pursue. You don't need your good works to be noticed, though, you simply need to know that you're doing all you can to make a difference, even if it's only for one other person. Keep working at it until you can step back and honestly say, "It's all good."

IN THE FLOW

Lord, help me do the kind of good you want me to do. Sometimes I intend to do good things, but I get caught up in my own day and discover at the end of it, I didn't take time to reach out to anyone else. Help me always pursue the good in myself and others. Amen.

The Sound of the Spirit

Don't suppress the Spirit. Don't brush off Spirit-inspired messages, but examine everything carefully and hang on to what is good.
—1 Thessalonians 5:19-21

It's not likely that you would ever intentionally ignore the Spirit of God. You wouldn't consciously turn your back or simply suggest you don't have time to listen. Would you?

The problem comes, though, when we don't have our ears well enough tuned to the Spirit to actually listen, so we don't connect to his efforts to inspire our hearts and minds. Most of the time we're a lot more connected to the voices and the noises coming in through our cyberspace networks. How can we hear the Holy Spirit then? How can we hear that still quiet voice so we don't end up giving him the brush-off?

Listen carefully and take note of what you hear. You may find some instruction that you would have missed, some opportunity that you didn't realize was there, simply because you chose to listen and not brush off the Spirit. Pray, meditate, give God your undivided attention today and see where he takes you. Love him with your heart, soul, and mind.

In the Flow

Lord, I know I need to spend more time resting in you. Please remind me to take the time as often as I can to simply sit at your feet and get to know more of you. Please help me never ignore your gracious and generous Spirit. Amen.

THINK ABOUT WHAT YOU'RE THINKING ABOUT!

*Therefore, submit to God. Resist the devil, and he will run
away from you. Come near to God, and he will come near to
you. Wash your hands, you sinners. Purify your hearts, you
double-minded. Cry out in sorrow, mourn, and weep! Let
your laughter become mourning and your joy become sadness.
Humble yourselves before the Lord, and he will lift you up.*
—James 4:7-10

In the stillness and the quiet hours, we find ourselves awake and
poised, ready to learn more of what God would have for us. We
listen carefully, desiring above all else to submit to his will.

The noise of the world occupies our minds. It is the work of
the evil one that you should not realize how little time you spend
in prayer and contemplation. He's a wily one, after all, cunning
and deceitful, and all you have to do to get him to flee is resist
him. Resist him and he will run from you.

He runs because the closer you get to God the less he can
stand the company you keep. So watch what you're thinking,
what you're listening to, and what you're perceiving as real. Wait
in the stillness for the voice of the One who loves you more than
life itself. He alone can lift you up over all the noise.

IN THE FLOW

*Lord, it is often noisy inside my head. I know that I need to quiet the
stress and the anxiety that hover around me, waiting to take over
when my spirit is weak. I submit myself to you and to your love for
me. Amen.*

COUNTING OUR BLESSINGS

Let the people thank you, God! Let all the people thank you! The earth has yielded its harvest. God blesses us—our God blesses us! Let God continue to bless us; let the far ends of the earth honor him.
—Psalm 67:5-7

It's hard to imagine that we could ever come to an end when we are counting our blessings. Miracles of life surround us and everywhere we look there are reasons to sing God's praises. We have a report card full of A's and every reason to celebrate.

Strangely, we often choose to count our sorrows first. We look at that same report card with just one D and all A's, and can only see the D. We then go to God and try to get an explanation. How is it we don't have all A's all the time? Why do we have to suffer through an occasional D?

It's an oversimplification to be sure, and yet, we need to take an honest assessment and look at the amount of time we spend thanking God for all we have compared to the time we spend complaining to him about what we don't have. We are blessed and God is good all the time. He watches over us and cherishes us so much that he provided not only the gifts we need to sustain life on this planet, but the Gift we need to be able to come home again to heaven. He provided all that we have and so it is only right to thank him and praise him.

IN THE FLOW

Lord, I am grateful for all you have done to provide for me, and I praise you for the gifts beyond measure that are mine. You are an awesome God! Amen.

WHEN THE WELL RUNS DRY

*Everything that has been created by God is good, and
nothing that is received with thanksgiving should be rejected.
These things are made holy by God's word and prayer.*
—1 Timothy 4:4-5

A certain French proverb reminds us that "we never know the
worth of water until the well runs dry." Most of us are used to
having good drinking water. We're used to turning on the tap
and filling up our glass or taking a shower and being totally
oblivious to the good water we have or the amount we use. We
are blessed with abundance when it comes to water.

These days, though, we often see clips of people around the
world where water is not abundant. People are doing their best
to drink water that runs somewhat brown and muddy from the
tap, or boiling water to make it safe to drink.

Whether we discuss water or clean air or a cozy home and a
comfortable bed, the truth is that we have come to expect those
things in our lives. We've convinced ourselves that we deserve
them and that we've earned them. We almost forget that God
provides for our well-being in every way, until the day things
change.

Today, let's thank him for the fresh water that comes easily
into our faucets and be grateful that he provides all that is good
for our bodies and our souls.

IN THE FLOW

*Lord, I guess I do take the drinking water for granted. I thank
you for taking such good care of me and ask that you would bless
families around the world with safe and clean water. Amen.*

THANKS FOR THE DISASTERS, LORD!

Rejoice always. Pray continually. Give thanks in every situation because this is God's will for you in Christ Jesus.
—1 Thessalonians 5:16-18

Have you ever tried to consciously go through the day giving thanks to God for every situation in which you find yourself? Let's say you're in a traffic jam and it's barely moving and you have a presentation to give at work in fifteen minutes. Do you sit there giving thanks to God in that situation?

Perhaps you walked into work in the morning ready to take on the world, only to be called into the boss's office and told that there's been a company-wide downsizing and you're about to lose your job. Oh, you were in line for a promotion, but all of that has changed. Is it your first inclination to take this news to God and say "thanks" for this circumstance?

We are not in control. We are in God's care and keeping, and he alone knows the whole picture, the reason why something we hoped for didn't materialize. He knows because he is working out all things for our good. That is the reason we can honestly be grateful. That is the reason we can go to him and say, "Lord, I may not understand, but I believe you are working on my behalf, and I trust you with my life. I am grateful even now that you are with me in this circumstance."

IN THE FLOW

Lord, you are so good to me. When I lose sight of that, when things fall apart, please help me to know that I'm not alone. Thank you for taking care of me so well. Amen.

AND THEN SHE SAID . . .

Without wood a fire goes out; without gossips, conflict calms down.
—Proverbs 26:20

Nothing spreads faster than a little gossip. It's amazing how often we fuel the flames of someone else's misfortune, or someone's unwise decisions. We get involved in office chatter or neighborhood smoke and don't even really know why we do it. What is it that makes us so willing to keep someone else's misery alive and well in conversation?

What God wants is for us to be kind, always kind. If being kind means you gently turn aside from the gossips in your neighborhood, then so be it.

Gossip can destroy someone. It rarely lifts them up. If we go back to 1 Corinthians 13 and look at what we are admonished to remember about love, then we can determine how to handle something like gossip. It reminds us that "love is patient, love is kind, it isn't jealous, it doesn't brag, it isn't arrogant, it isn't rude, it doesn't seek its own advantage, it isn't irritable, it doesn't keep a record of complaints, it isn't happy with injustice," and we might add, it doesn't listen to gossip.

Today is a good day to be kind and to love. That is the path to all that is good.

IN THE FLOW

Lord, help me recognize when I need to pass on listening to the conversations that hurt others. Help me be strong in you and be kind in all I do. Amen.

FINDING A LIFEBOAT!

LORD, the floods have raised up—the floods have raised up their voices; the floods raise up a roar! But mightier than the sound of much water, mightier than the sea's waves, mighty on high is the LORD!
—Psalm 93:3-4

November winds whip up the cool frosty air in some parts of the country, making us glad for family and friends and warm fires. Flood waters rage in other parts of the world, spilling over the banks and causing homes to float away.

The psalmist knew these moments. He too experienced the flood of discontent that erupts and washes away the spirit, causing people to question God's power in their lives. He knew something else, though, too, he knew that no matter how powerful the forces of nature might be, the God of the Universe who designed it all was mightier still.

Your life may be a disaster. It may cause you to feel like you're drowning. These things can seem insurmountable and leave you wondering if God is indeed still in control. You may wonder if he will ever send a lifeboat your way.

Hang on! He will reach out to you with his mighty hand and take care of you. Though you may bend with the winds and the powerful waves, you will not break. You are his, safe in his hand at all times.

God is your lifeboat. Reach out to him no matter what.

IN THE FLOW

Lord, thank you for rescuing me when the flood of worries come rushing in. Help me trust you in every way. Amen.

NOVEMBER 26

THE KNOWLEDGE OF THE LORD

The earth will surely be filled with the knowledge
of the LORD, just as the water covers the sea.
—Isaiah 11:9

The harvest time spills over with abundance. We see God's hand
in every living thing, the colors of the falling leaves, and the
bounty of the earth. We gather in gratefulness with our families
and friends to thank God for all he has given us.

We can see his grace and goodness across the landscape and
we come together rejoicing. God's blessings are unending, and
if we were to try to count each one we would see that they are as
endless as the waters across the seas.

Imagine your work without his guidance and direction.
Imagine your family without his love and grace. Imagine the
things you enjoy and the people you love totally without the
Lord of all even for a moment. When you imagine these things
you start to see that everything you have is because of your
connection to the God of the harvest, the keeper of all that is
good.

Learn more of the Lord. Reap the harvest from the bounty
of his Word that he provided for you long ago, knowing you
would need a field guide to the planet you inhabit. Be his student
in all ways, for always.

IN THE FLOW

Lord, you have enriched my life in ways that I don't always
acknowledge. Today I am so grateful for all you've done to honor me
with such abundance. Amen.

THE FEAST OF HAPPINESS

An understanding heart seeks knowledge; but fools
feed on folly. All the days of the needy are hard,
but a happy heart has a continual feast.

—Proverbs 15:14-15

When we choose to feast on happiness more than folly, we are
blessed with abundance and always satisfied. We have a banquet
of opportunities to fill us with delight. We smell the savory
goodness of all that is before us, appreciating the beauty of what
God has done to bring us to this place. Our happiness then
comes from the heart, and the more our hearts seek to know
God, the more knowledge we receive and our hearts are happy.

If we want to have a menu of happy choices, then we must
learn more about what it means to love, so that hate and its
cronies all fade away. If we want to lift others up, we build their
confidence and courage, leaving the words that bring destruction
far behind. We keep choosing to be happy.

We wonder sometimes about what it means to be happy.
We question how anyone can live in the world and still maintain
a spirit of joy, a child-like faith. The answer is that people are
happy who have taken God at his word, trusting in him for the
circumstances they don't understand.

It's a new day and the table is set. What will you choose to
feast on today?

IN THE FLOW

Lord, thank you for feeding me so well. Thank you for helping me
make good choices. I choose to remain forever in your love, for that is
the only thing that really makes me happy. Amen.

November 28

Real Love Never Fails

Love is patient, love is kind, it isn't jealous, it doesn't brag, it isn't arrogant, it isn't rude, it doesn't seek its own advantage, it isn't irritable, it doesn't keep a record of complaints, it isn't happy with injustice, but it is happy with the truth. Love puts up with all things, trusts in all things, hopes for all things, endures all things. Love never fails.
—1 Corinthians 13:4-8

Relationships fail. People fail. We mess up and we don't handle things well. At the same time, we love, and when we love in truth, we love for always. Love then never fails.

First Corinthians 13 is often quoted in marriage ceremonies to remind the new couple of what love really is. Whether we're married or single, it shows us how to behave in any relationship. If we act in ways that are counter to love, we need to look within ourselves, not to the other person. We need to assess what it is that causes us to be selfish or rude or irritable. We need to put away the score pad of who did what and let go of the need to be right all the time.

As you imagine the things you have to put up with in your relationships, take those thoughts a step further and imagine what someone else puts up with because of you, because they love you. Imagine what God puts up with in order to love any of us. Today, let's approach each other with the truth, the joy, the possibility that comes from real love. It will never fail us.

In the Flow

Lord, thank you for your real love. I know that I have a lot to learn before I love in the unconditional ways that you love me. I praise you and thank you for teaching me so well. Amen.

YOUR ATTENTION, PLEASE!

*From now on, brothers and sisters, if anything is excellent
and if anything is admirable, focus your thoughts on these
things: all that is true, all that is holy, all that is just, all that
is pure, all that is lovely, and all that is worthy of praise.*
—Philippians 4:8

Does your mind wander? Do you lose focus sometimes,
forgetting just where you were going and why you were going
there? You may have too much stress, too many worries, too
many bills to pay or family squabbles to patch up, and so you lose
your focus and direction. You wonder how you'll manage all the
things that cause you to fear each new day.

One remedy is to put your attention on the things that give
you new hope. Think about the good things. Don't just think
about them for a moment; write them down or list them in the
corners of your heart so you can refer to them often.

Stay alert for those holy moments in your day when you get
an "aha" and things you didn't understand before suddenly make
sense. Look for the opportunities to seek the good in others, to
discover the integrity of heart and mind that makes truth a reality.
Pay special attention to the good things of God and meditate on
them for as many minutes each day as you can muster.

You have an oasis, a place you can go for refreshment. Go
there and thank God for giving you all that you need.

IN THE FLOW

*Lord, you have given me so many amazing things and my life
is truly blessed. Please help me cast off the fears and worries that
occupy my mind and pay special attention to you. Amen.*

The Mean Gene

Be glad in the Lord always! Again I say, be glad! Let your gentleness show in your treatment of all people. The Lord is near. Don't be anxious about anything; rather bring up all of your requests to God in your prayers and petitions, along with giving thanks. Then the peace of God that exceeds all understanding will keep your hearts and minds safe in Christ Jesus.
—Philippians 4:4-7

You know you don't really have a mean gene in your body. God created you to be a loving person and to handle others with your heart and to handle your own life with your head. You're his example and he needs you to reflect his kindness wherever you are.

What happens when you're consumed with self-doubt or worry, though? Worry comes at you from every side. It disguises itself as conscientious thought and then it nosedives into utter despair. You're in the process of wondering how much you can take care of yourself because it's important to be independent and show God what you can do.

The truth is that he wants you to come to him with every issue that's on your plate, the big ones and the small ones. You can still go out and deal with them, but the difference is that now you'll go connected to him and he can guide your steps.

Today give every ounce of worry to God, and he'll give pounds of peace back to you.

In the Flow

Lord, you have always taken care of me, and it makes me wonder why I get caught up worrying. Remind me today to keep sharing my concerns with you so we can handle all things together. Amen.

December

May you have more and more

grace and peace through the knowledge

of God and Jesus our Lord.

2 Peter 1:2

IN THE REFLECTION OF YOUR ATTITUDE

Therefore, you should treat people in the same
way that you want people to treat you.
—Matthew 7:12

When we come at the world with a nasty disposition, somewhat like Scrooge before his change of heart, we often find the world treats us with a nasty disposition as well. When we arrive with a smile on our faces and an open heart, we usually get a matching reception.

The pattern of our friendships matches that of our relationship with God. When we approach God with the intention of getting to know him better and drawing near to him with love and gratitude, we show him what we want from him too. We've let him know that a relationship with him is important to us.

Step back to see how people respond to you today. If the response is not the one you want, then help people look at you in a new way. Help them treat you better by giving them the best you have to offer.

IN THE FLOW

Lord, please be with me today and help me learn more about how to build our relationship. Help me also give my best self to those you have put in my path. Amen.

BEING A GOOD FOLLOWER

Those who love their lives will lose them, and those who hate their lives in this world will keep them forever. Whoever serves me must follow me. Wherever I am, there my servant will also be. My Father will honor whoever serves me.
—John 12:25-26

If you follow people, you have the opportunity to observe them from a distance. You can stay comfortably back and just absorb what you can about them. Some people choose to follow Jesus that way, comfortably, from a distance.

You can also follow someone by imitating them in every possible way. You can try to do everything the leader does, giving your best impression of what you understand of the way they behave. Some people follow Jesus like that, imitating his every move as best they can.

These days you can follow someone on Twitter. You can see what they are thinking or feeling today based on the few words they might post. The person you've chosen to follow may not realize you're there most of the time. Some people follow Jesus like that.

Serving the Lord means that you follow him with dignity, doing what you can to bring honor to his name. Follow him today with all your heart.

IN THE FLOW

Lord, it is my intention to follow you all the days of my life. On those days when I don't make an effort to imitate you and the love you give others, please remind me to step back and start again. Amen.

December 3

So Close . . . and Yet, So Far!

*God made the nations so they would seek him, perhaps
even reach out to him and find him. In fact, God isn't far
away from any of us. In God we live, move, and exist. As
some of your own poets said, "We are his offspring."*
—Acts 17:27-28

You've probably had moments in your spiritual walk where you
thought God was so close you could touch his hand or feel his
presence. You were elated to know that the God of the Universe
was willing to come whenever you reached out for him.

What is it then that causes us to shift our bearings,
sometimes so much that we can hardly sense the Spirit no matter
how hard we try?

The answer may lie in the fact that we as his children
continue to wander off on our own, forgetting where home is.
We get lost in insignificant things and give them more power
than they deserve. We make our own gods just like the Israelites
did. We are just like they were.

We live and move and have our being in the God of the
Universe. Without him we are only dust blown around by the
winds of confusion. We are without the strength to withstand the
world's pressures. With him, we can do all things.

Give thanks and praise to the one who lives in you and
around you in every moment. Reach out in love and joy to him!

In the Flow

*Lord, it's a new day and I am in great need of you. Help me see you
at every turn and let others see you through me. Help me be worthy
of being called your child. Amen.*

BRING ON THE LOVE

Dear friends, let's love each other, because love is from God,
and everyone who loves is born from God and knows God.
—1 John 4:7

When it comes to love, we're all merely students. We must sit
at the feet of the Master. God has loved us beyond measure,
given his Son for us, provided for our well-being, and yet we still
are fledglings. We look to him to help us understand the grace,
the forgiveness, and the divinity of love, for we cannot create it
ourselves. He is the sun and we are just reflections of his light.

St. Francis de Sales wrote, "You learn to speak by speaking,
to study by studying, to run by running, to work by working;
and just so you learn to love God and man by loving."

We have an assignment. Let's begin today by doing the things
that help us learn more about what it means to love others. Let's
get out our notebooks and jot down some little things we can do
to become better at the art of love. We must study diligently, listen
attentively, and practice, practice, practice. Then we must observe
our own results to see just how far we've come.

Loving others is easy when they are nearby and love us in
return. Loving others also urges us forward when we hear of
natural disasters or neighbors in need. Loving each other is a
mission. God has set each one of us on that mission no matter
where we are.

IN THE FLOW

Lord, you have loved me in more ways than I can ever understand.
You have given me everything I need. Help me be generous and
loving to those around me. Amen.

December 5

Facing the Place of Grace

May you have more and more grace and peace through
the knowledge of God and Jesus our Lord.
—2 Peter 1:2

God's got you covered. He's got your back. He bought the
added insurance and the protection plan that will bring you back
to him as the future unfolds. You live every day under his grace.

Though grace may seem like a simple concept, it's not easy
for us to always grasp the gift it truly is and to thank God for it.
Abraham Lincoln wrote: "We have forgotten the gracious hand
which has preserved us in peace and multiplied and enriched and
strengthened us, and have vainly imagined in the deceitfulness
of our hearts that all these blessings were produced by some
superior wisdom and virtue of our own. Intoxicated with
unbroken success, we have become too self-sufficient to feel the
necessity of redeeming and preserving grace, too proud to pray
to the God that made us."

We are nothing without the love and protection of our
Creator and Redeemer. Our job is to call on his name, thank him
for all he gives us, and serve him so that others may recognize
him and call on him as well. Go in mercy and peace and serve
your heavenly Father.

In the Flow

Lord, you have blessed us so abundantly we hardly realize all you've
done. Give us grateful hearts to live well according to your grace
and mercy. Amen.

You'll Sleep Like a Baby

Therefore, get rid of all ill will and all deceit, pretense,
envy, and slander. Instead, like a newborn baby, desire the
pure milk of the word. Nourished by it, you will grow into
salvation, since you have tasted that the Lord is good.
—1 Peter 2:1-3

You know, it may not be the best thing to "sleep like a baby."
Babies wake up several times every night needing care and feeding.
They have to be assured that someone is there watching over them.

You probably have been sleeping through the night for some
time now and like it that way. However, if you're worried about
something, you may find sleeping to be more difficult.

Peter has an answer. He says to get into the Word. Pour it
on your heart and mind like milk on your cereal. Give yourself a
healthy portion every morning and every other chance you get.
Your heavenly Parent will feed you with everything that will make
life feel good and help you sleep better. As only a good shepherd
can, he watches over you all through the night. He wants you to
grow strong and capable and he longs to give you his peace.

As you begin your night-time prayers, make sure you invite
Jesus to be with you while you sleep. Know that he is there ready
to comfort you at any time. If you can't sleep, he has a really
Good Book. Sleep well!

In the Flow

Lord, thank you for being with me and helping me give my mind a
rest from all the worries and frustrations that linger there from the
day. Watch over all the people I love always. Amen.

You Can Be Right . . . or Righteous!

Don't let something you consider to be good be criticized as wrong. God's kingdom isn't about eating food and drinking but about righteousness, peace, and joy in the Holy Spirit. Whoever serves Christ this way pleases God and gets human approval.
—Romans 14:16-18

Do you ever catch yourself trying a little too hard to be right? You want the other person to acknowledge that your way is the right way. What you believe is what you believe and it's just that black and white to you. The problem is that we all come from different cultures. Some of us think it's okay to eat squid and snails. Some of us don't. But we just love to debate our "right-ness."

What's right in God's view, though, has little to do with what we eat or drink. God is after our righteousness. He wants our hearts to be right because then our actions follow. Martin Luther said: "Paul teaches us that the righteousness of God revealed in the gospel is passive, given to us in Christ. As this truth dawned, I felt I was born again, and was entering . . . paradise itself. The whole face of scripture changed. Just as much as I had hated the phrase 'the righteousness of God,' I now loved it—it seemed the sweetest and most joyous phrase ever written."

As you seek to know more of God and his ways, give him thanks for his righteousness and his great love that allows you to be right in your own circumstances.

In the Flow

Lord, thank you too for showing us what it means to be righteous in you. Amen.

A MATTER OF THE HEART

The one who searches hearts knows how the Spirit thinks,
because it pleads for the saints, consistent with God's will.
—Romans 8:27

You probably don't think of yourself as a "saint," but in the
bigger picture, you are because you are a redeemed child of God
and you have the Spirit of Jesus within you. That Spirit is the one
who prays for you, keeping you connected to God in every way,
working tirelessly for your good. Isn't it wonderful to have such
an advocate always in your corner?

Your connection with God is a matter of the heart. It's a
relationship that only you and he can share—the most significant
relationship of your life. When your heart is aligned with the will
of God, you can make a difference in the world; you can do good
in the name of Jesus and you are a saint. Watch your motives,
the reasons behind the things you do for good. Those that come
truly from your heart are the ones you do by God's will.

We may not understand how the Spirit of God thinks; yet,
we are beloved and protected, watched over by God himself so
that we have the strength and the opportunity to do good and to
enrich the work of his kingdom. Open your heart even more to
him today.

IN THE FLOW

Lord, thank you for taking care of me even when I'm not conscious
of the work of your Spirit. Help me always align my life and my
intentions with your will. Amen.

December 9

It's a Good Thing You're Here!

We know that God works all things together for good for the ones who love God, for those who are called according to his purpose.
—Romans 8:28

After the Potter created, he threw away the mold. You were perfect for what he designed you for and exactly what he wanted. He knew what you could do and looked forward to seeing you in action. You were created for a unique purpose.

John Henry Newman shed light on this idea when he wrote: "Everyone who breathes, high and low, educated and ignorant, young and old, man and woman, has a mission, has a work. We are not sent into this world for nothing. . . . God sees every one of us; He creates every soul . . . for a purpose."

You have a purpose every day. You have a reason for being that is bigger than your own set of goals. It's the mission you were sent here to do, and before you're beamed back up to God, you will strive to get it accomplished. He knows the distractions that will take you off the path, the trial and error that you'll go through. The thing is, he's always aware of you, always doing what he can to keep you pointed in the right direction. He supports the work you do to fulfill the purpose for which you were born. Give him thanks and praise today.

In the Flow

Lord, I have a sense of mission even though I don't always know what it is I'm supposed to do. Please keep working with me, helping me discover the path that will accomplish the goal for you. Amen.

A DIVINE APPOINTMENT

God promised this good news about his Son ahead of time through
his prophets in the holy scriptures. His Son was descended from
David. . . . This Son is Jesus Christ our Lord. Through him we
have received God's grace and our appointment to be apostles.

—Romans 1:2-5

Take a look at your business card. Is there anything that indicates
who you really are? Does it mention your status at work, your
mission, the reason you're here? If it doesn't you might wonder
why. You are here by divine appointment to do the work of God.
You have only one real boss. You have only one job to complete
before you go on to your next assignment. No matter where you
live, where you work, what title you list on your card, you have
one real job—to do the Will of God.

When did you sign up? You signed up the day you declared
that Jesus was your Savior, the day you realized that the Son of
God had the power to change your life. It was the best news you
had ever heard. He signed the contract with you, offering to
mentor you and train you for the job.

As you start your work today, stop to check in with your boss.
Make sure you undertand all the messages in your inbox so you
can make a difference. You're the one he named to get the job
done, and he's very proud of you. It's going to be a great day.

IN THE FLOW

Lord, thank you for hiring me to do the job you have in mind for
me. Help me do the work you've assigned me with great love and
integrity. Bless my work today in you. Amen.

DECEMBER 11

YOU ALREADY HAVE THE GOOD WORD!

*In the beginning was the Word and the Word was with God
and the Word was God. . . . Everything came into being through
the Word, and without the Word nothing came into being.*
—John 1:1-3

As you prepare for the Advent season, reflect on these words
from the Gospel of John. Imagine the beauty and the holiness of
the eternal God, who started it all and was in control then
and is now.

What does that mean as we get out the Christmas tree and
start decorating? How does it change our hearts and minds so
that we focus on the gift of Christmas, the Word made incarnate?
It helps us see the beauty around us with the eyes of our hearts.
We see the symbols of Jesus' birth and heave a sigh of relief. It's
the good news and it's eternal. We have God's Word on it.

Martin Luther said: "So tenaciously should we cling to the
world revealed by the gospel, that were I to see all the angels of
heaven coming down to me to tell me something different . . . I
would shut my eyes and stop my ears, for they would not deserve
to be either seen or heard."

At the Advent season, God shines a light on all that you
mean to him and all that he wants you to know through
his Word.

IN THE FLOW

*Lord, thank you for your Word and for your Son, Jesus. As I get
ready for the Christmas season, I ask you to touch my heart and the
heart of everyone who comes into my home with your love. Amen.*

Standing in the Light

What came into being through the Word was life, and
the life was the light for all people. The light shines in the
darkness, and the darkness doesn't extinguish the light.

—John 1:3-5

A woman had a vision of Jesus. In her vision, she sat by his feet
at a campfire, listening to his teachings. After a while, he invited
her to walk with him into the woods behind the camp. The eerie
blackness of night made her uncomfortable. Jesus asked the
woman, "Can you see me?" When she replied that she could not,
he asked, "Can you hear me?" She responded that she could. He
replied, "You can always hear me if you choose to listen."

At that point, Jesus said, "Put out your hand and reach
around you." The woman reached out her hand and was startled
to realize they were surrounded by people. These people were
down on their knees in the blackness of the night. Jesus said, "I
want you to touch these people, to be a light for them." The
woman was stunned that so many people waited in the darkness
for someone to touch them, and she agreed to do what she was
asked—to be a light in the darkness, to shine the light of Jesus.

St. Augustine said, "Do not believe that you are a light to
yourself. The Light is that which illumines every person coming
into this world." In this season of light and love, may you shine
for others.

In the Flow

Lord, help me share your light and love with anyone who is yet in the
darkness. Amen.

December 13

When the Blind Lead the Blind

The light was in the world, and the world came into being through the light, but the world didn't recognize the light. The light came to his own people, and his own people didn't welcome him.
—John 1:10-11

The stores are crammed with people, some aiming to secure the perfect present for someone on their list. Others wander about, just hoping to spot something that fits their budget and the person they are shopping for.

It's the season of light and love, yet the darkness persists. It's the one time of year when people are more often focused on the needs of others, on the opportunity to give generously. It's joyous, and yet it all goes unnoticed by many, by those who have never gotten the Word, never heard the voice of God echo in their hearts.

The light of the World has indeed come, and yet we walk past our brothers and sisters who are blind. We tell ourselves that it's not really our job to change them. We blind ourselves to their needs. Yet, Jesus comes and stands in our midst, shining for all to see. He asks those of us who see him to let others know about him. He desires that none should be blind, that all should know the light. It's Advent, the season of his coming into the world. Let's help light the way for those who do not yet recognize the gift of his presence.

In the Flow

Lord, I'm so comfortable with you that I sometimes don't realize how blinded I am to the fact that I don't shine your light as joyfully as I might. Help me spread the gift of your love to everyone. Amen.

GOD'S SEAL OF APPROVAL

But those who did welcome him, those who believed in his name,
he authorized to become God's children, born not from blood
nor from human desire or passion, but born from God.
—John 1:12-13

Jesus came to earth as a child of Joseph and Mary, but he was the Son of God. You came to earth as the child of your parents also, and because of God's love for you, you too are a child of God. As we approach Christmas, it's a great idea to ponder—that we are on the edge of all that God has planned to bring us back to himself one day. His Redeemer is about to be born.

As we embrace his infant Son, delighting in the gift of his presence, it's a good opportunity to look at the people around us, because each of them will have the opportunity to gain God's favor, to choose his Son and get his great stamp of approval. How amazing it is to realize how much we mean to our Father, that he provided for us through the beauty of a simple birth in Bethlehem.

When you were born to your earthly parents, they did their best to care for you and provide for you. When you were born to God, you received an entrance into all that he has to offer. You are a gift that is completely redeemed, signed, sealed, and delivered. At Christmas, celebrate his birth and your new life.

IN THE FLOW

Lord, you have done such marvelous things, it's hard to take them
all in. You're the King of this universe, and I am awed that you
have given even me your stamp of approval. Amen.

December 15

Your Unseen Guest

The Word became flesh and made his home among
us. We have seen his glory, glory like that of a
father's only son, full of grace and truth.
—John 1:14

Christmastime is difficult for many people. Some feel even more
of the pain of this world as they ponder the meaning of Jesus'
birth. They feel lonelier than usual because their families have
grown and gone away, their friends have moved on, and they
have nowhere to go. A joyous season for many, it's a challenge to
others.

What can we do to help and to share love and light? We can
work in homeless shelters, donate to charities, pray for those
who have less than we do, and look for chances to serve. We can
spread the cheer we receive through our faith in Christ.

We can also remember that none of us is actually ever alone.
We have an unseen guest who is part of all we do. At the time we
accepted Jesus' offer of love and salvation, we invited him into
our hearts and lives and homes. He is with us every moment; he
never leaves us. He is as close to us as a thought and a prayer.

It's a great time of year to pray for those who don't feel his
presence and the gift of his love. Help them come home to him.

In the Flow

Lord, thank you for living in my home as an unseen guest. I feel
your presence and I'm overjoyed at knowing you're always near me.
Bless those who have yet to invite you in and give them peace. Amen.

AN AMAZING BABY BOY

*The angel said, "Don't be afraid, Zechariah. Your prayers
have been heard. Your wife Elizabeth will give birth to your
son and you must name him John. He will be a joy and delight
to you, and many people will rejoice at his birth, for he will be
great in the Lord's eyes. He must not drink wine and liquor.
He will be filled with the Holy Spirit even before his birth. He
will bring many Israelites back to the Lord their God."*

—Luke 1:13-16

At this time of year, we happily prepare for Christmas. We
decorate the yard, we sing in the choir, and we bake bread for
the homeless shelter. We shop till we drop and we plan elegant
dinners. We prepare for the big day we'll celebrate with family
and friends and the great miracle of God's Son being born to us.

Zechariah and Elizabeth must have been reeling from their
own news a few months before Jesus' birth. They were long
past the child-bearing years when the angel told them God had
answered their prayers. God had a plan, and he used these two
servants to get things in order.

Zechariah and Elizabeth's baby boy was filled with the
Holy Spirit before he was even born. He made the path ready
so that Jesus would be seen and heard. He planted the seeds of
everlasting life. As we come to Christmas, let's consider all we
might do to let the light of the Spirit shine through and prepare
the way for our Lord.

IN THE FLOW

*Lord, I am your humble servant, and I'm willing to serve you in
any way I can. Thank you for preparing a way for me to see and
love you. Amen.*

DECEMBER 17

MAKING ROOM FOR THE BABY

While they were there, the time came for Mary to have
her baby. She gave birth to her firstborn child, a son,
wrapped him snugly, and laid him in a manger, because
there was no place for them in the guestroom.
—Luke 2:6-7

Remember what it was like when a new baby was coming into
your life? There was planning about where to have the baby, where
the baby's room would be, and what things would be needed.

Many preparations go into making way for a new baby.
Jumping back two thousand years, try to imagine a young
teenage girl doing her best to understand the God of the
Universe, riding into Bethlehem on a donkey, suddenly faced
with yet one more obstacle. There's no room anywhere for this
baby to be born. Did Mary get to have the help of midwives
and other women of her hometown as was customary for Jewish
women in her day? Did she simply have to deliver the baby all on
her own?

The Bible is sketchy about the delivery itself, but one thing
is sure—this was a delivery unlike any before or since. Not only
did this baby need room to come into the world, but he grew up
to be One still looking for a room. This baby, as the Lord of All,
seeks a room wherever he can find it. He is looking at you today,
hoping you are prepared to give him more room in your heart.

IN THE FLOW

Lord, I am awed by the circumstances surrounding your humble
birth. It fills my heart with great joy each time I picture you lying in a
manger. I pray that I always have room for you in my heart. Amen.

THE SHEPHERD OF ALL SHEPHERDS

Nearby shepherds were living in the fields, guarding their
sheep at night. The Lord's angel stood before them, the
Lord's glory shone around them, and they were terrified.
The angel said, "Don't be afraid! Look! I bring good news
to you—wonderful, joyous news for all people. Your savior
is born today in David's city. He is Christ the Lord."
—Luke 2:8-11

In Bible times, shepherds lived in the fields with their sheep.
They watched over them and protected them from predators.
They moved them around so they could get the best grass, took
care of the newborn lambs, and searched for those that wandered
away. It was a full-time job and a lonely occupation. As shepherds
watched over the sheep, God watched over the shepherds.

Perhaps he visited them in the fields on that night of Jesus'
birth because they were men of integrity and were an example of
the way his son, the Lamb of God, would take care of the world.

The shepherd rarely got news of any sort, and now he was
being told by an angel that something big was happening in
David's city. It had to leave him in total awe. He had known
since he was just a boy that the Messiah would someday be born.
But here it was—happening right before his eyes.

The shepherd discovered that God had a plan for him to have
a protector, an advocate, a Shepherd as well. It was a day of great
rejoicing—and the heavens have not ceased to declare its wonder.

IN THE FLOW

Lord, thank you for bringing the Good Shepherd to watch over us.
Help us grow strong in you. Amen.

December 19

Visited by Angels!

When the angels returned to heaven, the shepherds said to each other, "Let's go right now to Bethlehem and . . . confirm what the Lord has revealed to us." They . . . found Mary and Joseph, and the baby lying in the manger. When they saw this, they reported what they had been told about this child. Everyone who heard it was amazed at what the shepherds told them. Mary committed these things to memory and considered them carefully.
—Luke 2:15-19

We might have wondered about those starstruck shepherds, full of tales. But when God does something big, he lets more than a few people in on his plans.

Not only had God prepared for the angels to visit the shepherds in the field, he had prepared the way in Mary's heart long before. He had let her in on the secret with an angel visit as well. Mary knew that angels didn't just come calling for no real reason. Joseph had talked with angels in his dreams and he had told Mary those stories too, so her heart was full of the work of the Lord as those excited sheep herders came to visit.

Mary knew that God was working out the salvation of the world and had determined to use her to get the job done. She had been awed. Mostly, she held all her thoughts close to her heart, sharing them only with her husband. She would be committed to her task from that day forward. God wants the same kind of commitment from us too.

In the Flow

Lord, as we ponder what you've done in giving us the baby Jesus, may we be awestruck like the shepherds of long ago. Amen.

WHAT SHALL WE CALL THE BABY BOY?

*A child is born to us, a son is given to us, and authority
will be on his shoulders. He will be named Wonderful
Counselor, Mighty God, Eternal Father, Prince of Peace.*

—Isaiah 9:6

Mary and Joseph didn't have to go through the baby name book
to come up with a name. Their infant son would be called Jesus
just as the angel had told them from the beginning. Over his
lifetime, though, Jesus would have many names, and Isaiah gives
us a glimpse of those here. We could add some of the others:
Bread of Life, Name above all names, Lamb of God, Light of the
World.

As you get closer to Christmas, see how you feel each time
you speak the name of Jesus or hear his name sung or praised
in church. Look at all you do in the name of Jesus. Pray in the
name of Jesus. Offer your heart and your help to others in the
name of Jesus.

God named his Son, just as he named John the Baptist,
Abraham, and Sarah. He knew your name too even before you
were born, and you've been on a first-name basis with him ever
since.

As you come to the manger, carrying the little blue blanket
and matching booties to keep him warm, stop and admire him.
Give him all your love at this Christmas season and always. Bless
his holy name.

IN THE FLOW

*Lord, you are so awesome, I can hardly take it in. The Christmas
season brings abundant joy to my heart as I reflect on your beautiful
and everlasting name. Amen.*

THE CALL OF COMPASSION

When Mary [Jesus'] mother was engaged to Joseph, before they were married, she became pregnant by the Holy Spirit. Joseph her husband was a righteous man. Because he didn't want to humiliate her, he decided to call off their engagement quietly. . . . An angel from the Lord appeared to him in a dream and said, "Joseph son of David, don't be afraid to take Mary as your wife, because the child she carries was conceived by the Holy Spirit."
—Matthew 1:18-20

Most couples agree to keep the intimate parts of their relationship exclusive, a celebration belonging to just the two of them. In Joseph's case, he and Mary had not yet formed their intimate relationship, but as an engaged couple they were totally committed to the contract of marriage. Going outside the bounds of that agreement meant the relationship was broken. Joseph must have felt relief when the angel came to him in a dream to let him know the truth. He must have been glad he had not done anything to destroy Mary's name or her family.

It's not easy to be compassionate, especially when we feel wronged. Yet, this lesson in compassion from Joseph to Mary reminds us that we don't always have enough information to simply react. We must always wait for God to reveal the next steps. Let compassion fill your heart for others as you come to the Christmas season.

IN THE FLOW

Lord, sometimes we jump to conclusions and make rash judgments. Help me always seek your face when I deal with others. Amen.

STARSTRUCK

*When they heard the king, they went; and look, the star they
had seen in the east went ahead of them until it stood over the
place where the child was. When they saw the star, they were
filled with joy. They entered the house and saw the child with
Mary his mother. Falling to their knees, they honored him.*

—Matthew 2:9-11

The scholars of the day, the astronomers, those men wise enough
to be looking for the birth of the Christ child, were filled with
awe as they witnessed the movement of the star. It seemed to
guide them exactly where they were meant to go. They had
waited for this moment most of their lives, the answer to their
prayers.

That star of wonder is still leading us, still calling to us to
look up in the night sky and open our hearts to the possibility of
our Savior. It's still reminding us that no matter where we are,
we can follow that star and find peace and life and truth.

Wherever you are this Christmas season, may you look up
with the wisdom of those ancient surveyors of the heavens to
discover that wondrous sight whose meaning the angels declared
with songs of joy. May you stand in awe, starstruck by what God
has done to give you the gift of his Son. The stars are shining
brightly, declaring God's love for all who search the skies with
expectant hearts.

IN THE FLOW

*Lord, you have given us so many ways to try to find you. Help us
always look for the signs of your love. Amen.*

THE HELP OF THE ANGELS

*When the magi had departed, an angel from the Lord appeared
to Joseph in a dream and said, "Get up. Take the child and his
mother and escape to Egypt. Stay there until I tell you, for Herod
will soon search for the child in order to kill him." Joseph got up
and, during the night, took the child and his mother to Egypt. He
stayed there until Herod died. This fulfilled what the Lord had
spoken through the prophet:* I have called my son out of Egypt.
—Matthew 2:13-15

The work of angels may well be a mystery to most of us. We may
not have been aware of their presence, and yet we know of angels
from reading the Word, which informs us of their role in God's
universe. The angels were certainly at work in Joseph's life as he
stepped in to protect his infant son.

It stands to reason that God would have messengers in spirit
form. After all, he is working with human beings who need all
the help they can get, and much of the time we don't understand
him clearly. The beauty of angels is that they are even more
efficient than FedEx since they can visit at any time via dreams or
in the shapes of creatures great and small.

If you're open to the messages of angels, then listen carefully
for their voices. If nothing else you may hear them simply
praising the Lord just so you can join them in the chorus.

IN THE FLOW

*Lord, I'm grateful for the work of the angels and awed by the service
they perform for you and your children. I ask that you would bless
my life with angels whenever they can guide me to your will and
purpose. Amen.*

THE BIRTH OF JESUS, HOPE OF THE WORLD

Without question, the mystery of godliness is great: he
was revealed as a human, declared righteous by the
Spirit, seen by angels, preached to throughout the nations,
believed in around the world, and taken up in glory.
—1 Timothy 3:16

At Christmas Eve, we become part of the story. We walk through
the incredible saga of a young teenage girl giving her heart over
to God's plans, doing all things to bring to life her infant Son.
She knew she carried the story of salvation, and though she
probably didn't understand it fully, it was a mission given to her
and she accepted it.

The mystery continues for us as we strive to embrace God's
Son more fully. We honor his birth at Christmas, read about his
adventures, and are blessed by his words and teachings as well.
Jesus is the hope of all the world, and we, like Mary, are asked to
carry his message forward, helping others come to know him.

Imagine that God has called you to carry his Son in your
heart all the days of your life. Every time you allow his light to
shine you have the chance to give someone else the hope that
came to all of us that Christmas Day.

IN THE FLOW

Lord, I thank you and praise you for coming to earth to help us
learn of the things of God. Help me shine your light as surely as any
star that every topped a Christmas tree. Thank you, Jesus. Amen.

CHRISTMAS IS ALL ABOUT LOVE

This is how we know we remain in him and he remains in us, because he has given us a measure of his Spirit. We have seen and testify that the Father has sent the Son to be the savior of the world. . . . God is love, and those who remain in love remain in God and God remains in them.
—1 John 4:13-16

You may have grown up with mixed messages about Christmas. You knew about the baby born in Bethlehem. You had your nativity set, heard stories of his birth, and sang songs like "Joy to the World."

You may also have dreamed of what Santa Claus might leave under the tree. You might have had an inkling that Santa wasn't real, but it was fun to imagine the jolly old elf.

The truth is that both of these stories—the one that God gave us and the one that Clement Moore gave us—are stories of generosity, hope, and sharing love. When you outgrew Santa Claus, you were left with the amazing tale of the infant Jesus, born to save the world, blessed by God to bring us back to him.

As you celebrate the love of Jesus, mixed with gifts exchanged in the spirit of Kris Kringle, remember that God loves you so much, he sent his baby boy to earth just for you. Now that's the gift of Christmas!

IN THE FLOW

Lord, thank you for all the beauty of Christmas. Thank you for bringing joy to the world through your Son, Jesus, and for all the gifts we have come to know because of his love. Amen.

THE GIFT THAT KEEPS GIVING

*God made his Son the heir of everything and created the world
through him. The Son is the light of God's glory and the imprint
of God's being. He maintains everything with his powerful
message. After he carried out the cleansing of people from their
sins, he sat down at the right side of the highest majesty.*
—Hebrews 1:2-3

You may be experiencing a sense of let-down now that
the celebration of Christmas Day has passed. You may be
remembering stories that were told as gifts were unwrapped and
dinners prepared. You may be musing about the joys of family
and friends and how much this season means to you.

If you are, then keep your spirits up and your hopes high.
Step over the boxes and bows and open your arms to the One
who made it all happen.

You can see his work all around you. You can connect to him
any time you choose and tap into his powerful message of joy and
peace and deliverance. He was born for you. He died for you. He
loves you, and that is the message he wants you to take with you
wherever you go. You may be eating leftovers, re-gifting some
presents that didn't quite work out, and saying good-bye to your
company, but Christ is the gift that will be with you forever.

IN THE FLOW

*Lord, it is so amazing to realize that after the last gift is opened and
the guests have gone home, I am still able to sit near you, right by
the tree, and receive your gifts of love forever. Thank you so much for
loving me. Amen.*

SIMPLY BECAUSE YOU ARE FAITHFUL

All you who are faithful, love the LORD! The LORD protects those who are loyal, but he pays the proud back to the fullest degree. All you who wait for the LORD, be strong and let your heart take courage.
—Psalm 31:23-24

Loyalty and *faithfulness* seem like archaic words these days. We seldom see them in action. Companies are not loyal to their workers even after years of service. Friends are not loyal to each other. So how do we become loyal and faithful to those we've made a commitment to, and especially to God?

Remember that faithfulness is not really a goal or a destination, but a manner of traveling. It's the things we always carry with us. It's packed with power when it serves in little ways. We are faithful in little things all the time. Mother Teresa said she did not pray to be successful, she prayed to be faithful—a good prayer for any of us. There are many biblical stories of those who were faithful in small matters being elevated then to watch over greater things. Even when the job was no longer pleasant, even when it was fearful, even unto death, Jesus remained faithful.

As his children, we are directed to complete the mission God gave us. His work cannot be done without our faithful willingness to continue to do it. He protects, strengthens, and supports all we do in his name because we are faithful.

IN THE FLOW

Father, thank you for being the anchor to my life, the steadfast support, and the one I can always trust to be there. I treasure your loyalty to me and pray I will always be loyal to you in return. Amen.

PROCLAIMING THE YEAR OF THE LORD'S FAVOR

He unrolled the scroll and found the place where it was written:
The Spirit of the Lord is upon me, because the Lord has
anointed me. He has sent me to preach good news to the
poor, to proclaim release to the prisoners and recovery of
sight to the blind, to liberate the oppressed, and to proclaim
the year of the Lord's favor. *He rolled up the scroll, gave it
back to the synagogue assistant, and sat down. Every eye in
the synagogue was fixed on him. He began to explain to them,
"Today, this scripture has been fulfilled just as you heard it."*
—Luke 4:17-21

As you unroll the scroll of the New Year, remember all the
assignments Jesus was given when he came to earth. As the
Savior, he was ready to serve God in every way. Delivering the
good news and healing the sick were just part of it. One of the
outstanding aspects of his ministry was that he could proclaim
the year of God's favor. He could tell a starving world that the
Bread of Life would be with them forevermore. Jesus fulfilled
his mission using all that was available to him. He was our living
example of what it means to be filled with the Spirit.

So what does he want from us? What work are we here to
do? Perhaps we could discover just one idea—to love. Imagine
if we fulfilled the mission to love the Lord with all our heart and
mind and soul and to love one another as well.

IN THE FLOW

*Lord, keep my mind and heart open to your leading. Thanks for
empowering me to do your work. Amen.*

THERE'S ONLY ONE SAFE PLACE

The LORD's eyes watch all who honor him, all who wait for his faithful love, to deliver their lives from death . . . during a famine. We put our hope in the LORD. He is our help and our shield. Our heart rejoices in God because we trust his holy name.
—Psalm 33:18-21

There's another devastating earthquake in Asia, another tornado ripping lives apart in Oklahoma. The planet heaves and sighs and we feel so vulnerable we wonder what to do. We doubt whether God knows all that we're going through. The truth is, we have a deliverer and every reason to be confident in him.

Martin Luther said, "The Holy Spirit is no skeptic. He has written neither doubt nor mere opinion into our hearts, but rather solid assurances." In other words, we can't trust all the appearances of the world—natural disasters and threats of terrorists. We know the one truth, and that is we are always in the care and keeping of God.

John Newton declared, "Assurance grows . . . by our repeated experimental proof of the Lord's power and goodness to save; when we have been . . . sorely wounded and healed, cast down and raised again; . . . and when these things have been repeated . . . a thousand times over, we begin to learn to trust."

As one year ends and another one begins, rest in the assurance that your God reigns and that he is in control.

IN THE FLOW

Lord, thank you for being in control of this world. Thank you for taking care of me. Help me rest in you today. Amen.

GOD'S PROMISES FOR THE NEW YEAR

*I raise my eyes toward the mountains. Where will my
help come from? My help comes from the* LORD, *the maker
of heaven and earth. God won't let your foot slip.
Your protector won't fall asleep on the job. No! Israel's
protector never sleeps or rests! The* LORD *is your protector; the*
LORD *is your shade right beside you. The sun won't strike you
during the day; neither will the moon at night. The* LORD
*will protect you from all evil; God will protect your very
life. The* LORD *will protect you on your journeys—whether
going or coming—from now until forever from now.*

—Psalm 121

We often struggle with the belief that God is with us, watching over us and comforting us in our sorrows. It is good to remind ourselves that he is indeed with us.

What evil will the Lord protect you from? Perhaps he'll safeguard your thoughts so you won't wander too far away from him. Perhaps he'll send angels to guide you so you will walk on solid ground.

Come to him whenever you have doubts. Engage him in conversation as you would a close friend. Bring him into your heart so nothing can come between you. When you do, you'll feel his presence in everything. You'll be aware of his helping hand and loving embrace. Give him thanks and praise.

IN THE FLOW

*Lord, thank you for keeping watch over me. Protect me from
anything that could harm my relationship with you. Help me be all
that you want me to be in the coming year. Amen.*

GOD CREATED THE RIVERS OF LIFE

*You put gushing springs into dry riverbeds. They flow between
the mountains, providing water for every wild animal—
the wild donkeys quench their thirst. Overhead, the birds in
the sky make their home, chirping loudly in the trees.
From your lofty house, you water the mountains. The
earth is filled full by the fruit of what you've done.*
—Psalm 104:10-13

As we reach the end of the old year and head toward the new,
it is good to remember the Creator, who is with us from the
beginning to the end of all things. He set all that we have into
motion and brought us to the place we are in today.

The psalmist fills us with images of God's endless love, his
life-giving waters. He cares for all of his creation, providing
everything needed to sustain life fully. He quenches the thirst
of each living thing, and he quenches our thirst with the living
water of his Son's love. He gives us reason to sing with the birds,
and he hears the songs of our hearts.

Whatever you need, he has provided. He knows what will
make you prosper, what will please your heart, what will feed
your soul and bring you back to his place of peace and joy. Cling
to him so that his face may shine upon you and give you peace.
He will be your wellspring of hope and wisdom all through the
coming year whenever you call his name.

IN THE FLOW

*Lord, you have washed me with blessings and grace, holding me up
and giving me all that I need. Help me start anew, refreshed in you
as the year begins. I thank you and praise you for all you do to give
me hope and peace and joy. Amen.*

2/20/15

G

DISCARD